CONTENTS

T0385900

Focus 2 Workbook walkthrough

UNITS (pp. 4–115)

UNITS 1–8

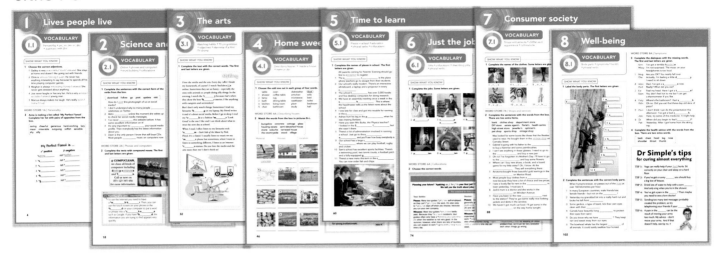

BACK OF THE BOOK (pp. 116–160)

The VOCABULARY BANK is a topic-based wordlist including vocabulary from all units. It is followed by exercises which provide more vocabulary practice.

Focus 1 Grammar Review contains grammar explanations and revision of the grammar taught in level 1.

The GRAMMAR: Train and Try Again section provides more grammar activities for self-study.

The WRITING BANK provides a list of the useful phrases from the WRITING FOCUS boxes in the Student's Book.

The answer keys to the Focus 1 Grammar Review, Self-check and GRAMMAR: Train and Try Again sections support self-study and promote student autonomy.

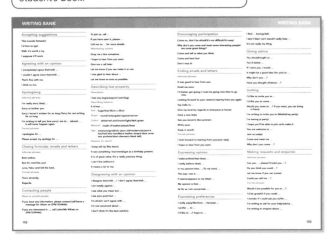

DON'T MISS

The SHOW WHAT YOU KNOW tasks in the Vocabulary and Grammar lessons serve as a warm-up and revise vocabulary or grammar students should already know.

SHOW WHAT YOU KNOW

1 Complete the sentences with the correct form of the verbs from the box.

> download follow go post update visit

How do I _post_ this photograph of us on social media?
1 I don't understand why so many people _____ celebrities on Twitter.
2 Akito _____ online the moment she wakes up to check her social media messages.
3 I've never _____ this website before. It has some excellent information on it!
4 It's very important to _____ your social media profile. Then everybody has the latest information about you.
5 Dean is the only person I know that still buys CDs. Most people _____ music on computers now.

The SHOW WHAT YOU'VE LEARNT tasks in the Vocabulary and Grammar lessons help students to check their progress and be aware of their own learning.

SHOW WHAT YOU'VE LEARNT

6 Write questions for the underlined parts of the answers.
> _Who usually cleans the bathroom at the weekend_?
> Dad usually cleans the bathroom at the weekend.
1 _____?
The girls are cooking mushroom soup.
2 _____?
Dean has brought his new guitar.
3 _____?
Michelle has forgotten to close the door.
4 _____?
Nicola is doing her homework.
5 _____?
Craig wants a motorbike.
6 _____?
People are listening to the band.

/6

GRAMMAR: Train and Try Again page 144

The SHOW THAT YOU'VE CHECKED section in the Writing lessons is a useful checklist that accompanies the final writing task.

SHOW THAT YOU'VE CHECKED

Finished? Always check your writing. Can you tick ✓ everything on this list?

In my story:

- I have given information to set the scene, e.g. _I was ten years old …_, _It was a cold dark evening_. ☐
- I have used the Past Simple and Continuous, and perhaps _used to_ to describe what happened, e.g. _It started to rain as I was climbing the mountain_. ☐
- I have used different words and phrases to make my story interesting for the reader, e.g. _What was going on? It was awesome!_ ☐
- I have included adverbs to add interest, e.g. _Suddenly, Luckily, incredibly_. ☐
- I have given my story a strong ending, e.g. _I'll never forget when I first went …_, _… was an event I'll never forget_. ☐
- I have checked my spelling and punctuation. ☐
- My text is neat and clear. ☐

The REMEMBER BETTER boxes provide tips on learning, remembering and enriching vocabulary.

REMEMBER BETTER

When you learn phrasal verbs, check in the dictionary or online and find the antonym. We often (but not always) use the opposite preposition, e.g _switch on ≠ switch off_.

A Write the opposites. Use a dictionary if necessary.
scroll up   ≠   _scroll down_
1 turn up (the volume) ≠ _____
2 turn on   ≠ _____
3 log on   ≠ _____

B Complete the sentences with phrasal verbs from Exercise A.
The information you need is at the bottom of the webpage. You need to _scroll down_.
1 I can't study with that loud music playing. Please will you _____ the volume.
2 Use your username and password to _____ to the website.
3 _____ the TV before you go to bed.

The REMEMBER THIS boxes focus on useful language nuances.

REMEMBER THIS

When you learn new nouns, use a dictionary or go online and check if they are countable or uncountable. Remember some nouns can be both countable and uncountable depending on the context:
You need lots of experience to become a professional footballer.
(uncountable – knowledge and skill learnt from the time spent doing something)
Working in the USA was a great experience.
(countable – something memorable that happened to you).

The star coding system shows the different levels of difficulty of the activities in the Grammar lessons.

2 ★ Choose the correct quantifiers to complete the dialogue between a researcher and Lynn.
R: Excuse me, may I ask you a few quick questions about your experience in the shopping centre today?
L: Er … will it take long?
R: No, not at all. Just [1]_a few / a little_ minutes.
L: OK then.
R: Thank you. [2]_How much / How many_ shops did you visit today?
L: Oh, I'm not sure exactly. Certainly [3]_too much / too many_. My feet hurt!
R: Oh dear. Poor you. I'll write more than 10 on the form then. [4]_How much / How many_ time did you spend in the food zone today?
L: Oh, [5]_very few / very little_. I stopped for a cup of coffee, but only for ten minutes.
R: OK, thanks. Just one more question, if you don't mind. [6]_How much / How many_ money did you spend today?
L: Only [7]_a few / a little_. Most of the time I was window shopping.

3 ★ ★ Use _not much_ or _not many_ to make the sentences negative.
Frieda has a lot of friends.
Frieda _doesn't have many_ friends.
1 Peter goes to a lot of parties.
Peter _____ parties.
2 Nick and Nancy watch a lot of news.
Nick and Nancy _____ news.
3 Jenny drinks a lot of juice.
Jenny _____ juice.
4 Edward and Eve write a lot of emails.
Edward and Eve _____ emails.
5 Francis eats a lot of fruit.
Francis _____ fruit.

The SPEAKING BANK lists the key phrases from the Speaking lesson.

SPEAKING BANK

Giving an opinion
I think he … _____
I don't think it's … _____
Personally, I think … _____
I really believe … _____
In my opinion, … _____
If you ask me, … _____

Agreeing
I couldn't agree more. _____
_____
That's a good point. _____

Disagreeing politely
I see what you mean, but … _____
That's true, but … _____
I'm not so sure. _____

Disagreeing
I totally disagree! _____
Oh come on! That's nonsense. _____

Speaking tasks in the exam format help students to prepare for their exams.

EXAM SPEAKING

1 In pairs, ask and answer the questions.

2 Look at the photos of people doing voluntary work.

Lives people live

VOCABULARY

1.1

Personality • un-, in-, im- ir-, dis-
• questions with *like*

---

1 Choose the correct adjectives.

1 Gabby is very *unsociable* / *loud* / *stressed*. She stays at home and doesn't like going out with friends.

2 Chris is *serious* / *boring* / *quiet*. He never has anything interesting to say because he spends all his time playing computer games.

3 Meghan is always *interesting* / *funny* / *relaxed*. She never gets stressed about anything.

4 Joe never laughs or has any fun. He's a very *serious* / *sociable* / *relaxed* young man.

5 Marcus always makes me laugh. He's really *quiet* / *funny* / *loud*.

WORD STORE 1A | Personality

2 Anna is making a list called 'My Perfect Fiancé'. Complete her list with pairs of opposites from the box.

> caring   cheerful   generous   hard-working   lazy
> mean   miserable   outgoing   selfish   sensible
> shy   silly

My Perfect Fiancé is ...

✓ positive	✗ negative
ᵃcaring	not ᵇselfish
1 ᵃs_____	not ᵇ_____
2 ᵃc_____	not ᵇ_____
3 ᵃo_____	not ᵇ_____
4 ᵃh_____	not ᵇ_____
5 ᵃg_____	not ᵇ_____

3 Complete the conversation between Anna and Laura with the correct adjectives from the box. There are two extra words.

> caring   cheerful   generous   hard-working
> mean   miserable   selfish   shy   silly

A few months later ...

L: So, how are things with Simon? Is he the perfect fiancé?

A: Well, nobody's perfect, but you know what? He's really great. First of all, he's really *cheerful*, you know, always happy and smiling. And he's very
¹_____ . He wants to be a teacher and he does lots of studying in the evenings.

L: Does he have any time for you then?

A: Oh sure. He's a very ²_____ guy. He calls me every night and asks about my day.

L: Wow. Lucky you! Dave never asks about my day. He only thinks about himself. He's so ³_____ . Dave also thinks he's the best fiancé in the world, but he never buys me anything nice and he doesn't like paying for us when we go out. He's really
⁴_____ .

A: Poor you. Simon is exactly the opposite. He takes me to a restaurant sometimes and he pays for the food. And he often buys me flowers. He's very
⁵_____ . I'm really happy, you know.

L: Well, good for you. Unfortunately, I'm not. I'm unhappy; really ⁶_____ . I don't know what to do. Does Simon have a twin brother?

WORD STORE 1B | un-, in-, im-, ir-, dis-

4 Add negative prefixes to adjectives a–g. Complete sentences 1–4 with some of the adjectives in their negative or positive form.

_un_popular

a ___sensitive
b ___honest
c ___polite
d ___responsible
e ___adventurous
f ___wise
g ___dependent

Try to be generous. Nobody likes mean people. They are nearly always _unpopular_.

1 Mum trusts my older brother Peter to look after our little sister. He's extremely _____ . He never does anything dangerous or silly.

2 Katie never lies. She is a very ᵃ_____ person. Katie's also ᵇ_____ – she knows a lot of things.

3 David doesn't say 'please' or 'thank you'. He's ᵃ_____ . He's extremely ᵇ_____ too and likes doing everything without any help.

4 I was unhappy because I didn't pass my driving test. I told Tom and he laughed! Is he always so _____ ?

> **REMEMBER THIS**
>
> You can use personality adjectives before a noun:
> A _caring_ **friend**
> or after the verb _be_:
> My friend **is** _caring_.

5 Read REMEMBER THIS. Put the words in the correct order.

has / very / parents / Pauline / serious
Pauline has very serious parents.

1 last / was / hairdresser / cheerful / Zoe's

_____

2 two / I / dishonest / had / friends

_____

3 new / Jamie's / loud / friend / extremely / is

_____

> **REMEMBER BETTER**
>
> To help you learn the personality adjectives from this lesson, try to remember them with people you know:
> My dad is usually _cheerful_. He's not a _miserable_ man.

Choose five pairs of opposite personality adjectives from this lesson. Write sentences about people you know. Use the model sentences.

My little sister is shy. She's not an outgoing girl.

1 Our History teacher is _____ . He's/She's not a _____ man/woman.

2 My best friend is _____ . He/She is not a _____ person.

3 _____ .

4 _____ .

5 _____ .

WORD STORE 1C | Questions with _like_

6 Look at the dialogues. Correct the mistake in each question.

A: Do you ~~looks~~ like your parents? _Do you look like your parents?_
B: People say I look a little like my mum.

1 A: What flavour ice cream you like?
B: I love vanilla.

2 A: Are Gareth and Liu like dogs?
B: I think they like cats more.

3 A: What is your sister look like?
B: She's tall and has small brown eyes.

4 A: What does Tracy like?
B: She's caring and sensitive.

5 A: What does your English teacher look?
B: He's short and wears glasses.

> **SHOW WHAT YOU'VE LEARNT**

7 Choose the correct answers A–C.

1 A person who is __ is outgoing and likes meeting other people.
   A relaxed   **B** funny   **C** sociable

2 A person who is __ does not do silly things.
   A sensible   **B** selfish   **C** sensitive

3 A person who is __ loves doing new and crazy things.
   A independent   **B** adventurous   **C** irresponsible

4 A person who is __ is somebody who is not loud.
   A sociable   **B** silly   **C** quiet

5 A person who is __ is somebody that not many people like.
   A unwise   **B** unpopular   **C** outgoing

8 Complete the sentences with adjectives. The first letters are given.

Mike is **g**_enerous_. He gives half of his pocket money to the local charity.

1 Please don't be **s**_____ . Share the chocolate with me.

2 My older sister doesn't talk to people she doesn't know well. She's extremely **s**_____ !

3 Mia is very **i**_____ and doesn't like asking for help or advice from anybody.

4 Amy is **w**_____ . She knows the answer to every question I ask her.

5 Lucy is extremely **u**_____ . She never wants to try new things. Fortunately, her younger sister is quite the opposite!

/10

1.2 Present tenses
– question forms

1 Complete the sentences with the correct present forms of the verbs in brackets.

1 It's 11:00 and the bus *hasn't arrived* (not/arrive) yet. Oh! Wait ... there it is. I can see it now.
It _____ (come) round the corner.

2 I ᵃ_____ (never/try) sushi.
I ᵇ_____ (not/like) fish.

3 Sorry, Emily ᵃ_____ (not/be) here now. She ᵇ_____ (run) in the park. Can you call back later?

4 Your dad ᵃ_____ (already/have) breakfast. He ᵇ_____ (walk) the dog. He'll be back in ten minutes.

5 Leroy ᵃ_____ (read) a very good book at the moment. He always ᵇ_____ (buy) his books online.

2 ★ Complete the questions with the correct forms of *do*, *be* or *have*.

Why *are* you always so selfish?

1 _____ Carl ever had long hair?

2 What _____ an appropriate birthday present for my five-year-old nephew?

3 _____ doctors need to be caring and sensitive people?

4 Why _____ Kelly so miserable today?

5 Which sports _____ Phil's sister like?

6 How much _____ they pay for their children's dance lessons?

3 ★★ Complete the questions about the ᵃsubject and the ᵇobject of each sentence.

1 ᵃEmma has eaten ᵇeggs.
a Who *'s eaten eggs*?
b What _____ ?

2 ᵃLawrence and Lucy are living in ᵇLondon.
a Who _____ ?
b Where _____ ?

3 ᵃRay reads ᵇbiography books.
a Who _____ ?
b What _____ ?

4 ᵃCharles has chosen ᵇchips for lunch.
a Who _____ ?
b What _____ ?

5 ᵃHelen is helping ᵇHarry.
a Who _____ ?
b Who _____ ?

6 ᵃFreddie feels ᵇfantastic.
a Who _____ ?
b How _____ ?

4 ★★ Write questions for the underlined parts of the answers.

What is he playing?
He's playing chess.

1 _____ ?
James is watching *The Da Vinci Code*.

2 _____ ?
Sandra follows Natalie Portman on Twitter.

3 _____ ?
Oscar has bought a new DVD.

4 _____ ?
I have visited Edinburgh and London.

5 _____ ?
Basketball is my brother's favourite sport.

5 ★★★ Complete the questions in the dialogues.

1 S: Who *loves writing*?
P: My brother loves writing.
S: What ¹_____ ?
P: He's writing a short story now.
S: Why ²_____ ?
P: He's writing it because he wants to win a competition at school.
S: Do ³_____ ?
P: Yes, I like writing.
S: Have ⁴_____ ?
P: No, I haven't written a story for the competition.

2 P: What ⁵_____ ?
S: I'm baking a cake.
P: Why ⁶_____ ?
S: It's brown because it's a chocolate cake.
P: Have ⁷_____ ?
S: No, I haven't baked a cake before.
P: Do ⁸_____ ?
S: No, I don't want any help. Thank you.

6 Write questions for the underlined parts of the answers.

Who usually cleans the bathroom at the weekend?
Dad usually cleans the bathroom at the weekend.

1 _____ ?
The girls are cooking mushroom soup.

2 _____ ?
Dean has brought his new guitar.

3 _____ ?
Michelle has forgotten to close the door.

4 _____ ?
Nicola is doing her homework.

5 _____ ?
Craig wants a motorbike.

6 _____ ?
People are listening to the band.

/6

GRAMMAR: Train and Try Again page 144

1.3 Word building • voluntary work • -ive, -ative, -able, -ing

1 Choose the correct words to complete the interview with two volunteers, Karen and Martin.

Extract from Students' Book recording 🔊 1.9

I: What sort of people volunteer?

K: ¹Fantastic / Fantasy people! No. Um, volunteers are ²care / caring people. Of course, a lot of people are […], but volunteers are more likely to do something about it.

I: So why do you do this ³voluntary / volunteer work?

M: I am ⁴passionate / passion about the environment, and I'm interested in ⁵responsible / responsibility farming. I believe that organic farming is very important for the future. I also like working in a team. I learn important life skills and I'm more ⁶confidence / confident than before. Also, I want to study farming and agriculture, so this is good experience.

I: What about you, Karen?

K: Well, there are problems in my community and I want to help.

2 Complete the sentences with the correct words in capitals.

1 FANTASY / FANTASTIC
a This book is _____ . It's the best thing I've ever read.
b Marcus loves _____ books. He's read The Lord of the Rings four times!

2 CARE / CARING
a I can pay for child _____ for my baby daughter now that I have a job.
b My sister is a very _____ person. When I'm feeling sad or ill, she's always really kind to me.

3 VOLUNTARY / VOLUNTEER
a Janet has decided to become a _____ for a charity that helps children in Africa.
b I'm afraid we don't pay you. It's all _____ work.

4 PASSIONATE / PASSION
a I have a real _____ for politics. I'm thinking of joining the Green Party.
b Arthur is very _____ about music. He's got over 600 CDs and often goes to concerts.

5 RESPONSIBLE / RESPONSIBILITY
a It's not my _____ to clean your room. It is your room!
b Who is _____ for that noise? Please, be quiet.

6 CONFIDENT / CONFIDENCE
a Morris isn't a very _____ child, so try to be very positive about his homework.
b People that have too much _____ can be difficult to work with.

REMEMBER THIS

We often form adjectives with suffixes:
care + **-ing** = caring, passion + **-ate** = passionate.

3 Read REMEMBER THIS. Choose the correct adjectives. Use a dictionary if necessary.

Many people find Steve Jobs' life and work ¹inspire / inspiring / inspiration. His ideas to change the world were ²admirable / admire / admiring.

VOCABULARY PRACTICE | Voluntary work

4 Look at the vocabulary in lesson 1.3 in the Students' Book. Complete the sentences with the correct word or phrase from the box.

developing country   farm   hospital   library
nursery   old people's home   prison   soup kitchen

I've decided I want to work in a(n) library because I love books so much.
1 Tim's mother is a volunteer in a local _____ . She doesn't get paid, but she likes helping the homeless people who eat there.
2 Ella's grandfather lives in a(n) _____ because he's 87 years old and can't do everyday things like cooking and washing by himself.
3 I'm learning to be a doctor and part of my course is in a real _____ where I can watch people with experience.
4 Have you ever been in a(n) _____ ? Yes, I have. I visited Alcatraz when I was in San Francisco in the States.
5 James and Amanda met when they were at a(n) _____ and then they went to the same school. They're both 17 and best friends now.
6 Helen grew up on a large _____ where her family had lots of sheep and cows.
7 In a(n) _____ , many people are poor and do not have enough food or water.

WORD STORE 1D | -ive, -ative, -able, -ing

5 Complete the sentences with the correct forms of the words from the box.

act   adapt   communicate
imagine   inspire   protect

I've decided I need to be more active, so I'm going to join the school basketball team.
1 Mario is very _____ – you can ask him to do anything and he always does it well.
2 Michal is _____ , so why don't we ask him to create the new charity event?
3 Lucy isn't very _____ , so it's not easy to get her to share her opinions.
4 Parents shouldn't be too _____ of teenagers. Young people need to become independent.
5 This biography of Nelson Mandela is extremely _____ . You should read it!

7

READING

1.4

Classroom psychology • verbs & nouns • verb + preposition

1 **Read the text quickly and choose the best title.**

1 Where you sit is how you feel ☐
2 Where you sit is where you are ☐
3 Where you sit is how you fit ☐

HOME | ARTICLES | FORUM | CONTACT

Today's hot article

1___ For more than 70 years, psychologists and teachers have studied the link between the place where students <u>choose</u> to sit in class and what they are like as people and learners. Where do you usually decide to sit? Have you ever really thought about the reasons for your <u>decision</u>?

I At the back
People often think that students who sit at the back are lazy. But is this really true? Well, some researchers say it is not. In fact, shy students often choose the back row because it is far away from the teacher and they don't want to answer questions or be involved* in discussions. At the back, students probably won't speak much, but in big classrooms, it can be hard to see the whiteboard and hear what the teacher is saying. **2**___ . For students with poor <u>sight</u> or <u>hearing</u>, a seat at the back of the classroom is definitely not a good choice.

II On one side
Students who sit on one side of the class, are normally interested in lessons, but they like watching and listening rather than joining in. These students are usually also very good at taking notes. **3**___ . On the sides of the classroom, you will generally find modest* and thoughtful people. These people usually get good marks at school and are keen* on learning.

III In the middle
Do you sit in the middle of the classroom? Yes? Then the statistics say you probably like your teacher. **4**___ Caring, outgoing and cheerful people usually sit in the middle. They are normally serious about learning and feel disappointed* with low marks in tests and exams.

IV At the front
Are you passionate about <u>knowledge</u>? Do you like being in control? Are you worried about missing important information in lessons? Yes? Then you probably sit right at the front of the class. Students at the front usually want to <u>discuss</u> things with the teacher and are often very enthusiastic about school. They want to be in the best place to see and hear everything the teacher does and says. The only problem with sitting at the front is that it can be difficult to see and hear what other students do and say in class. **5**___

We need YOUR opinion. Tell us what you think of this article. Add your comments below.

GLOSSARY

involved (adj) – someone who is involved in an activity or event gives it a lot of time, attention
modest (adj) – someone who is modest doesn't like talking about their abilities, skills, success, talents, etc.

keen (adj) – someone who is keen on something is very interested in it or enjoys doing it very much
disappointed (adj) – unhappy because something you hoped for did not happen, or because someone or something was not as good as you expected

2 Read the text. Match sentences A–F with gaps 1–5. There is one extra sentence.

A You probably also have a good relationship with your classmates.

B This could be the reason why students who sit here often get lower marks in tests and exams.

C So, if you really want to hear what everyone says in class, choose a different place to sit.

D Research suggests that the chair you choose in the classroom says a lot about you and your personality.

E This means it's a good idea to sit in a different place every day.

F Next time you miss a lesson, borrow notes from someone who sits here.

3 Read the text again. Match questions 1–6 with the correct part of the text I–IV.

In which part of the text do you learn …

1 where in the classroom you can find students who prefer thinking about what they see and hear during the lesson to discussing things? ☐

2 why those who would rather not respond to questions usually look for a place far from the whiteboard? ☐

3 where to find students who are positive about the person they learn mostly from? ☐

4 where in the classroom you should look for someone who has detailed written information on what the lesson was about? ☐

5 where in the classroom it could be hard to hear what the classmates say during the lesson? ☐

6 where you can find students who don't always have good results when the teacher checks what they learnt in the lessons? ☐

4 Complete the table with underlined nouns and verbs from the text.

Verb	Noun
choose	choice
1 know	_____
2 _____	discussion
3 see	_____
4 hear	_____
5 decide	_____

5 Complete the sentences with words from Exercise 4. Change the form of the verbs if necessary.

Sorry? What did you say? Could you repeat that please? My _hearing_ is terrible these days.

1 When Ollie takes Helen out for dinner, she always _____ the most expensive thing on the menu.

2 Stevie Wonder, the famous soul singer, is blind. He lost his _____ when he was a baby.

3 Peter is very wise. He really _____ a lot of things.

4 Today in class we had an interesting _____ about politics.

5 We can't _____ if we like Kevin's new haircut or not. It is certainly very … different.

When you learn a new word, e.g. a verb, look in a dictionary and see if you can also learn another form of the word, e.g. a noun or an adjective. They often look similar and because of that are easy to remember, e.g _feel – feelings._

A Check the noun forms of the adjectives in a dictionary.

popular = _popularity_
1 polite = _____
2 sensitive = _____
3 honest = _____
4 lazy = _____

B Complete the sentences with words from Exercise A. The first three letters are given.

Everyone likes Mrs Jackson. She's a very **pop**_ular_ teacher.

1 **Pol**_____ is very important when you meet new people.

2 Be careful what you say to Rachel. She's very **sen**_____ about her appearance.

3 What makes a good friend? Well, **hon**_____ is very important.

4 I think **laz**_____ is a very bad thing. Everybody should work hard.

WORD STORE 1D | Verb + preposition

6 Choose the correct prepositions.

1 Lazy people do not believe _in / on / about_ working hard.

2 I'm trying to focus _at / with / on_ my homework. Please be quiet.

3 It's a good idea not to worry _on / about / in_ your exam. Study hard and you will be fine.

4 How do you deal _in / at / with_ your work and study at the same time?

5 Janice doesn't like to depend _on / from / with_ anybody. She's very independent.

6 I prefer to connect _on / at / with_ friends by meeting them, not through social media.

7 Pauline listens _at / on / to_ music on her way to school every morning.

8 Oliver really cares _on / about / with_ his friends. He's always kind and generous to them.

9 Are you still thinking _at / on / about_ the dress in the shop window?

GRAMMAR

Verb + -ing form
or verb + to infinitive

SHOW WHAT YOU KNOW

1 Choose the correct answers A–C.

1 We ___ town on Saturday afternoons. We hate shopping when it's busy.
   A avoid   B miss   C decide

2 I ___ a burger, medium fries and a chocolate milkshake, please.
   A like   B 'd like   C love

3 They usually eat in the most expensive restaurants, but we ___ it. We don't have enough money.
   A don't mind   B enjoy   C can't afford

4 My little brother ___ that he's riding a motorbike. He makes motorbike noises and runs around the house.
   A enjoys   B pretends   C spends time

5 Dad still goes running in the winter, but Mum ___ to. She won't go because it's too cold.
   A prefers   B refuses   C agrees

6 I don't know how I'll ___ to finish all this homework before school on Monday, but I'll try.
   A hope   B consider   C manage

2 ★ Choose the correct forms.

1 Christopher doesn't mind *to pay* / *paying* for English lessons. He goes on holiday to England every year.

2 Amy avoids *to sunbathe* / *sunbathing*. She has blonde hair and very fair skin.

3 Do you want *to go* / *going* camping at the weekend? The weather forecast is good.

4 Marco and his mum choose *flying* / *to fly* when they visit their family in Italy.

5 Carly pretends *to be* / *being* cheerful when she's away, but I really think she misses home.

6 Do we really need *to take* / *taking* four big bags with us? We are only going away for three days.

3 ★ ★ Complete the sentences with the *-ing* form or the *to* infinitive of the verbs in capitals.

1 **SHOP**
   I don't like *shopping* with my dad. He hates
   ᵃ_____ and I refuse ᵇ_____ with him.

2 **SWIM**
   Lola loves ᵃ_____ . Yesterday, she managed
   ᵇ_____ 500 metres. Next weekend, she hopes
   ᶜ_____ a full kilometre.

3 **BUY**
   Can you afford ᵃ_____ this expensive coat?
   You should consider ᵇ_____ a cheaper one.
   You need to save money.

4 **MEET**
   Simon enjoys ᵃ_____ his friends at the skate park. This weekend they've agreed ᵇ_____ at the skate shop because he wants to buy new wheels for his board.

4 ★ ★ ★ Complete the forum post with the -ing form or the to infinitive of the verbs from the box. There are two extra words.

> cook   eat   find   ~~live~~   miss
> see   shop   write   visit

Are you a foreigner living in Estonia? Tell us what you think about living here and what you miss from home.

Araya Estonia writes:

My family comes from Thailand, but we live in Tallin because my dad works for an Estonian electronics company. I like *living* in Estonia, but I'm not keen on the food.
I miss ¹_____ for fresh food in the markets in Bangkok. Luckily, my mum is always busy in the kitchen. She spends a lot of time ²_____ our favourite Thai meals. Unfortunately, she can't always manage ³_____ the right ingredients, and we can't afford ⁴_____ Thailand every time we do our shopping! Anyway, I'm happy to say that there are always chillies in the shops in Estonia. My dad won't consider ⁵_____ a meal without chillies! Are there any other Thai teenagers out there? Would you like ⁶_____ to me and tell me what you miss about Thailand? I promise to reply.

SHOW WHAT YOU'VE LEARNT

5 Complete the sentences with the words in brackets in the correct form. Do not change the order of the words. You may need to add words. Use no more than six words.

Marie's grandparents are rich – they can *afford to have a flat* (afford / have / flat) in the centre of Paris and a house in southern Provence.

1 Why _____ he / refuse / use) social media? Everyone is on Facebook except him!

2 Giulia _____ (miss / meet) her friend, Stefano, at the café near their secondary school. They've lost contact with each other.

3 Maria usually _____ (spend / lot / time / talk) on the phone.

4 Felix and Eva _____ (avoid / talk) politics – they prefer discussing other topics.

5 _____ (you / mind / open) the window for a while? It's really hot in here.

6 My sister _____ (not / stand / clean / window). She says it's dead boring.

/6

GRAMMAR: Train and Try Again page 144

USE OF ENGLISH

1.6

so and such

1 ★ Choose the correct words.

1 There are eight people living in my house: it's *so / such* crowded!
2 My school is *so / such* a long way from my house.
3 Buses and trains are *so / such* expensive in the UK.
4 This car is really large for *so / such* a small family.
5 We were *so / such* lazy that we stayed home and watched TV.
6 My baby brother is very small, but he makes *so / such* a lot of noise.

2 ★ ★ Complete the sentences with *so, such* or *such a/an.*

My brother is *so* serious. He never laughs.

1 Gabby is _____ hard-working person. She's always busy.
2 I love my uncle Greg. He tells us _____ funny and imaginative stories.
3 Peter is _____ shy. He doesn't say very much and doesn't like going to parties.
4 My grandparents are _____ old that we help them cook and clean.
5 We had _____ fun at the park yesterday. We're going again today.
6 It was _____ interesting class and the teacher was very cheerful.
7 You have _____ beautiful furniture in your house. I really love the green sofa.
8 Why is it _____ hot in here? Can we open a window, please?

3 ★ ★ Choose the correct answers A–C.

Why I **love** living at home

Living with your parents really isn't ¹___ bad thing. Firstly, living at home is inexpensive. I have a friend who lives in a flat and it costs ²___ money that it's hard to believe! Another problem is that she lives ³___ long way from the city centre and our school. She has to travel every day for over one hour. But living with amazing people is the most important thing for me. My parents are ⁴___ caring and generous. They help me with my homework, they give me advice and they often drive me places in the car. My brother is really great too! He's funny, sensitive and enthusiastic about everything. He's my best friend. At weekends we all play games and just focus on having fun and spending time together as a family. I feel ⁵___ lucky to live at home and have ⁶___ positive people close to me.

1 A so   B such   C such a
2 A so many   B so much   C such a
3 A such   B such a   C so
4 A such   B so   C such a
5 A so   B such   C such a
6 A so   B so much   C so many

4 ★ ★ ★ Complete the sentences with one word in each gap. In one sentence, you don't need to add a word.

Ann: It's *such* a beautiful day! Let's go to the beach.
Liz: That's an excellent idea. We can have a picnic!
1 Mum: There are such ___ elegant suits in this shop. I can't decide which one to buy for Dad.
Daughter: I prefer the dark blue suit. That one looks really nice.
2 Jill: Amanda is such ___ sensible girl. She never does anything silly or irresponsible.
Tina: Yes, and she's wise too.
3 Tom: It's really loud. Why are there so ___ children in the cinema?
Bill: I think the new *Madagascar* film starts today.
4 Ella: This song is ___ energetic that I just want to dance here and now. Listen to it.
Matt: Sorry. I don't really like this kind of music.
5 Eva: Ben is such ___ unsociable guy. Do you think he's miserable?
Jess: I don't know. Maybe he's just shy.

5 ★ ★ ★ Complete the second sentence so it has a similar meaning to the first. Use between three and five words, including the word in capitals.

The weather is so beautiful that I want to go swimming in the sea. **IS**
It *is such beautiful weather* that I want to go swimming in the sea.

1 I'm bored because of my work and I want to find a new job. **BORING**
My _____ that I want to find a new job.
2 John and Sandra are so insensitive that I'm surprised they have any friends. **AN**
I'm surprised John and Sandra have any friends because _____ couple.
3 I got such negative results in the test. I don't want to try again. **THAT**
The test _____ don't want to try again.
4 Jack was disappointed with Abby's answer. She's normally such a generous person. **SO**
Abby _____ that Jack was disappointed with her answer.
5 You can't trust Mike because he is so dishonest. **PERSON**
Mike _____ that you can't trust him.
6 These hoodies were really inexpensive, so I bought two. **CHEAP**
These hoodies _____ that I bought two.

11

WRITING

1.7

A personal email/letter

1 Choose the correct words to complete the tips on writing personal emails.

1 Start the email with a *formal* / *friendly* greeting, e.g. *Dear Mark* or *Hi Ruby*.
2 Use *full forms* / *contractions*, e.g. I am I'm.
3 It's *OK* / *not OK* to use emoticons ☺ and abbreviations, e.g. *Bye for now = Bye4now*.
4 It's a *good* / *bad* idea to ask some questions if you want a reply.
5 Finish the email with a friendly goodbye such as *Yours sincerely* / *Cheers*.

2 Put the words in order to make phrases.

Becky / Hi *Hi Becky*

1 writing / I'm / about / to / tell / you / more / bit / a / myself.

_____

2 now. / I / going / be / must

_____

3 hearing / to / forward / from / you. / Looking

_____

4 U / month. / C / next

_____

5 you / your / are / doing? / How / and / family

_____

6 was / hear / to / good / It / from / you.

_____

7 hello / Say / your / family. / to

_____

3 Choose the correct phrase 1–7 from Exercise 2 to replace the underlined formal phrases a–g in the email.

Dear Ms Jones, *Hi Becky*

ᵃI enjoyed reading your recent email. _____
ᵇI hope you and your family are very well. _____
I'm excited ¹*about* / *for* / *at* your visit next month, and ᶜI am writing to give you some information about myself and my life. _____

I'm sixteen and I live with my parents in Kraków. I'm not crazy ²*at* / *to* / *about* living here but it's OK.

I go to school in the city and I'm involved ³*in* / *with* / *on* lots of after-school activities. I'm not keen ⁴*at* / *on* / *to* studying, but I'm worried ⁵*for* / *at* / *about* my exams – I don't want Dad to be disappointed ⁶*on* / *with* / *at* me, so I work hard. Do you like school?

Sorry it's only a short email, but ᵈI need to stop writing now. _____ ᵉPlease give my best wishes to your family. _____ ᶠI look forward to receiving a reply from you soon. _____ ᵍI will see you next month.

_____

Kamila

4 Read the email again and choose the correct prepositions.

5 Complete the sentences with the missing prepositions.

I'm really bad <u>at</u> cooking but I am looking forward to trying some Spanish food.

1 I hear that you're good _____ chess. Maybe you can teach me how to play when I visit you?

2 Are you serious _____ taking me to the Louvre? I'd really love to go.

3 My sister is completely obsessed _____ motorbikes. Do you like them too?

4 I believe that you're mad _____ art. Who's your favourite artist?

5 Did you know that I'm afraid _____ dogs? You don't have one, do you?

6 Do you like tennis? Unfortunately, I'm useless _____ all sports.

7 Well, I was disappointed _____ the street art festival last year. I hope this year it will be different.

8 I'm not really keen _____ motor racing but of course we can watch the racing show if you want.

9 Are you involved _____ any sports club? Could I go to training with you when I come?

6 Find and correct the mistakes.

What do you enjoy to do?

What do you enjoy doing? `4`

A Bye 5 now.
_____ ☐

B I write to tell you about the plans for Saturday.
_____ ☐

C How are you going?
_____ ☐

D Hay Steven,
_____ ☐

E Waiting forward to hearing from you soon.
_____ ☐

7 Put the sentences in Exercise 6 in the order they are usually used in an email.

8 Read the task below. Then read the email and complete the questions with the missing question words.

> You have received an email from your English-speaking friend. Read the excerpt below.
>
> *Thanks for inviting me to visit you next month. I'm really excited about coming to Spain for the first time. Please tell me more about what sort of things you do there in your free time. Do you like going to the cinema or doing sports? What places do you like visiting with your friends?*
>
> **Write an email with a reply. Include and develop these points:**
>
> - Say how you feel about your friend visiting you.
> - Tell him/her about some of the things you do in your free time.
> - Write about some of the places you visit with your friends.
> - Ask about your friend's interests.

Hi Barry,

A _____ are you? I'm really excited about your visit. I'd love ¹*to tell* / *telling* you about what I spend my free time ²*to do* / *doing* and the places I like visiting.

As you know, I'm keen on ³*do* / *doing* sports. I hope you don't mind ⁴*to wake* / *waking* up early to go running ☺.
B _____ you like sports? Of course, I also enjoy ⁵*to go* / *going* to the cinema but I refuse ⁶*to watch* / *watching* romantic films! **C** _____ kind of films do you like? **D** _____ you have a favourite film?

E _____ you ever heard of la Barceloneta? I hope ⁷*to take* / *taking* you there with my friends. I'm sure we'll have fun.

All the best,

Miguel

9 Read the email again. Choose the correct forms of the verbs.

10 Some family friends from the UK and their teenage son are coming to stay with you and your family this summer. You would like to learn something about him before their visit. Write a personal email to him giving some information about yourself. Include and develop these points:

- Introduce yourself and say why you are writing.
- Tell him some basic information about yourself (age, the place where you live, etc.)
- Tell him about your hobbies.
- Ask him about his interests.

Finished? Always check your writing. Can you tick √ everything on this list?

In my personal email:

• I have started with a friendly greeting e.g. *Dear Nick* or *Hi Kate*.	☐
• the first paragraph says why I am writing.	☐
• the second paragraph gives some basic information about me (age, home town, etc.).	☐
• I have included some information about my likes/dislikes/hobbies, etc.	☐
• I have included some questions to show that I want a reply.	☐
• I have used contractions (e.g. *I'm* / *aren't* / *that's*).	☐
• I have perhaps used some emoticons ☺ and abbreviations (*info* / *CU* / *gr8*), but not too many!	☐
• I have finished with a friendly goodbye, e.g. *CU (= See you) soon* / *next week* / *in a few months*.	☐
• I have checked my spelling and punctuation.	☐
• My text is neat and clear.	☐

SPEAKING

Showing interest

1 Translate the phrases into your own language.

SPEAKING BANK

Showing interest

A: I've got loads of friends
and they want to meet you.   _____

B: Really? That's cool!   _____

A: I've just got one sister.   _____
She's a model.   _____

B: Is she?

A: She's training to be a pilot.   _____

B: Wow, that's interesting!   _____

Saying you are similar

A: I love travelling and meeting   _____
new people.

B: Me too.   _____

A: I don't really like rock or   _____
heavy metal.

B: Me neither.   _____

Saying you are different

A: I'm not very keen on tea.

B: Really? I love it.   _____

A: I don't like travelling.   _____

B: Don't you? Oh, I do!   _____

A: I play the violin.   _____

B: Do you? Right ...   _____

2 Mark and Diane are at a music festival. They meet in a queue to buy a T-shirt. Complete their conversation with expressions from the bank.

D: Excuse me. Do you know how much the T-shirts cost?

M: Er ... no ... I mean ... yes ... I ... I think the white ones are £10 and the coloured ones £15. That's what it says on the sign.

D: Oh yeah! You're right. I didn't see the sign. Well, I want a blue one.

M: Oh ... er ... m<u>e</u> t<u>oo</u>. I don't like white.

D: Ha! ¹M_____ n_____ . I'm Diane by the way.

M: Er ... hi. I'm Mark.

D: What do you think of the festival? I love it. I saw six bands yesterday. My friend is here too. Somewhere!

M: Oh ... right ... ²I_____ s_____ ?

D: Yeah. She's a DJ. She's playing tonight at 10 o'clock, in tent number 4.

M: ³R_____ ?... er ... W_____ , that's i_____ .

D: Yeah. She plays techno mostly and a bit of house.

M: Oh right. I see. Well, I ... er ... don't really like techno.

D: ⁴R_____ ? I l_____ it . I dance to any kind of music really.

M: Oh ... er ... That's ⁵c_____ . Actually, I don't dance.

D: ⁶D_____ y_____ ? Oh, I d_____ . I want to be a professional dancer one day. So, what do you do when everyone is dancing then?

M: Er ... well ... I stand at the back and listen to the music. I'm quite shy really.

D: Are you? ⁷R_____ ... Well ... er ... oh, look there's my friend!

M: What about your T-shirt?

D: Er ... yes, that's my friend over there. Time to go ...

M: Oh, er ... OK. Bye then.

3 Put the words in order to make phrases. Then complete the conversations. There is one extra phrase in each group.

A   she? / Hasn't
       too / Me
       ~~That's / Really? / cool~~

Ryan: My sister is having a baby in December.

Emma: *Really? That's cool*. My sister hasn't got any children yet.

Ryan: _____ Well, maybe one day. I'm really looking forward to being an uncle.

B   you? / Right ... / Do
       interesting / that's / Wow
       you? / Can't

Karen: My parents are keen on music. Dad plays the piano and Mum is a great singer.

Ken: ¹_____ . I would like to hear them play. Unfortunately, I don't play any instruments and I can't sing.

Karen: ²_____ Well, don't worry, I'm not musical at all. I think my parents are a bit disappointed with me.

C   love / Really? / it / I
       Do / Right / you?
       too / Me

Gita: It's getting cold again. This morning there was ice on our car. I hate the winter.

Miko: ¹_____ . Everything looks so beautiful in the winter. I hope it snows soon. I love building snowmen.

Gita: ²_____ .... I prefer to stay inside and watch films.

D   don't / I / Oh / do / you?
       too / Me
       they? / Are

Phil: I've finally saved enough money and this weekend I'm buying a new phone.

Paul: ¹_____ . Shall we go to the shops together?

Phil: Sure. How much have you got to spend?

Paul: Er ... well ... my parents are paying for it.

Phil: ²_____ Lucky you.

1 In pairs, ask and answer the questions.

PART 1

Talk about the environment.
1 What is your dream birthday meal?
2 Would you prefer to work long hours in a job you enjoy or short hours in a job you hate? Why?
3 Is there an extreme sport you would like to try? Why?
4 What can tourists do and see in the area where you live?
5 How is the weather changing? Should we try to stop it from changing? How?

PART 2

Talk about personalities.
1 What adjectives can you use to describe yourself? Why?
2 When you meet new people, are you outgoing or shy? Why?
3 What sort of a personality should a good teacher have?
4 Which person in your family do you admire because of their personality? Why?
5 How important are clothes for your identity? Why?

2 Look at the photos of people doing voluntary work.

PART 1

Take turns to describe the photos.

A

B

PART 2

In pairs, ask and answer the questions about the photos.

Student A's photo
1 What is the woman with short hair doing?
2 How can you describe the woman's personality?
3 How are the volunteers helping the people standing opposite them?
4 What skills do the volunteers need to do this work?
5 Would you like to do this voluntary work? Why?/Why not?

Student B's photo
1 What are the young people in this photo doing?
2 How are they helping the elderly people?
3 Why do you think this is useful for the elderly people?
4 What skills do you need to do this sort of voluntary work?
5 Would you like to do this voluntary work? Why?/Why not?

3 Read the instructions on your card. In pairs, take turns to role-play the conversation.

Student A

You are getting to know Student B, an exchange student at your school. Ask questions and find ways you are similar/different.

- Introduce yourself and ask Student B what his/her favourite hobby is.
- Show interest. Say if you are similar or different. Ask Student B about his/her personality.
- Say if you are similar or different. Ask Student B if he/she is from Generation Z.
- Say if you are similar or different. Ask Student B if he/she prefers films, music or books.
- Say if you are similar or different. Summarise ways that you're similar to Student B.
- End the conversation.

Student B

You are an exchange student visiting Student A's school. Listen, answer and find ways you are similar/different.

- Tell Student A about your favourite hobby.
- Describe your personality.
- Say if you are from Generation Z.
- Tell Student A if you prefer films, music or books.
- Summarise ways that you're different to Student A.

VOCABULARY AND GRAMMAR

1 Choose the negative adjective in each group.

	honest	(selfish)	funny	relaxed
1	caring	cheerful	mean	hard-working
2	unpopular	outgoing	sensible	sociable
3	interesting	silly	generous	independent
4	responsible	adventurous	lazy	polite
5	wise	sensitive	popular	dishonest

/5

2 Complete the sentences with the correct words. The first and last letters are given.

It's hard to talk to Brian because he's so **b**_orin_**g**. I want to sleep when I speak to him.

1 I'll help you with your homework after I **d**_____**l** with this logic problem.
2 John is **s**_____**h** and doesn't like to share anything.
3 James is very **a**_____**e**. He likes swimming, running and playing basketball.
4 Amanda is extremely **i**_____**t** and likes working alone.
5 Jen's dad is a very **c**_____**e** person. He finds it easy to speak to anybody.

/5

3 Complete the sentences with the correct words. The number of letters is given in brackets.

Annette worked on a fruit _farm_ (4) last summer. She earned good money picking apples all day.

1 There are two _____ (9) near my flat, so you can hear the sound of young children playing throughout the whole day.
2 Lia still borrows books from _____ (9). I only read books on my e-reader.
3 James helps serve the food in a soup _____ (7) at weekends. Do you do any voluntary work?
4 Did you know that in most developing _____ (9), public schools are not free? That means parents need to pay for their children's education.
5 People in the UK often put their parents or grandparents into an old people's _____ (4). It's not very common to do this in my country.

/5

4 Choose the correct answers A–C.

___ you ever tried yoga?
A Do   (B) Have   C Are

1 Do they ___ their car every weekend?
   A washing   B washes   C wash
2 Which singer ___ a number one hit?
   A have never had   B is never having
   C has never had
3 ___ is he talking to on the phone?
   A Who   B What   C What time
4 ___ do you usually clean your room?
   A Who   B When   C What
5 What TV series ___ at the moment?
   A do you watch   B are you watching
   C have you watched

/5

5 Complete the sentences with the -ing form or the to infinitive of the verbs in brackets.

My sister has decided _to celebrate_ (celebrate) her birthday after her exams.

1 Kelly would like _____ (learn) how to play the violin.
2 Sam doesn't enjoy _____ (play) football when it's cold and rainy.
3 Will you manage _____ (carry) the shopping on your own?
4 Have you considered _____ (study) English at university?
5 Jeanette's dad sometimes drives her to school, but really, she prefers _____ (walk).

/5

6 Choose the correct answers A–C.

JOIN THE POLICE

Would you like to _A_ something to help society and the community you live in?

Have you ever ¹___ about a career in the police?

Police work is challenging – our officers are often in difficult situations and accept ²___ for their actions. Our national police force wants ³___ crime and we need ⁴___ people to help us do this. Choose ⁵___ for the police and help make your town a safe place to live.

	A	B	C
	(A) do	B doing	C done
1	A think	B thinking	C thought
2	A responsible	B responsibility	C irresponsible
3	A stop	B to stop	C stopping
4	A unadventurous	B boring	C adaptable
5	A to work	B working	C works

/5

Total   /30

7 Choose the correct answers A–C.

Who ___ ?
A does Janet enjoy to meet?
(B) does Janet enjoy meeting?
C Janet enjoys meeting?

1 Patrick is ___ person that it's impossible to be friends with him.
A so irresponsible
B such irresponsible
C such an irresponsible

2 Peter, ___ Arthur yet? He plays on my football team.
A did you meet
B are you meeting
C have you met

3 I haven't agreed ___ shopping with you.
A to going
B to go
C going

4 That music sounds interesting. ___
A What are you listening to?
B What do you listen to?
C What have you listened to?

5 I don't know anything about his hobbies. What ___
A does James like?
B is James like?
C likes James?

/5

8 Choose the correct answers A–C to replace the underlined part of the sentence.

Would Katie like to come to my party?
(A) Does Katie want to come
B Is Katie coming
C Does Katie like coming

1 What is your cousin Jon like?
A What things does your cousin Jon like?
B What kind of person is your cousin Jon?
C What is your cousin Jon's appearance?

2 I can't afford to buy this hoodie.
A I don't have enough money to buy
B I don't mind paying for
C I am considering not buying

3 I'd prefer to order pizza for lunch.
A I want to order
B I hope to order
C I agree to order

4 What sports are you passionate about?
A don't you mind doing?
B do you choose to do?
C do you really enjoy doing?

5 Does this tie belong to Paul?
A Is this Paul's tie?
B Does Paul have a tie?
C Does this look like Paul's tie?

/5

9 Complete each pair of sentences with the same answer A–C.

Which of your friends do you depend ___ for good advice?
How can you focus ___ your work with that loud noise outside?
A at   B from   (C) on

1 I'm not going to take this job because I ___ to work on Sundays.
James is such a polite person that he would never ___ to help you.
A refuse   B want   C avoid

2 There are ___ many people in here. I can't move my arms.
Does it take ___ much time to become a doctor?
A so   B such   C such a

3 ___ are you visiting in London?
___ has broken my new laptop?
A What   B Why   C Who

4 What kind of music ___ she like?
Why ___ Jane look so miserable?
A is   B does   C has

5 Dan cares ___ what people say about him.
Why are Jill's parents so worried ___ her?
A with   B for   C about

/5

10 Complete the text with the correct word.

Are you mad _about_ chess? Yes? Great!
Then you are welcome to come to Charlie's Chess Club and play a game or two with us!

We have people here who are very serious players and can't ¹_____ losing, but also lots of people who just like playing for fun. We are sure you will find the perfect chess partner to connect ²_____ at your level.

Are you good at chess? No? Ha, me neither! But always remember, chess is ³_____ a fun game and you can choose ⁴_____ have free lessons with one of our very friendly club members! We believe ⁵_____ having a good time and developing your chess skills.

We hope to see you soon!

/5

Total /20

2 Science and technology

VOCABULARY

Online • phones and computers • word building • collocations

REMEMBER THIS

Log on and *log in* both mean start using a computer system or website (you often have to enter a username and password to do this, but not always).
Their antonyms are *log off* and *log out*.

SHOW WHAT YOU KNOW

1 Complete the sentences with the correct form of the verbs from the box.

(download   follow   go   post   update   visit)

How do I *post* this photograph of us on social media?

1 I don't understand why so many people _____ celebrities on Twitter.

2 Akito _____ online the moment she wakes up to check her social media messages.

3 I've never _____ this website before. It has some excellent information on it!

4 It's very important to _____ your social media profile. Then everybody has the latest information about you.

5 Dean is the only person I know that still buys CDs. Most people _____ music on computers now.

WORD STORE 2A | Phones and computers

2 Complete the texts with compound nouns. The first and last letters are given.

REMEMBER BETTER

When you learn phrasal verbs, check in the dictionary or online and find the antonym. We often (but not always) we use the opposite preposition, e.g
switch on ≠ switch off.

A   Write the opposites. Use a dictionary if necessary.

scroll up   ≠ *scroll down*
1 turn up (the volume) ≠ _____
2 turn on   ≠ _____
3 log on   ≠ _____

B   Complete the sentences with phrasal verbs from Exercise A.

The information you need is at the bottom of the webpage. You need to *scroll down*.

1 I can't study with that loud music playing. Please will you _____ the volume.

2 Use your username and password to _____ to the website.

3 _____ the TV before you go to bed.

@ **COMPUCLEAN**, we clean all kinds of computers including **d**e**s**k**to**p **c**omputer**s** and **¹l**_____**s**. Call us now on 073 123 345 456 for more information.

---

howitworks.com – Internet searches

To use the Internet you need to have a **⁵w**_____ **b b**_____**r**. Then, you can use the touch screen on your phone or the **⁶k**_____**d** on your computer to put a word or phrase into a **⁷s**_____**h e**_____**e** such as Google. If you have **⁸b**_____**d**, the information you are trying to find appears very quickly.

Thank you for joining **www.english4U2learn.com**, the number one website for language learners. We have sent you an email with your **²u**_____**e** and other login details. Follow the link in the email and choose a **³p**_____**d** of nine characters or more. And remember, you can use a **⁴l**_____**r p**_____**r** to print your personal daily wordlist, so you can study any time, anywhere!

---

our comments on the topic of **teenage communication**

will328 says:

Most young people do not use their phones for speaking to people. We either look for information on the Internet or we send **⁹t**_____**t m**_____**s** to family and friends.

WORD STORE 2B | Word building

3 Complete the sentences with the correct form of the words in capitals.

Charles Darwin, the world famous _biologist_, travelled to many exotic places such as the Galapagos Islands. **BIOLOGY**

1 Galileo Galilei, a famous _____ , was the first person to see the rings of Saturn. He did this using his telescope in 1610. **ASTRONOMY**

2 The famous _____ Isaac Newton was born on Christmas Day 1642. And it's not true that an apple hit him on the head. **PHYSICS**

3 Larry Page, the _____ who helped start the company Google, is now worth $44.5 billion. **COMPUTER SCIENCE**

4 The Nobel Prize is named after Alfred Nobel. He was a _____ and he is famous for making dynamite. **CHEMISTRY**

5 Euclid was a _____ and many people call him the Father of Geometry. He wrote one of the first textbooks for teaching Maths. **MATHEMATICS**

WORD STORE 2C | Collocations

4 Choose the correct verbs.

1 When you _do / make_ an experiment, it's not always a success.

2 I prefer _collecting / taking_ specimens. It's better than working in the laboratory.

3 Was it Maria Skłodowska-Curie that _invented / discovered_ radium?

4 The Scottish man, John Logie Baird, _invented / discovered_ television in 1925.

5 Please _take / do_ the important measurements this afternoon, Adam.

6 Famous scientists often _develop / observe_ important theories.

7 Do you prefer _taking / doing_ notes on a computer or a piece of paper?

8 Today we can _do / make_ research on the Internet. In the past it wasn't so easy.

9 Scientists spend a lot of time just _observing / discovering_ their experiments.

5 Choose the correct answers A–C.

1 I can't enter the website. Something is wrong. Am I using the correct ___ ?
A keyboard
B password
C text message

2 I've started using a new ___ . I type in what I'm looking for on the Internet and it finds the websites I want really quickly.
A broadband
B username
C search engine

3 Sarah spends a lot of time ___ specimens in the countryside. She truly enjoys being a biologist.
A collecting
B developing
C inventing

4 Kevin wants to be a computer ___ when he is older.
A science
B scientist
C biologist

5 Ben emailed the document to me. I made a copy of it on paper with the ___ for you.
A keyboard
B web browser
C laser printer

6 I'm busy at the moment. I'm ___ notes on this film about astronomy.
A making
B doing
C taking

7 Most people have a ___ Internet connection now because it's fast.
A web browser
B broadband
C desktop

8 I need a new ___ for my desktop computer. The 'Enter' key doesn't work.
A keyboard
B laptop
C username

9 You must be very creative to ___ something completely new and useful for people to use.
A invent
B discover
C observe

10 James' father is a(n) ___ . He develops new drugs for people who are sick.
A astronomer
B chemist
C physicist

/10

19

SHOW WHAT YOU KNOW

1 Complete the sentences with the Past Simple forms of the verbs in brackets.

1 Graeme ^a_went_ (go) online this morning and
   ^b_____ (buy) tickets for the concert.

2 Simone and Kay ^a_____ (be) very busy all
   day yesterday. They ^b_____ (not/have)
   time for a break.

3 ^a_____ (Carly/be) at the Science club last
   week?
   ^b_____ (she/give) her presentation?

4 ^a_____ (you/download) those games
   recently?
   ^b_____ (they/be) free?

2 ★ Complete the dialogue between a policeman and Steve with the Past Continuous forms of the verbs in brackets.

At the police station …

P: What _were you doing_ (do) at six o'clock on the 23rd
   of October?

S: Erm … I don't remember. I think I was at home. Yes,
   I ¹_____ (watch) TV.

P: Was anyone at home with you?

S: No, nobody. It was just me. I ²_____
   (not/work) that day.

P: I see. So nobody saw you at home at 6 p.m. that day?

S: Oh … er … yes of course. Silly me! My wife was there
   too. She ³_____ (make) dinner in the
   kitchen.

P: And what about your children?

S: Oh yeah, the kids! They ⁴_____ (do/
   homework) upstairs in their bedrooms.

P: And your mother-in-law?

S: Oh yes, of course. Er … She ⁵_____
   (stand) in the kitchen.

P: I see. So, can you explain why we have pictures of
   you waiting in your car outside the bank at 6 p.m.?

3 ★ Complete the sentences with the Past Continuous forms of the verbs in brackets.

Alexander Graham Bell _was experimenting_
(experiment) in his laboratory when he made the first
successful telephone call.

1 _____ (Archimedes/have)
   a bath when he shouted 'Eureka!'?

2 Mark Zuckerberg _____ (study)
   at Harvard University when he created Facebook.

3 _____ (Isaac Newton/sit)
   under an apple tree when he thought of his theory of
   gravity?

4 Maria Curie _____ (not/live) in
   Poland when she won her first Nobel Prize in 1903.

4 ★ ★ Choose the correct forms.

1 Sorry, I ^a*had / was having* a shower when you
   ^b*called / were calling.*

2 ^a*Did Lola stand / Was Lola standing* outside when it
   ^b*started / was starting* to rain?

3 When the car ^a*crashed / was crashing* into us, we
   ^b*waited / were waiting* at the traffic lights.

4 Fortunately, we ^a*didn't ski / weren't skiing* when the
   bad weather ^b*came / was coming.*

5 ★ ★ ★ Complete the story with the Past Simple or Past Continuous forms of the verbs in brackets.

What _were you doing_ (you/do) the last time
you ¹_____ (see) something truly
amazing? Well, fisherman and journalist Al
McGlashan ²_____ (fish) with friends in
his private boat when he ³_____ (find)
something very, very strange. At first the group of
fishermen ⁴_____ (not/know) what it was,
but when they ⁵_____ (look) closely, they
saw the body of a giant squid – almost 4 metres long!

Al got out his video camera and then another amazing
thing ⁶_____ (happen). He ⁷_____
(film) the squid when a large blue shark
⁸_____ (arrive) and began eating the dead
squid for lunch!

Al ⁹_____ (tell) an Australian newspaper
that in all his years of fishing he'd never seen
anything like it.

SHOW WHAT YOU'VE LEARNT

6 Find and correct the mistakes.

He ~~was clicking~~ on an icon and nothing happened.
clicked

1 Tom was downloading music when his computer
   was getting the virus. _____

2 Annabelle visited the zoo when she saw
   an elephant for the first time. _____

3 Grandma, were you watching television when
   Apollo 11 was landing on the moon? _____

4 They were waiting for the bus when it was starting
   to snow. _____

5 The girls were playing tennis when Helen was
   breaking her arm. _____

6 Was the computers working this morning when you
   arrived? _____

/6

GRAMMAR: Train and Try Again page 145

2.3

Science and scientists
• collocations

1 Read the extracts of interviews with two people and choose the correct answers.

1 Speaker A is *a child psychologist / a children's doctor.*
2 Speaker B is *a deep sea diver / a marine biologist.*

2 Complete the text with the correct verbs from the box. Change the form of the verb if necessary.

analyse   collect   do (x2)   explore   protect

Extract from Students' Book recording 🔊 **1.32**

A: I always want to understand why people do what they do – why do they behave that way? What are they thinking? I'm interested in how we develop from birth to the age of seven. […] I love *doing* research and ¹_____ data. When I finish my studies, I want to work in a children's hospital. […]

B: The first time I went scuba diving, I saw a little fish swimming away into the distance, and at that moment I thought 'Oh yes, that's what I want to do – I want to ²_____ oceans, ³_____ evidence about global warming and help to ⁴_____ marine life.' I love my work – I can't understand why everybody isn't ⁵_____ my job.

3 Choose the word which does <u>not</u> form a collocation. Use a dictionary if necessary.

1 **explore**   *oceans / planets / people / countries*
2 **analyse**   *chemistry / data / evidence / research*
3 **do**   *experiments / solutions / research / business*
4 **collect**   *evidence / signatures / information / science*
5 **protect**   *marine life / the environment / wildlife / biology*

4 Complete the sentences with collocations from Exercise 3.

Even simple things like not throwing rubbish in the sea help to protect *marine life*.

1 I don't like beach holidays. I prefer to explore different _____ and to visit places where tourists don't usually go.
2 The police analysed the _____ but weren't able to solve the crime.
3 My dad is travelling for work again. His company is doing _____ with a Japanese car company.
4 Emma's got a summer job with a marketing company doing _____ in a shopping centre. She has to stop shoppers and ask them a few questions.
5 Our class is collecting _____ for a petition against scientific experiments on animals.
6 The government should not build a new road here. We need to protect _____ and the natural environment in this area.

VOCABULARY PRACTICE | Science and scientists

5 Look at the vocabulary in lesson 2.3 in the Students' Book. Choose a word or phrase from each pair in the box to complete the sentences.

archaeology / an archaeologist
conservation / a conservationist
geology / a geologist   ~~linguistics / a linguist~~
marine biology / a marine biologist
psychology / a psychologist

Did you know that *a linguist* studies how languages work?

1 You must be able to swim if you want to be _____ . You will probably work in the sea a lot of the time.
2 Haley has _____ that she meets. He helps her to talk about her feelings.
3 There's an interesting course on _____ in the local youth centre. Maybe I can do it and then help people learn more about saving the planet.
4 Rafaele wants to be _____ because he's always liked looking for old things buried in the ground.
5 I don't think I'd like _____ – you often examine rocks and stones and get your clothes and hands dirty all the time.

WORD STORE 2D | Collocations

6 Complete the sentences with the missing verb in the correct form. The first letters are given.

Allan **a**nalysed the data yesterday and sent me the results this morning.

1 It's important to **c**_____ lots of data before making any hypothesis.
2 Next week, Margaret will **p**_____ her first research paper in a science journal. She's very excited.
3 Everybody is responsible for helping to **p**_____ the environment. So turn off the computer when you are not using it!
4 Dr Brown often **s**_____ hours looking at test results before he finds a problem.

READING

All about passwords • antonyms • nouns and verbs • the temperature

1 Read the text quickly and choose the best title.

1 How to create a secure and easy-to-remember password
2 How to remember all your passwords
3 How to guess someone's password

1 _____

We all know the <u>basic</u> rules for choosing good passwords and keeping them secret. Rule number one: use numbers, symbols and a good mix of letters – upper case (A, B, C) and lower case (a, b, c). Rule number two: use a <u>different</u> password for each of the devices you use or for each website you visit. Rule number three: change your passwords regularly. Rule number four: never write your passwords down. These rules sound easy to follow, right?

2 _____

Well, not really. The rules say that a secure password should look something like this: 'N0r@5%_fpO&47d1nk'. Do you think you can <u>remember</u> that? Don't forget you should have several different ones, you shouldn't write them down AND you have to change them every few weeks. Does this sound like an <u>impossible</u> task? Well, for most people, it is. So what do most of us do?

3 _____

Recently, researchers had a chance to analyse secret information about passwords. They found that many of us totally ignore the experts' advice and choose <u>simple</u>, easy to remember and extremely insecure passwords. Data shows that one out of every ten people uses '1234' as the pin number for their bank cards, and that the passwords 'welcome', '123456', 'ninja' and of course 'password', are some of the most popular choices.

Even governments choose <u>terrible</u> passwords. It seems hard to believe, but in the 1980s, the American government actually used the 'secret code' '00000000' to unlock its nuclear missiles.

4 _____

So how can we make our passwords secure and memorable*? Well, first, the length of your password is important. For a hacker with a computer that can make 1000 guesses per second, a lower case, 5-letter password like 'ftmps' takes only around 3hrs and 45 minutes to crack*. A similar password with 20 letters takes a little longer – around 6.5 thousand trillion centuries*!

5 _____

Hackers are very good at guessing when we choose symbols and numbers instead of letters. For example, the password 'M@nch3st3r' seems like a good one, but the code is actually very simple – first letter = upper case, @ = a, 3 = E. It is easy for hackers to program their computers to look out for these kinds of codes. Because the length of the password is so important, a group of words written in lower case, e.g. 'help cheese monkey swimming' is much more secure than something like 'M@nch3st3r', and probably a bit easier to remember (think of a monkey – it is shouting for help and swimming towards some cheese!).

6 _____

One day, we probably won't have to worry about all this because we won't need passwords. Some laptop computers already have fingerprint* readers. Recently, scientists in the US have designed a prototype ring for your finger that sends electricity through your skin to a touch screen to tell computers and phones who you are. For now though, we still need passwords, and if you want one that is secure and memorable, the best advice is to make it loooooooooo oooooooooooooooooooooooooong.

GLOSSARY

memorable (adj) – easy to remember
crack a code or a password (v) – work it out or solve it
century (n) – 100 years

fingerprint (n) – a mark made by the pattern of the skin on the end of your fingers

2 Read the text again. Match headings A–H with paragraphs 1–6. There are two extra headings.

A NuM83rs @nd sYmB0ls
B How to become a hacker
C No more passwords!
D Passwords for beginners
E Dangerous choices
F How they did it in the US
G How good is your memory?
H Short = bad, long = good

3 Read the text again. For questions 1–6, choose the correct answer A–D.

1 Which basic rule for passwords is <u>not</u> mentioned?
  A Use a mix of letters, numbers and symbols for passwords.
  B Use different passwords for different websites.
  C Never tell another person your password.
  D Change your passwords often.

2 The article says that most people
  A don't know how to choose a secure password.
  B use the same password for everything.
  C don't follow experts' advice when they choose a password.
  D forget passwords easily.

3 The most popular password is
  A not mentioned.
  B 'password.'
  C '1234.'
  D '00000000.'

4 In the 1980s, the US government
  A had a secure password for unlocking its nuclear missiles.
  B didn't have a password for unlocking its nuclear missiles.
  C lost the password for unlocking its nuclear missiles.
  D didn't have a secure password for unlocking its nuclear missiles.

5 The article says that hackers
  A choose passwords with symbols and numbers.
  B program their computers to look for symbols and numbers in passwords.
  C choose lower case passwords.
  D program their computers to look for long passwords.

6 According to the article, scientists in the US recently designed
  A fingerprint readers for phones.
  B a prototype keyboard.
  C something people can wear to identify them.
  D a touch screen laptop.

4 Find the opposites underlined in the text.

fantastic	≠	_terrible_	3	forget	≠ _____
1 advanced	≠	_____	4	possible	≠ _____
2 similar	≠	_____	5	complicated	≠ _____

VOCABULARY PRACTICE| Nouns and verbs

5 Look at the vocabulary in lesson 2.4 in the Students' Book. Complete the sentences with the missing verbs or nouns. The first and last letters are given.

My grandmother always has a **j**_igsa_**w** on her living room table. I like to help her when I visit, but I often put the pieces in the wrong place.

1 You'll need to put on another **l**_____**r** of clothing. It's really cold outside today.

2 My father never takes food to work because he eats at the company's **c**_____**n** every day.

3 How long will it take to **r**_____**h** the top of the hill? I'm already really tired.

4 Annie wants to **r**_____**n** her own computer games shop when she finishes school.

5 In many towns here you can still see the **r**_____**s** of the old city walls made from large stones.

6 We can't land on the island. There's no **a**_____**p** there.

WORD STORE 2E | The temperature

6 Complete the telephone conversation between Warmomatic and a customer with the words from the box. There are two extra words.

> above   below   boiling   chilly   ~~cold~~
> degrees   falling   freezing   rising

In the year 2033 …

W: Good afternoon. This is Warmomatic. How can I help you?

C: Hello? Warmomatic? Oh, thank goodness you've answered. HELP!

W: What is the problem, madam?

C: My computer-controlled heating system isn't working. My home is really _cold_! It is ¹_____ zero in every room in the house and the temperature is still ²_____ . It's minus ten now.

W: OK madam, please try to calm down. I'll try to fix the problem from my desktop computer. Please call me again in 20 minutes.

20 minutes later …

W: Good afternoon. This is Warmomatic. How can I help you?

C: It's me again! Now the house is too hot. In fact, it's ³_____ . It's plus 35 ⁴_____ centigrade and the temperature is ⁵_____ . Help me!

W: Oh dear. There is one very easy solution, madam.

C: Anything. Please. Tell me what to do.

W: Open a window madam. It's ⁶_____ outside.

GRAMMAR

2.5 *used to*

SHOW WHAT YOU KNOW

1 Tick the sentences that describe routines. Choose the time expressions that show regularity.

> Alastair played computer games <u>every evening</u> before bed. ☑

1 Karen bought a new laptop last weekend. ☐

2 Patricia and Matt called each other every Friday night. ☐

3 Dean always watched football on Saturday afternoons. ☐

4 Mary dropped her mobile phone down the toilet. ☐

2 ★ When they went to university, two friends, Carl and Owen, moved into a student flat together. Write sentences about them with *used to* or *didn't use to* and the verbs in brackets.

When they lived with their parents ...
> they *didn't use to eat* (eat) unhealthy food. Now they only eat kebabs and pizzas.

1 they _____ (do) any cleaning at home. They still don't do much and their flat is a mess.

2 their parents _____ (pay) the bills. Now they pay their own bills.

3 Carl _____ (use) his dad's computer. Now he uses Owen's.

4 Carl and Owen _____ (argue). Now they argue about the computer.

3 ★ ★ Write positive sentences (+), negative sentences (–) and questions (?) about mobile phones in 1983. Use the correct forms of *used to* from the box and the words above each line.

(did   didn't use to   used to   use to)

> mobile phones / have cameras (?)
> *Did mobile phones use to have cameras?*

1 mobile phones / cost a lot of money (+)

_____

2 most normal people / own a mobile phone (–)

_____

3 people / make fewer phone calls (+)

_____

4 mobile phones / be bigger (?)

_____

5 mobile phones / have touch screens (–)

_____

6 mobile phones / send text messages (?)

_____

4 ★ ★ ★ Tick the correct sentences. Sometimes both sentences are correct.

When I was in the Science club at school, ...

1 a we met every Thursday at 4 p.m. ☑
  b we used to meet every Thursday at 4 p.m. ☐

2 a we watched videos about great discoveries. ☐
  b we used to watch videos about great discoveries. ☐

3 a one week, a physicist came to speak to us. ☐
  b one week, a physicist used to come to speak to us. ☐

4 a our group went on a trip to the Science Museum in London. ☐
  b our group used to go on a trip to the Science Museum in London. ☐

5 a my friend Emma once gave a talk about the sun. ☐
  b my friend Emma once used to give a talk about the sun. ☐

SHOW WHAT YOU'VE LEARNT

5 Complete the dialogue between Jodie and her dad with the correct forms of *used to* and the verbs in brackets.

J: Dad, *did you use to own* (you/own) a smartphone when you were my age?

D: Did I what?

J: **1** _____ (you/use) a smartphone or a laptop when you were a teenager?

D: What?! No I didn't. I was 14 in ... er ... wait a minute ... in 1981. We **2** _____ (have) laptops back then.

J: So, how **3** _____ (check) your messages?

D: Jodie?! There were no messages or texts; no Facebook or anything. We **4** _____ (send) letters or faxes.

J: I see. Wow ... Dad, what's a fax?

D: Er ... well ... it was a bit like a photocopier. You **5** _____ (write) your message on a piece of paper, then put it in the fax machine ...

J: And then?

D: Well, then you **6** _____ (dial) the number and wait. The machine er ... well ... it read the piece of paper and sent it to your friend.

J: What, the piece of paper?

D: What? No! Not the same piece of paper, Jodie – just the message.

J: I see. Wow.   /6

GRAMMAR: Train and Try Again page 145

1983   today

1 ★ **Choose the correct words.**

1 I read the biography of Martin Luther King *during* / *while* I was at home sick.

2 They didn't have smartphones *when* / *by* my father was a student.

3 *As soon as* / *While* we downloaded the song, we listened to it six times.

4 I learned a lot about web browsers *during* / *while* the weekend computer course.

5 It was minus ten every day last week *until* / *by* Friday.

2 ★ ★ **Complete the second sentence so it has a similar meaning to the first. Use between two and five words, including the word in capitals.**

You can take my laptop now but I need it on Wednesday. **BY**
You can take my laptop now but return it *by Wednesday*, please.

1 The moment you get home, send me a text message. **SOON**
Send me a text message _____ home.

2 Susie drove to Manchester and listened to the CD in the car. **WHEN**
Susie listened to the CD _____ to Manchester.

3 I was watching the film and began to feel cold. **DURING**
I _____ the film.

4 We had something to eat and waited for the program to download. **WHILE**
We had something to eat _____ downloading.

5 James did the experiment then showed me his notes. **AFTER**
James showed me _____ the experiment.

6 I read my book and waited for you to arrive. **UNTIL**
I _____ your arrival.

3 ★ ★ **Choose the correct answers A–C.**

4 ★ ★ **Complete the sentences with one word in each gap. Use each word only once.**

Dad: Jono, I don't want you to use my laptop *while* I'm washing the car. Wait until I finish, OK?

Jono: Yes, Dad. I promise.

1 Tess: Let's play a game _____ the flight to Madrid.
Bill: Good idea. How about Scrabble?

2 Matt: I had to speak to my Physics teacher. Why didn't you wait _____ the end of our conversation?
Vic: I didn't know where you were or who you were with. Sorry.

3 Al: I decided to take a year off _____ I went to university to study Chemistry.
Gina: Really? What did you do for a year?

4 Phil: I stopped downloading the game as ____ as I realised it was illegal software.
Chris: Good idea. Why don't we try a different game?

5 Ella: I need to finish this report _____ tomorrow morning. Can we meet in the afternoon?
Jon: No problem. I'll send you a text message.

5 ★ ★ ★ **Complete the sentences with the words in brackets in the correct form. Do not change the order of the words. You may need to add words. Use no more than six words in each gap.**

I listened to *the song before I knew* (the song / before / know) who sang it.

1 Adrian sent the text message _____ _____ (while / drive), which is dangerous.

2 I _____ (not fall / asleep / during) the Biology class. I was just resting my eyes.

3 _____ (after / I / speak / Mandy) I decided not to lend her my smartphone.

4 The children all _____ (go / sleep / by / midnight) on the school trip last week.

5 Yesterday, I called my mum _____ _____ (while / travel) home on the bus.

A modern genius

Stephen Hawking was one of the most famous scientists in the world. He was born in Oxford in 1942 and lived there [1]__ the moment he moved to Cambridge to complete his PhD. [2]__ this, however, people already knew that he was intelligent. He enjoyed Maths and Science at school very much. He found both subjects very easy, and it was [3]__ he was studying there that his friends began to call him 'Einstein', for fun.

Stephen's first university was actually Oxford, where he studied Physics and Chemistry. [4]__ his studies there, at the age of 21, he became very sick and had problems speaking and moving. [5]__ he realised he was extremely ill, he decided to work harder. This was because he really wanted to finish his PhD [6]__ he died.

Hawking finished his PhD when he was only 24. Later he wrote over 15 very popular science books. His doctors didn't expect him to live long. He died at the age of 76 – definitely too early, as many say.

1 A till	B by	C while
2 A After	B Before	C Until
3 A during	B while	C as soon as

4 A During	B While	C As soon as
5 A Till	B While	C When
6 A before	B by	C for

WRITING

2.7

A story

5 Read the story *Lost in New York* below. Cross out one incorrect word in each underlined sentence a–h. Then write the correct word.

6 Complete the story with the correct form of the verbs in brackets.

1 Read the tips for writing a story. Tick the useful advice.

1 Set the scene by introducing who is in the story and where they are. ☑
2 Include at least three main characters. ☐
3 Use different past tenses and structures in the story. ☐
4 Use adjectives, adverbs and phrases to make the story interesting. ☐
5 Use linkers and time expressions to show the order of events. ☐
6 Try not to repeat the same words. ☐
7 Write a happy ending. ☐
8 Write four paragraphs. ☐

2 Match suitable parts ofuseful phrases for writing a story. There are two extra endings.

It was four years   *i*
1 What a ☐
2 I'll never ☐
3 It was a few ☐
4 It was a lovely day ☐
5 What ☐
6 Meeting my husband was ☐

a years later when …
b in trouble
c a surprise!
d nightmare!
e forget …
f going on?
g for a walk …
h an event I'll never forget.
i ago when …

3 Read the story *Hitting the Jackpot* below. Complete gaps 1–4 with a suitable phrase from Exercise 2.

4 Read the story again. Choose the correct words.

BLOG

Lost in

New York

I was 14 years old ~~while~~ **when** I got lost in New York. I <u>was</u> (be) on a school trip and on the last day we went to a museum before our flight home. We ¹_____ (travel) by city bus when I ²_____ (begin) to feel sleepy.

ᵃ<u>All of the sudden</u>, someone ³_____ (start) shaking me. I was the only person left on the bus. ᵇ<u>What was going up</u>? I slowly realised I was lost. ᶜ<u>I have to saying I was scared</u>. I ⁴_____ (not/have) any money and my phone was dying. ᵈ<u>I was by trouble</u>.

While I ⁵_____ (think) what to do, I ⁶_____ (see) a woman. She was wearing a pilot's uniform. ᵉ<u>Lucky, she helped me</u>. ᶠ<u>She was incredible kind</u> and told me how to get to the airport and even gave me ten dollars for the ticket.

When I finally ⁷_____ (get) on the plane, the pilot ⁸_____ (make) an announcement. I recognised her voice immediately. It was the woman from the bus. She ⁹_____ (invite) me to the front of the plane and ¹⁰_____ (explain) how everything worked. ᵍ<u>I'll always forget the day I travelled with the pilot</u>.

Hitting the JACKPOT* 🎱24 🎱12 🎱14 🎱32

<u>*It was four years ago when*</u> my luck started to change. I was walking home from work when a man rushed out of a newsagent's and jumped on a bus. ᵃ*Unfortunately / Incredibly*, a small piece of paper fell from his pocket.

It was a lottery ticket. I put it in my bag and forgot all about it until a few weeks later when I found it again in my handbag. I checked the ticket. ¹_____ It wasn't the winning ticket, but it won a small amount of money.

ᵇ*Anyhow / I must admit* I thought about taking the money, but I decided to keep the ticket for good luck instead. ᶜ*Actually / While*, my luck did change after that. ²_____

I met my husband, Paul. On our wedding day, he said he felt like the luckiest man alive. At that moment, I decided to tell him the story of my lottery ticket to show him I was lucky too. ᵈ*Then / Unfortunately* Paul started to laugh.

³_____ the next thing he told me. He used to play the lottery and the numbers on the ticket were his lucky numbers. ᵉ*During / Suddenly* I knew who he was. It was Paul who dropped the ticket. I couldn't believe it! We weren't rich, but we were very happy ᶠ*anyway / luckily*.

🎱47 🎱9 🎱6

* Hit the Jackpot – to be very successful or lucky

7 Read the task below. Then complete gaps 1–6 in the story with the phrases from the box. There is one extra phrase.

> Your school is holding a competition for the best short story about a surprising event. Write a story. Include and develop these points:
> - Give information to set the scene.
> - Describe what happened on that day using different past tenses and structures.
> - Use different words and phrases to show the order of events and add interest.
> - Give your story a strong ending.

> didn't use to care   didn't use to smile
> used to have   used to laugh   used to see
> didn't use to take   used to tell   used to walk

An unexpected gift

I was 17 years old ᵃ*when* / *while* I moved to my village. Every day I ¹_____ the same way home from school and every day I ²_____ an old man. He ᵇ*was* / *were* sitting quietly under the same tree. He always looked miserable and children ³_____ at him.

During the next few weeks I ᶜ*started* / *was starting* to say hello when I saw him under the tree and later we actually became good friends. I ⁴_____ him about the exams I was taking at school and he told me all about the job he ⁵_____ as a conservationist. I ᵈ*have* / *must* admit ⁶_____ about the environment, but thanks to him, I started to think about it more carefully.

Anyway, one day he wasn't there. And he wasn't there the next day. What ᵉ*was going* / *went* on? I went to his house to look for him. Unfortunately, I found out he died the day before.

Then, a few weeks later when I ᶠ*wasn't* / *was walking* home from school, a young woman came and gave me a letter. It was from the old man's wife. He told her about our conversations and that he felt cheerful when he was talking to me. He decided that he ᵍ*was wanting* / *wanted* to give me a gift.

He ʰ*gave* / *was giving* me his special bracelet. He ⁷_____ it off. Now I do the same. The old man is a friend I'll never forget.

8 Read the story again. Choose the correct words a–h.

9 Look at the story in Exercise 7 again and find examples for some of the tips in Exercise 1.

> **Tip 3** 3 examples of the Past Continuous:
> _____
>
> **Tip 4** 2 adjectives to describe the old man:
> _____
> 2 adverbs: _____
> 1 phrase: _____
>
> **Tip 5** 4 linkers and time expressions showing the order of events: _____
> _____

10 You see a short story competition in your favourite magazine and decide to enter. Write a story with the title 'A day to remember'. Include and develop these points:
- Give information to set the scene.
- Describe what happened on that day using different tenses and structures.
- Use different words and phrases to show the order of events and add interest.
- Give your story a strong ending.

Finished? Always check your writing. Can you tick √ everything on this list?

In my story:

- I have given information to set the scene, e.g. *I was ten years old …*, *It was a cold dark evening.* ☐
- I have used the Past Simple and Continuous, and perhaps *used to* to describe what happened, e.g. *It started to rain as I was climbing the mountain.* ☐
- I have used different words and phrases to make my story interesting for the reader, e.g. *What was going on? It was awesome!* ☐
- I have included adverbs to add interest, e.g. *Suddenly, Luckily, incredibly.* ☐
- I have given my story a strong ending, e.g. *I'll never forget when I first went …*, *… was an event I'll never forget.* ☐
- I have checked my spelling and punctuation. ☐
- My text is neat and clear. ☐

1 Translate the phrases into your own language.

SPEAKING BANK

Telling a story

Use the right tenses

• Past Continuous is used to describe the background for the main events:

The sun was shining and I was _____
enjoying myself. _____

• Past Simple is used to describe a problem and the main events.

The weather changed. _____
I couldn't see the path. _____

Use linkers

• Beginning: **To start with/** _____
At first _____

• Middle: **Suddenly/All of** _____
a sudden/Luckily/Fortunately/ _____
Unfortunately

• End: **In the end/Eventually/** _____
Finally _____

Say how you felt

I was excited/frightened/ _____
relieved/surprised/shocked/ _____
worried. _____
_____

Make a 'final comment'

It was the best/worst day _____
of my life! _____

I'll never forget the look _____
on his face! _____

I'll never do it again. _____

Listening to a story

Neutral response

Really?/Oh dear./Oh no. _____

Strong response

That sounds amazing/funny/ _____
frightening. _____

What a great _____
story/a nightmare! _____

Respond with questions

What happened? _____

What did you do? _____

2 Complete the dialogue between Felix and Eva with the words from the box. There are two extra items.

> ~~except for~~ excited happened Luckily
> Next time nightmare relieved shocked
> sounds Suddenly to start with

F: We had a fantastic time on our summer holiday – _except for_ the day we went to the island.

E: What ¹_____ ?

F: We were travelling on a fast boat to visit a beautiful little island. The captain of the boat was going very fast and the waves were really big. ²_____ , the boat hit a giant wave.

E: Oh no!

F: There was a loud bang, the front window broke and lots and lots of water rushed in.

E: Wow! That ³_____ really frightening.

F: Yeah, well, we were ⁴_____ because it happened so quickly and the water hit us really hard. ⁵_____ , nobody was seriously hurt.

E: What did you do?

F: Well, in the end we got to the island – wet but very ⁶_____ to be back on dry land.

E: What a ⁷_____ !

F: ⁸_____ , we'll take the slow boat.

3 Complete each gap with one word.

Conversation 1: Alice and Cindy

A: I once met someone famous.

C: Really? Who?

A: Well, I was sitting in Manchester Airport, waiting for a flight to Warsaw. I remember, I was reading *Harry Potter* <u>at</u> the time. Suddenly, the lady next to me said 'Excuse me, ¹_____ you enjoying that book?'

C: Who was it?

A: Well, I looked at her and I thought, 'I know you', and then I realised it was J. K. Rowling.

C: What? The author of the book you ²_____ reading? That's amazing! What did you say?

A: Well, to start ³_____ I didn't know what to say, but fortunately, she was really friendly. ⁴_____ the end, we chatted for about ten minutes and I told her how much I love her books.

C: What a great story.

A: I know, and she signed my book!

Conversation 2: Andrew and Nancy

A: I'm afraid ¹_____ horses.

N: What? Why?

A: Well, when I was twelve years old, my neighbour took me riding on her horse.

N: ²_____ happened?

A: It was my first time on a horse. ³_____ first, everything was OK. We ⁴_____ going very slowly. My neighbour was holding the horse and I was sitting ⁵_____ its back. I was enjoying the ride, but then all ⁶_____ a sudden, there was a loud noise and the horse got scared and started running ... really fast!

N: That sounds really frightening.

A: It was. Luckily, I didn't fall off. I stay away from horses these days.

1 In pairs, ask and answer the questions.

PART 1

Talk about personalities.
1 What is your best friend like?
2 Are you generous or mean? Why?
3 What qualities would you like to have? Why?
4 What is a good travelling companion like? Why?
5 Do you think students should wear school uniforms? Why?/Why not?

PART 2

Talk about technology.
1 What do you mostly use your smartphone for? Why?
2 How do you feel in a place with no wifi? Why?
3 Would you prefer to give up your smartphone for a week or your laptop for a month? Why?
4 Have you ever had a problem with technology? What happened and how did you feel?
5 What is bad about living in the technological age?

2 Look at the pictures that show different types of scientists.

PART 1

Which of these jobs do you think is the most interesting? Discuss in pairs.

PART 2

In pairs, ask and answer the questions.
1 Have you ever watched the night sky like an astronomer?
2 Would you prefer to be a physicist, biologist or chemist? Why?
3 Do you like Mathematics? Why?/Why not?
4 What things can conservationists do to help our planet?
5 How do you think archaeologists feel when they find something important? Why?
6 Do you like studying Science? Why?/Why not?
7 Which of these jobs do you think is the best for you? Why?

3 Discuss this question together. 'Do you think scientists do a more important job than artists?' Why?/Why not?

For scientists:

Scientists ...
- find ways to make us feel better when we are sick.
- discover ways we can communicate with each other.
- help us to understand the world.
- find ways to help us travel.

For artists:

Artists ...
- create culture in society.
- help us to understand ourselves.
- create things that touch our emotions.
- bring colour to our world.

VOCABULARY AND GRAMMAR

1 Complete the sentences with the words from the box in the correct form. There are two extra words.

> jigsaw keyboard laser printer layer
> password ~~search engine~~ specimen username

For more information, check online using a _search engine_.

1 We need another two _____ of paint on the wall. I can still see the graffiti.

2 This new _____ is excellent. Look at the high quality of these pictures.

3 Luther is in the garden collecting _____ for our project on plants.

4 I can't find the last piece of the _____ . Maybe it's under the sofa.

5 Did you know that the most used _____ in the world is '123456'?

/5

2 Complete the sentences with the correct words. The first letters are given.

Sir Isaac Newton is probably the most famous **p**_hysicist_ in the world.

1 My favourite subject is **C**_____ because I love working in the lab.

2 Patrick is very good with numbers. Does he want to study **M**_____ at university?

3 **C**_____ **s**_____ make a lot of money. And with robots becoming more popular, they will earn more in the future.

4 I know I'm a plant biologist, but it's ten degrees **c**_____ outside. Let's stay in the lab today, OK?

5 In January 1971, experts observed temperatures of 80 degrees **b**_____ zero. Now THAT is cold!

/5

3 Use the beginnings from the box to make words and complete the sentences.

> archaeo- astro- ~~conserva-~~ geo- lingui- psycho-

Theodore Roosevelt was an early _conservationist_. He protected over 150 million acres of American forests for public use.

1 Many people say that John Aubrey (1626–1697) invented _____ when he studied Stonehenge in England.

2 Philip Zimbardo is a contemporary American _____ . His 'prison experiment' showed how people behave in extreme conditions.

3 Did you know that _____ don't only work with materials on Earth? Some of them work with rocks from the moon and other planets.

4 In 1610, Galileo discovered the four largest moons of Jupiter using a telescope. For this reason, people call him the father of _____ .

5 You don't have to speak a foreign language to be a good _____ , but it probably helps.

/5

4 Choose the correct verb forms.

Peter ⟨didn't go⟩ / wasn't going to school on Thursday.

1 Adam ᵃdid / was doing his homework when Simon ᵇcalled / was calling.

2 We ᵃslept / were sleeping when the postman ᵇrang / was ringing the doorbell.

3 ᵃWere they finding / Did they find the pharmacy before it ᵇclosed / was closing?

4 Chloe and Kyle ᵃdanced / were dancing together when the music ᵇstopped / was stopping.

5 ᵃDid Shelly wait / Was Shelly waiting at the station when the train ᵇcrashed / was crashing?

/5

5 Find and correct the mistakes.

Did Auntie Kay ~~used~~ to cook a big meal on Sundays?

use

1 Beth used to go to Hong Kong for the first time in 2009. _____

2 Teenagers didn't used to have mobile phones in the 1980s. _____

3 Josh used to invent a popular video game. _____

4 Did use to be milk free at school when you were little? _____

5 When Grandpa was young, films used to were black and white. _____

/5

6 Choose the correct answers A–C.

Flat computers

_C_ are small, light personal computers for mobile use. They have most of the same components as ¹___ computers including a screen, speakers and a ²___ to write/type with. In the 1970s, IBM ³___ the first company to make and sell these mobile computers. At first, laptops didn't ⁴___ to have batteries and the screens were black and white and very small. Later, in the 1990s, colour screens ⁵___ more popular. Nowadays, laptops are more popular than any other type of computer.

	A	B	C
	Desktops	Websites	ⓒ Laptops
1	A broadband	B desktop	C Internet
2	A keyboard C web browser	B password	
3	A was	B used to be	C used to
4	A use	B used	C have
5	A were becoming C became	B used to become	

/5

Total /30

7 Choose the correct answers A–C.

Phil: My father ____ in a chemistry laboratory in Chicago last summer.

Vic: Cool. Did you visit him when he was there?

A used to work
B were working
Ⓒ worked

1 Amy: Why didn't you answer the phone?

Tony: Sorry, I ____ measurements of the room.

Amy: Ah, OK.

A took
B was taking
C 'm taking

2 Fiona: When I lived in Florence I often went to the Leonardo da Vinci Museum.

Cathy: Really? I didn't know ____ in Florence.

Fiona: Yes. I lived there for six years.

A you were living
B you used to live
C were you living

3 Dad: Sara! ____

Sara: Sorry. I just wanted to check something.

A Not to use my smartphone.
B You don't use my smartphone.
C Don't use my smartphone.

4 Pete: I had a great time ____ the visit to the Natural History Museum.

Jim: I'm not surprised. It's amazing!

A during
B while
C as soon as

5 Mark: Georgiana waited for me ____ I finished analysing data and then we had lunch.

Connie: That was kind of her.

A when
B until
C soon

/5

8 Complete the sentences with the words in brackets in the correct form. Do not change the order of the words. You may need to add words. Use no more than six words in each gap.

The American physicist James Russell *didn't invent the CD* (not / invent / the CD) in 1964, but in 1965.

1 Professor Phillips was _____ (plan / publish / research paper) when he suddenly became ill.

2 I _____ (not / use / like) computer games but then I discovered Minecraft.

3 He sent me the file _____ (soon / it / download) so that I could check it.

4 James _____ (use / work) for Microsoft. He thinks it is a good company.

5 Where _____ (you / go) when I saw you in the tram last night?

/5

9 Complete the text with the correct forms of the words from the box. There are two extra words.

collect   develop   do   follow
protect   remain   sit   walk

The Giants of Georgia

In 2008, a farmer *was walking* with his animals through the Caucasus Mountains in Georgia. He used ¹_____ this often, but on this day he saw the unusual ²_____ of an old stone structure. The farmer decided to explore the area. Inside the structure were two human skeletons. They ³_____ on chairs in front of a table. What was so interesting? The bodies were extremely large.

He contacted a team of archaeologists. On the way there, they saw some very large statues and what seemed to be a large stone road through the forest.

The scientists ⁴_____ evidence (i.e. some of the bones) and took it to Tbilisi, the capital city of Georgia. They asked Professor Vikua, famous for discovering Homo Erectus Georgicus, to help them, but he died before he could do any research. When the scientists looked for the bones that Professor Vikua had, they could not find them.

In 2014, the Science Channel opened a new investigation, but they haven't found any new evidence or ⁵_____ a theory to explain these mysterious giant bones.

/5

10 Choose the correct answers A–C.

A job advert from space

Are we in danger from visitors from other planets? Are the astronauts that we *B* into space making life on this planet dangerous?

Last week while I ¹__ a science magazine, I found this interesting article. NASA, it said, were looking for someone to help them ²__ experiments on the organisms that astronauts regularly collect during their trips into space. The job is to ³__ notes on what you observe during these tests, and then work with other scientists looking closely at the data.

Your research may help protect Earth against a future alien invasion. But, NASA hopes, one day the results of your work might help them to ⁴__ new life on other planets. They might also help mankind ⁵__ parts of the universe where no man or woman has ever visited before. What a great job!

	A	B	C
	A sent	Ⓑ send	C did send
1	A did read	B read	C was reading
2	A make	B do	C take
3	A take	B have	C do
4	A collect	B invent	C discover
5	A get	B reach	C go

/5

Total   /20

31

3 The arts

VOCABULARY

3.1

Watching habits • TV programmes • adjectives • elements of a film/ TV drama

SHOW WHAT YOU KNOW

1 Complete the text with the correct words. The first and last letters are given.

MyBlog

I love the media and the arts. Every day (after I finish my homework, of course!) I watch YouTube **c***lip***s** online. Sometimes they are so funny – especially the ones with animals or people doing silly things. In the evening, I watch the **¹t**_____**y** because that's when they show the best **²h**_____**r** movies. I like anything with vampires and werewolves!

But I don't only watch things. Sometimes I read my favourite **³b**_____**g** on my laptop. My friend writes it and it's about social media. Before I go to sleep I read my **⁴e-**_____**k** or a fashion **⁵m**_____**e**. 'Look Good' is the one I like and I can think about what to wear the next day at school.

When I read, I often listen to my favourite rock **⁶a**_____**m** – *Dark Side of the Moon* by Pink Floyd. It's a classic! I usually listen to music on my **⁷m**_____**e** phone but sometimes, when I want to listen to something different, I listen to an Internet **⁸r**_____**o** station. Do you love the media and the arts more than me? I don't think so!

2 Match the film titles to the type of film.

	La La Land	☐h
1	*The Hobbit*	☐
2	*Se7en*	☐
3	*Blade Runner 2049*	☐
4	*Angry Birds*	☐
5	*Bridget Jones's Baby*	☐
6	*The Exorcist*	☐
7	*Mr Bean's Holiday*	☐

a animation
b comedy
c fantasy
d horror
e thriller
f romantic comedy
g science fiction
h musical

3 Complete the sentences with a type of TV programme. Some letters are given.

I never watch <u>r e a l i t y</u> TV programmes because I don't think they are anything like real life.

1 Chiara loves a good **t _ l _ _ _ _ h _ w** – maybe one day she'll go on one, win the competition and then become a famous singer.

2 I watched this excellent **p _ _ _ o _ d _ _ m _** yesterday about King Henry VIII and his wives. The actors were fantastic!

3 My favourite **g _ m _ _ h _ _** is the one where you start with fifteen people but only one person wins the prize money.

4 Sir David Attenborough, famous for his excellent wildlife shows, has a new **d _ _ _ m _ _ _ _ r _** on TV called *Planet Earth 2*.

5 *Friends* is such a good **s _ _ c _ _** . It's quite old now, but it still makes me laugh.

4 Complete the sentences with the names of programmes. There are two words in each gap.

We saw Brad Pitt on a <u>chat show</u> last week. He's quite funny and answered some interesting questions about his life.

1 My cousin's mum watches all of the _____ _____ . I don't like them because everyone is so miserable all the time and has problems in their lives.

2 Trevor and Sharon are flying to Cuba next year. They watched a _____ about it and now they really can't wait to go there on holiday.

3 Did you just see that _____ ? There's been a big fire near the city centre.

4 Before we decide to go for a picnic, let's check the _____ to see if it's going to stay sunny.

5 Sam got this special pierogi recipe from a _____ _____ that she watched on TV yesterday.

6 Mum's watching a _____ about this criminal that used to be a police officer.

WORD STORE 3B | Adjectives

5 Choose the correct adjectives.

1 Evelyn doesn't understand what's happening in this crime drama. The story is too *complex* / *gripping* / *addictive* for her.

2 This comedy isn't funny – it's *excellent* / *embarrassing* / *entertaining*. We both feel silly and uncomfortable watching it.

3 Carrie isn't coming to the theatre. She's watching a really *addictive* / *imaginative* / *embarrassing* soap opera and she can't leave home.

4 A good crime drama needs to be *gripping* / *inspiring* / *moving*, which normally means you don't know how it will end.

5 Have you seen the animation film *The Lion King*? It's so *addictive* / *engaging* / *moving* that everyone usually cries at the end.

6 I thought the film was *fascinating* / *disappointing* / *gripping*, to be honest. I was expecting it to be much better.

7 Walter found the documentary very *inspiring* / *imaginative* / *addictive*. Now he wants to volunteer to help homeless people too.

8 That was one of the most *imaginative* / *embarrassing* / *complex* things I've ever seen. How is it possible to be so creative?

9 I watched a documentary about how to make glass bottles. I know it sounds boring, but it was actually really *moving* / *fascinating* / *disappointing*.

WORD STORE 3C | Elements of a film/TV drama

6 Jake and Angela have just watched a film at the cinema. Complete their dialogue with the missing words. The definitions in brackets are given to help you.

J: What did you think of the movie, Angela? Excellent, eh?

A: Erm. Not really. The *plot* (*what happens in the story*) was really silly. For example, why did they go to the island with no food, no water and no map?

J: Because it's a film! What did you think about the
¹_____ (*what the actors do*)? That was good. Some of the actors might even win an Oscar.

A: Well, I don't think they'll win any Oscars for the
²_____ (*the text in a drama*). What the
³_____ (*people in a drama*) said was clichéd and not very realistic. But I have to say that the
⁴_____ (*music during a drama*) was great. It created a very frightening atmosphere. And the
⁵_____ (*illusions created by computers*) were also very good. The monsters on the island looked real.

J: I agree. And I think all of the ⁶_____ (*clothes the actors wear*) were good. I thought the
⁷_____ (*the place or time of a drama*) was really original and the ⁸_____ (*how a drama finishes*) was a big surprise for me. I really enjoyed the film.

A: Really? They're showing Hitchcock's *The Birds* next week. Maybe you'd like to see a *really* good film?

REMEMBER THIS

Actors and actresses can *be*, *appear* or *star in films*, *plays* and *TV shows*, but the verb play is used with information about the character from the film. Compare

Johnny Depp **stars** in the Pirates of the Caribbean *films*.

vs

He **plays** a pirate called Captain Jack Sparrow.

7 Read REMEMBER THIS. Choose the correct words.

I really like director Peter Jackson's *Hobbit* films. They are fantasy films. Martin Freeman and Ian McKellen ¹*star* / *play* in them. Martin Freeman ²*appears* / *plays* Bilbo Baggins and Ian McKellen ³*is* / *plays* Gandalf the wizard.

SHOW WHAT YOU'VE LEARNT

8 Choose the correct words.

Conversation 1: Owen and Billy

O: Have you seen that new animation where all of the ¹*special effects* / *characters* / *acting* are funny animals that have a secret life at night?

B: No, I haven't. Let's watch it. It sounds ²*entertaining* / *moving* / *inspiring*.

Conversation 2: Mike and Ellie

M: I bought two DVDs for Laura for her birthday. One is a ³*horror* / *fantasy* / *thriller* about dragons, wizards and magic.

E: What's the other one?

M: It's a ⁴*romantic comedy* / *crime drama* / *period drama* about a woman who falls in love with a man from Mars. People say it's very funny.

Conversation 3: Olivia and Beth

O: Did you watch the latest episode of your favourite ⁵*weather forecast* / *news bulletin* / *soap opera*? I heard it was boring.

B: I did. And it was. So after half an hour, I changed channels and watched something with a better ⁶*acting* / *plot* / *special effects*.

Conversation 4: Jenny and Holly

J: Let's watch that new ⁷*talent show* / *chat show* / *game show* and try to answer the questions.

H: I don't watch those kinds of programmes. They're too ⁸*addictive* / *engaging* / *moving* for me and then I need to watch them all.

Conversation 5: Al and Ben

A: The ⁹*script* / *setting* / *acting* of this film is Birmingham in the 1960s.

B: I know. And I read in the newspaper that the ¹⁰*script* / *plot* / *soundtrack* was written by a real ex-gangster, so how the characters speak is quite authentic.

/10

SHOW WHAT YOU KNOW

1 Match two adjectives from the box with their opposites 1–4. There are two extra words.

confident   exciting   far   intelligent   interesting
loud   ~~noisy~~   outgoing   popular   sensible

1   quiet   ≠   _noisy_   / _____
2   silly   ≠   _____   / _____
3   boring   ≠   _____   / _____
4   shy   ≠   _____   / _____

2 ★ Complete the sentences about the London museums. Write *S* for the Science Museum and *N* for the Natural History Museum.

	The Natural History Museum	The Science Museum
Number of visitors per year	3.5 million	2.7 million
Started in	1881	1857
Distance from Victoria Station	2.2 miles	2.0 miles
Distance from Buckingham Palace	1.7 miles	1.8 miles
Opening hours	10:00 a.m. – 5:50 p.m.	10:00 a.m. – 6:00 p.m.

The ᵃ<u>S</u> Museum is not as popular as the ᵇ<u>N</u> Museum.

1   The ᵃ___ Museum is not as old as the ᵇ___ Museum.
2   The ᵃ___ Museum is not as far from Victoria Station as the ᵇ___ Museum.
3   The ᵃ___ Museum is not as far from Buckingham Palace as the ᵇ___ Museum.
4   The ᵃ___ Museum is not open as long as the ᵇ___ Museum.

3 ★ Complete the sentences with the superlative form of the adjectives in brackets.

Bob Marley is probably the _greatest_ (great) reggae artist of all time.

1   I think the violin makes the _____ (beautiful) sound of all the instruments.
2   The guitar is one of the _____ (easy) instruments to learn.
3   Their Greatest Hits (1971–1975) by the Eagles is one of the _____ (popular) albums ever written.
4   The Pacific Ocean is the _____ (big) ocean on our planet.

4 ★ ★ Complete the dialogue between Kristen and James with the comparative or superlative form of the adjectives in brackets.

In the modern art museum ...
K: What do you think of the exhibition, James?
J: Yeah, great actually. It's much _better_ (good) than I expected.
K: Yeah. I think it's ¹_____ (funny) than last year. Actually, it's the ²_____ (good) exhibition I've ever been to. I really liked the photos of the dogs in the water.
J: Personally, I thought the giant baby sculptures were the ³_____ (interesting) thing in the exhibition.
K: I didn't see those. Where are they?
J: Go back down this corridor and they are a bit ⁴_____ (far) along than the dog photos.

5 ★ ★ Complete the sentences with the correct form of the words in brackets. Add any other words if necessary.

Heavy metal music is _much louder than_ (loud) jazz music.

1   *Guardians of the Galaxy II* is just _____ (silly) the first film.
2   That film was much _____ (exciting) the one we saw yesterday.
3   The Apollo Theatre is a bit _____ (far) the cinema, so we should take a bus to get there.
4   Horror films are not _____ (popular / as) comedy films.

SHOW WHAT YOU'VE LEARNT

6 Complete the second sentence so it has a similar meaning to the first. Use the word in capitals.

Of course, for younger listeners, rap is more popular than opera. **POPULAR**
Of course, for younger listeners, opera is _not as popular as_ rap.

1   The actor is not as short as he looks in his films. **BIT**
The actor _____ than he looks in his films.
2   Henry's poem is longer than Bethany's. **LONG**
Bethany's poem _____ Henry's.
3   I don't know anyone more intelligent than Miko. **INTELLIGENT**
Miko is the _____ girl I know.
4   The screens in Central Cinema aren't as big as the screens in Empire Cinema. **THAN**
The screens in Central Cinema _____ the screens in Empire Cinema.
5   There isn't a photograph more beautiful than the one of the snowy mountains. **BEAUTIFUL**
The photograph of the snowy mountains _____ .
6   It's far noisier in the library at lunchtime. **MUCH**
When it's not lunchtime, it _____ in the library.

/6

GRAMMAR: Train and Try Again page 146

1 **Complete the dialogue between the presenter and Katy West with the correct form of the auxiliary verbs *do, be* or *have*.**

Extract from Students' Book recording 🔊 **1.49**

P: It's two thirty on Saturday afternoon, and you <u>are</u> listening to the <u>Culture</u> Programme. In this part of the <u>programme</u>, we invite a <u>guest</u> to talk about their 'Artist of the Week'. This week, we have Katy West in the <u>studio</u>. Katy is the Editor of *Photo Monthly Magazine*. Welcome to the *Culture Programme*.

KW: Thank you.

P: Katy, tell us about your 'Artist of the Week'.

KW: My 'Artist of the Week' is a French photographer. He takes photographs and makes them enormous. Then he pastes them in public places.

P: ¹_____ he have a name?

KW: Ah, well, he's called JR. [...]

P: So what kind of photographs ²_____ he take, and where can we see them?

KW: He takes black and white portraits of people and pastes them on buildings, walls and bridges. He ³_____ had exhibitions in museums such as the Pompidou Centre in Paris, but his favourite art gallery is in the street. He wants people who ⁴_____ usually go to museums to see his work.

2 **Complete the questions with the correct forms of the auxiliary verbs *be, do* or *have*. Match them with the answers a–d. There is one extra question.**

What <u>is</u> this street artist called?   (e)
1 What _____ his age?   ◯
2 _____ he paint people?   ◯
3 Where _____ he paint?   ◯
4 What _____ he do in his home town last month? ◯
5 _____ he worked in the United States?   ◯

a He spray paints images on the walls of old buildings in public places.
b He painted a graffiti picture of a running dog on the side of the local factory.
c No, he usually creates images of animals.
d No, he hasn't.
e We don't know his identity. He wants to be anonymous.

REMEMBER BETTER

Use diagrams to record groups of connected words. This will help you remember them better.

A **Complete the spider diagram with underlined words from Exercise 1 and words from the box. There are two extra words in the box.**

> CDs   chat   DJ   travel
> black and white   presenter

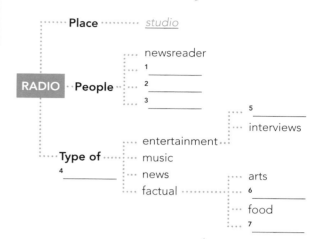

B **Draw your own spider diagram for the topic of art. Use words and phrases from this unit and add any others you know.**

WORD STORE 3D | Art and artists

3 **Choose the correct words.**

1 Good *painters / photographers / sculptors* need a wide selection of colours and brushes.

2 This *painting / sculpture / photograph* is made out of stone.

3 I like looking at pictures of people. Let's go to the *portrait / landscape / sculpture* section of the gallery.

4 Amy doesn't like *classic oil / modern abstract / black and white* paintings because she doesn't understand what they are about.

5 I love the picture that hangs in my parents' living room. It's an 18th-century *photo / painting / landscape* of a group of young children sitting in front of their house.

6 There's an exhibition of old movie posters *copied / taken / pasted* on walls and buildings in the city centre. Shall we go and see it?

7 Art *in public places / in an art gallery / at a museum* is great because everybody can see it for free – even when they walk to work. Yes, I love street art.

1 Read book reviews A–F. Mark them as *F* for fiction or *N* for non-fiction.

A ☐   B ☐   C ☐   D ☐   E ☐   F ☐

2 Read descriptions 1–5 about people's taste in books and book reviews A–F. Decide which book would be most suitable for each person to read. There is one extra review.

1 Gareth ☐   4 Sean   ☐
2 Karen   ☐   5 Jemma ☐
3 Nathan ☐

1 Gareth, 16

I'm training to be a professional chef, so I'm very busy. When I find time to read, I like books that help me forget about my work and studies. I love reading about the real lives of successful, famous people. I'm not really into romantic stories.

2 Karen, 18

I'm a student and I don't have much time to read for pleasure. I enjoy practical books – one of my favourites is *101 Things Every Student Needs to Know*. I hate books about monsters and space.

3 Nathan, 16

I love getting lost in great stories. I enjoy reading stories about the lives, love and relationships of people from the past. I like a book to make me laugh and cry, and to show me what life was like in other countries, at other times.

4 Sean, 15

I like books where the heroes are teenagers like me. I prefer stories that don't follow the rules of the real world. My favourite books have incredible people, strange aliens and amazing events. I don't like stories with romance in them.

5 Jemma, 18

I'm studying Science, but I prefer fictional books that make me forget about the real world. When I was a little girl, I used to imagine I had magic powers. I killed monsters and fought dragons – things like that. Now I'm older, I like stories that mix romance with fantasy.

A

The Great Gatsby by F. Scott Fitzgerald

The Great Gatsby is the story of rich, successful Jay Gatsby and his beautiful friend Daisy Buchanan. They live in a magical world of love, jazz and champagne in 1920s New York. There is romance and happiness, but like in many classic novels, there is also sadness and heartbreak.

B

Real Food, Real Fast by Sam Stern

Teenage chef Sam Stern introduces delicious healthy recipes which you can have on your plate in just a few minutes. This useful book is great for amateur chefs and busy students. Sam's recipes are cheap, fast and delicious.

C

Ritz Paris: Haute Cuisine

Do you want to learn to cook like a professional chef? Are you interested in the history of great French food? This is not a cookbook for the average home cook. The recipes are long and challenging, the ingredients are unusual and expensive and the food … is absolutely delicious!

D

Twilight by Stephenie Meyer

This is a fantastic story about a young student called Bella. She falls in love with Edward and then finds out he's a vampire. Vampires are usually found in stories of the past, but Stephenie Meyer's book brings them to modern America. This book will make you laugh, cry and dream of romance with vampires! We think it is a future classic.

E

Night of the Purple Moon by Scott Cramer

Scientists say a <u>comet</u> from deep space is passing Earth and it will make the moon purple. Teenager Abby Leigh is looking forward to watching this happen. But the <u>comet</u> carries a terrible secret – an alien virus that kills all the world's adults. Abby is suddenly responsible for her brother and young sister's survival in this world without adults.

F

Steve Jobs: The Exclusive Biography by Walter Isaacson

This is the life story of Apple's former boss Steve Jobs. Walter Isaacson tells us about the professional and personal life of one of modern America's most successful businessmen. We learn about Jobs' family, his loves and the ideas he had for the future of Apple before his sad death in 2011.

3 Book E is a science fiction book. Underline four more words in the review connected to this type of book. *Comet* is underlined as an example.

4 Books B and C are cookbooks. Match words from the reviews to these definitions.

    an adjective; delicious   *tasty*
1 an adjective; good for you   _____
2 a noun; instructions for how to make food   _____
3 a noun; you eat your dinner off a ...   _____
4 a noun; this person's job is to cook food   _____
5 a noun; the different foods you put together to make a meal   _____

REMEMBER BETTER

Go to an English language online bookshop and look at the different types of books in the best-sellers list. Read some of the reviews and make a note of useful vocabulary. Don't worry if you don't understand everything.

VOCABULARY PRACTICE | Books

5 Look at the vocabulary in lesson 3.4 in the Students' Book. Choose the correct types of book.

1 My dad reads a lot of *classic novels* / *poems* / *historical fiction* because he enjoys books from the past that are important and popular in our times.
2 Sarah and Vicky love scary stories. They both read *autobiographies* / *fairy tales* / *horror fiction*.
3 Chloe wants to join the police and be a detective. She enjoys reading *horror* / *classic* / *crime* novels about real modern-day murders and police investigations.
4 Emily is seven years old. Her mum reads *Pinocchio*, *Snow White* and other *fairy tales* / *classic novels* / *autobiographies* to her before she goes to sleep.
5 I really like *poems* / *historical fiction* / *horror fiction*. They're like music with words.
6 This *historical fiction* / *classic novel* / *crime novel* about Queen Elizabeth I falling in love with Shakespeare and going on holiday with him to Newcastle is really funny.

6 Complete the sentences with the missing words. The first letters are given.

    The best **t**hrillers involve complex crimes and maybe even a spy or two.
1 The Polish writer of **f**_____ **n**_____, Andrzej Sapkowski, created the *Witcher* – one of the best known characters among the fans of video games.
2 Hannah is reading the **b**_____ of Steve Jobs. Jobs didn't write it himself, but it has lots of interesting information about the life of this great man.
3 Jack has always loved **s**_____ **f**_____ . He enjoys reading about aliens, spaceships and the future.
4 Marie only reads **s**_____ **s**_____ . She says she doesn't have the patience to read anything too long.
5 The first superhero to appear in **c**_____ **b**_____ was Mandrake the Magician. That was in 1934 – four years before Superman started saving the planet.

VOCABULARY PRACTICE | Cinema

7 Look at the vocabulary in lesson 3.4 in the Students' Book. Read the comments on the film Arrival. Look at the words in bold and correct the mistakes.

filmfocus.com

Arrival
by Denis Villeneuve

your comments and ratings

jellybean_21 says: Some films in the science-fiction **gender** / *genre* are very unrealistic but I thought *Arrival* seemed very real – very human. Often with this kind of film you can't *relate* to the characters but *Arrival* was completely different. Plus, I had no idea how it was going to finish! Wonderful.

comedyfan246 says: I enjoyed *Arrival*, but I think every film should have funny moments and there was nothing to laugh at in this one. I also didn't like the main character very much – the one that ^A_____ on the job of talking with the aliens – even though she was played by an [1]**A-listed** / _____ actor. So, not a great film but it's OK.

LaraNYC says: I knew from the very beginning that the professor would ^B_____ up her job (and possibly her life!) to help the military, but the rest of the film was not easy to predict. During the film I felt scared, excited, happy and sad and I didn't expect to feel all those different emotions. A very entertaining and engaging film – not a [2]**blockboster** / _____ movie but I loved it!

debsterHK says: I watched the [3]**trainer** / _____ , so I was expecting something special. Unfortunately, *Arrival* is the same as all the other sci-fi films I've seen – I thought it was very predictable and unoriginal – in other words, nothing new. For example, there's always the bad military character who is ^C_____ up for the humans and too many [4]**computer generation images** / _____ in every scene. Boring. You also really need to ^D_____ yourself to watching this film because it's very slow and long.

ianbSMC says: Normally I enjoy relaxing films, and I often fall asleep before the end! *Arrival* was not this kind of film. It took me to another world for two hours. A very unusual film and a very good one. Well worth the price at the [5]**boxing office** / _____ . When does *Arrival 2* ^E_____ out?

WORD STORE 3E | Phrasal verbs

8 Look at the texts in Exercise 7 again. Complete gaps A–E with the correct forms of the verbs from the box. Use the particles after the gaps to help you. There is one extra verb.

    come   cope   dedicate   give   ~~relate~~   stand   take

---

SHOW WHAT YOU KNOW

1 Complete with the Past Simple or Present Perfect form of the verbs. Use the words in brackets.

Did the film win (the film/win) any Oscars at the ceremony last year?

1 _____ (you/ever/read) a play by Shakespeare?

2 Penny _____ (never/borrow) a book from the library.

3 _____ (know) that Peter wrote a novel in 2012?

4 Megan and Sam _____ (not/see) the *Twilight* films, but Kim has.

2 ★ Put the words in order to make sentences.

already / has / *Star Wars – The Last Jedi* / seen / Dylan
Dylan has already seen Star Wars – The Last Jedi.

1 *Iron Man III* / Has / yet / seen / Katie
_____ ?

2 *The Hobbit* / already / Carl / seen / has
_____ .

3 *The Hunger Games* / hasn't / yet / read / Mia
_____ .

3 ★ Write sentences with the Present Perfect forms of the verbs and *just*. Use the pictures to help you.

the play / finish
The play has just finished.

1 the concert / start
_____
_____

2 Dad / fall asleep
_____

3 The actor / forget what to say _____

---

4 ★ ★ Put *just, yet* or *already* in the right place (a or b) in each question or sentence.

Has the bus ᵃ*just* arrived outside the theatre ᵇ_____ ? (just)

1 Elliot hasn't ᵃ_____ listened to all the tracks on the new album ᵇ_____ . (yet)

2 The scary scene has ᵃ_____ finished, so you can open your eyes ᵇ_____ . (already)

3 London's newest art gallery has ᵃ_____ opened ᵇ_____ . (just)

4 Max has ᵃ_____ read seven chapters ᵇ_____ and it's only 10:00 a.m. (already)

5 Have you ᵃ_____ looked at the cookbook I bought you for Christmas ᵇ_____ ? (yet)

5 ★ ★ ★ Complete the sentences with the Past Simple or the Present Perfect form of the verbs in brackets.

Paola *acted* (act) in a play last Christmas. She *hasn't been* (not/be) in a film yet.

1 Marie ᵃ_____ (not/see) Madonna in concert. She ᵇ_____ (not/go) to the concert last time Madonna came to Paris.

2 Kurt ᵃ_____ (go) to the National Gallery in London last year. He ᵇ_____ (not/be) to Tate Modern yet.

3 Becky ᵃ_____ (read) *Game of Thrones*. She ᵇ_____ (read) it in 2019.

4 ᵃ_____ (you/speak) to Angela yet today? Believe it or not, she ᵇ_____ (win) first prize in a radio competition this morning.

5 The builders ᵃ_____ (start) work in spring. It's November now, and they still ᵇ_____ (not/finish).

SHOW WHAT YOU'VE LEARNT

6 Choose the correct answers A–C.

1 Your mum has ___ watched the game show. And again she got most of the questions right.
A yet   B just   C not

2 I ___ writing my poem yet.
A didn't finish   B have finished   C haven't finished

3 Alice has ___ been to Hollywood five times. Her aunt lives there.
A already   B just   C yet

4 ___ to the bookshop on Saturday?
A Have you been   B Did you go
C Were you

5 Have you finished reading the book about the history of Facebook ___ ?
A yet   B just   C next

6 Ken and Michelle ___ to Metallica's concert at the stadium last weekend.
A haven't been   B have been   C didn't go

/6

GRAMMAR: Train and Try Again page 146

1 ★ **Choose the correct answers.**

1 Alison was *too lazy / enough lazy / lazy enough* to walk to the theatre.

2 Jake isn't *enough strong / strong enough / too strong* to carry the guitar.

3 I think Patrick is *insensitive enough / enough insensitive / too insensitive* to write beautiful poems.

4 Jessica speaks *too quick / too quickly / quick enough* for us to understand her easily.

5 Zakary can win the talent show *easy enough / easily enough / too easy* in my opinion.

6 I don't think we've bought *too much / too many / enough* paper for making the concert posters. Look! It's just the perfect amount.

7 Detective Andrews didn't seem to be *fast enough / enough fast / too fast* to stop the crime.

8 Marta is worried that we won't have *enough chairs / chairs enough / too many chairs* for everybody to sit down.

2 ★ **Complete the sentences with *too* or *enough* and the correct form of the words in brackets.**

The book is *too long* (long). I don't have much time for reading.

1 Ken's MP3 player is _____ (loud). He can't hear his music on the bus.

2 This Russian novel has _____ (many) characters. I don't know who's who.

3 I'm _____ (young) to remember the band Nirvana. I was born in 2001.

4 If you learn to sing _____ (good), you could be a famous singer one day.

5 Your telly is _____ (small). I can't see the players on the pitch.

3 ★★ **Complete the sentences with *too* or *enough* and one of the adjectives from the box. There are two extra words.**

> addictive boring embarrassing funny
> moving old popular ~~serious~~

Ken Loach films are all *too serious*. I prefer more entertaining films where I can laugh and relax a bit.

1 This new *Harry Potter* book is _____ . I can't stop reading it.

2 Frank doesn't like jazz music. He says it's _____ and it all sounds the same.

3 You're _____ to watch this horror film. It's only for people over 18.

4 I loved The Kings of Leon before they became _____ . Now their music is more like pop than rock.

5 This romantic comedy is _____ . Can you hear anybody laughing? I can't.

4 ★★★ **Complete the second sentence so it has a similar meaning to the first. Use the word in capitals.**

Avatar isn't old enough to be called a classic film. **MODERN**

Avatar *is too modern* to be called a classic film.

1 Jemima is an elegant dancer and could join the ballet. **ENOUGH**

Jemima _____ to join the ballet.

2 The chat show had more guests than was necessary in my opinion. **TOO**

The chat show had _____ in my opinion.

3 I can't hear the news bulletin well because it's very quiet. **LOUD**

The news bulletin _____ for me to hear it well.

4 There are too few famous composers to organise a festival. **NOT**

There _____ to organise a festival.

5 This sofa isn't big enough for us to sit and watch the film. **SPACE**

There is _____ on this sofa for us to sit and watch the film.

5 ★★★ **Find and correct the mistakes. There are two correct sentences.**

It's to hot in this theatre and there aren't any windows. *too*

1 Claire hasn't got money enough to go to the Nick Cave concert. _____

2 It's not cold enough to watch the opera in the park event today. _____

3 The sculpture is too large to go in our living room. _____

4 The band didn't sell many enough CDs for them to become famous. _____

5 James read the poem too quickly for it to sound really beautiful. _____

6 This painting is too expensive enough for Thomas to buy. _____

1   **Put phrases a–g in the correct order.**

a   Bill Condon … / by / Directed *Directed by Bill*
      Condon …

b   was / character / played … / The / female / skilfully
      _____

c   fascinating … / The / is / plot _____

d   me, / word / is … / the / For / best / describes / this /
      movie / that _____
      _____

e   is / story / The / in … / set _____

f   for … / it's / In / view, / my / suitable _____
      _____

g   I've / one / seen / ever / It's / of / best / the / films
      _____

2   **Complete gaps 1–4 in the review below with suitable phrases from Exercise 1.**

Beautiful or Beastly?

Should you see the remake of Beauty and the Beast?

Beauty and the Beast, <u>starring</u> Emma Watson and Dan Stevens, <u>was released</u> in 2017 and was a big success around the world. <u>*a*</u>, the live action* musical <u>is based on</u> the original Disney animation. So, should you go and see it?

¹___ a castle in the small town of Villeneuve and follows the main character, Belle, as she tries to save her father from the Beast. The Beast was a selfish prince until a witch cast a spell on him. To break the spell, he must learn to love, and find someone who loves him too. <u>At first</u>, the Beast believes this is impossible. <u>Then</u> he meets Belle, and his opinion starts to change.

²___ , <u>the special effects are amazing</u>, and the songs superb. ³___ . But, unfortunately, <u>I didn't find the Beast very convincing</u>. I'm also not sure we needed a remake of this classic film.

⁴___ adults, teenagers and children alike. But if you know and love the original version, there is nothing new for you here.

* live action – a film that has real actors and animals instead of animations

3   **Match the underlined phrases in the review to the categories below. Then add extra phrases from Exercise 1. Some phrases match more than one category.**

1   **Background information:** *starring*, _____
      _____

2   **Plot:** _____
      _____

3   **Acting:** _____
      _____

4   **Personal opinion:** _____

4   **Read the review of the documentary *Free Solo*. Put paragraphs A–D in the correct order.**

1 _____   2 _____   3 _____   4 _____

FREE SOLO

Are you brave enough to watch?

A   The photography is fantastic and the ¹*remake / screenplay* holds your attention from beginning to end. Alex is very interesting and at times he is quite funny. The final thirty minutes is probably the most amazing thing I've ever watched on the big ²*screen / scene*.

B   I don't usually watch documentaries, but *Free Solo* has totally changed my opinion. The film stars American rock climber Alex Honnold as he prepares to climb a 900-metre vertical rock face without using a rope. ³*Directed / Starring* by Jimmy Chin and Elizabeth Chai Vasarhelyi, the film was ⁴*awarded / based* an Oscar for the best documentary in 2018.

C   In my view, *Free Solo* is ⁵*a masterpiece / suitable* for anyone who has a dream. Alex is one of the most inspiring people I've ever seen, so get up from the sofa and go watch it now!

D   The ⁶*screenplay / action* takes place in Yosemite National Park and in every ⁶*scene / plot* we see stunning mountains and fantastic views. At first you think this is a film only about climbing, but there is nothing unsurprising about this film. The ⁷*soundtrack / plot* also focuses on Alex's life and his relationship with his girlfriend, Sanni. Climbing without a rope is very dangerous, and it's fascinating to hear Alex and Sanni talk about their life together.

5   **Read the review in Exercise 4 again. Choose the correct words.**

6   **Match sentences 1–4 with a–d.**

      The word that best describes this movie is **amusing**.
1   The screenplay is very **engaging**.
2   The main character is **inspiring**.
3   The soundtrack is **superb**.
4   The story was so **predictable**.

a   She has a very successful job and four children.
b   I've listened to it hundreds of times!
c   It holds your attention from beginning to end.
d   I knew who the killer was from the beginning.
e   I was laughing a lot.

e   ○ ○ ○ ○

7   **Find synonyms in the review of *Free Solo* for the words below.**

      amusing   =   *funny*
1   engaging   =   _____
2   superb   =   _____ , _____ , _____
3   predictable   =   _____

8 Read the task below. Then read the review and choose the correct answers A–C.

A film review website is looking for writers and you decide to send them a review of a film you've seen recently. Write a review. Include and develop these points:

- An interesting title and background information on the film.
- The plot and main characters.
- Your opinion on different aspects of the film.
- A summary of your opinion and recommendations for potential viewers.

BLACK PANTHER:
The best superhero film in history?

This superhero film starring Chadwick Boseman as T'Challa can't disappoint. Directed ^A^*in / by / at* Ryan Coogler, the film is one of ^1^___ films of all time. It was nominated ^B^ *for / as / by* seven Oscars and eventually ^2^___ three!

Black Panther is set ^C^*in / as / on* the present day in a fictional African country, Wakanda. When the king of Wakanda dies, T'Challa (also called 'Black Panther') returns home to take his rightful place as king. Unfortunately, a new enemy ^3^___ for him, which puts the whole world at risk. ^D^*On / As / At* first, things do not look good. Black Panther needs to use all his skill and power to make the world safe again.

Bozseman gives a great performance ^E^*by / as / for* Black Panther, and the special effects are stunning. The plot is ^4^___ other superhero films. There are some amusing moments as well as lots of action.

The word that best describes this film is unforgettable. I absolutely loved it, and ^F^*in / at / as* my opinion it's suitable ^G^*by / for / with* teenagers and adults alike. *Black Panther* is a masterpiece and ^5^___ superhero film of the year!

1 A the more popular   B the most popular
   C more popular

2 A won   B was winning   C win

3 A are waiting   B is waiting   C has waited

4 A most engaging   B more engaging
   C more engaging than

5 A the best   B best   C the better

9 Read the review in Exercise 8 again and choose the correct prepositions.

10 You have been asked to write a film review for your school blog. Think of a film you have seen recently and write a review. Include and develop these points:

- An interesting title and background information on the film.
- The plot and main characters.
- Your opinion on different aspects of the film.
- A summary of your opinion and recommendations for potential viewers.

Finished? Always check your writing. Can you tick √ everything on this list?

In my film review:

- I have used an interesting title. ☐
- I have divided the review into paragraphs. ☐
- I have given background information, e.g. *Directed by…, The action takes place in … , etc.* ☐
- I have described the plot and the main characters, e.g. *At first/Then/Later on…, The acting is excellent/terrible, etc.* ☐
- I have given my opinion, e.g. *The special effects are amazing, It's one of the best films I've ever seen, etc.* ☐
- I have given information who should see the film, e.g. *The film is suitable for ....* ☐
- I have used the phrases and vocabulary from the lesson to make my text interesting, e.g. *engaging, amusing, convincing, etc.* ☐
- I have used some contractions (e.g. *I'm / aren't / that's*). ☐
- I have checked my spelling and punctuation. ☐
- My text is neat and clear. ☐

SPEAKING

Describing a photo

1 Translate the phrases into your own language.

SPEAKING BANK

Beginning a description

In this photo, I can see .../ _____
there is .../there are … _____

This photo shows … _____

Saying where (place)

There are … so I think they're _____
in a bookshop/art gallery/at _____
a concert, etc. _____

Saying where (in the photo)

in the background/in the _____
middle/in the foreground _____
_____

on the left/on the right _____
_____

in front of/behind/next to _____

Speculating

He/She looks shy/bored/ _____
tired, etc. _____
_____
_____

She's probably … _____
Perhaps/Maybe/I imagine/I'm _____
sure … _____
_____

Giving your opinion

I think .../I don't think .../ _____
Personally, .../In my opinion, … _____

2 Complete the descriptions with adjectives from the box. There are two extra words.

> empty   famous   miserable   noisy
> ~~proud~~   quiet   shy   tired

I think this man in the foreground has won first prize. He has a medal and he looks very _proud_.

1 They are standing in a forest and there is nobody else there. It's a very _____ place. I imagine there is only the sound of the wind in the trees.

2 There is nobody in the restaurant. It's completely _____ . The waiter has nothing to do and he looks bored.

3 She's sitting next to this handsome guy, but she looks very uncomfortable and her face is red. Perhaps she's _____ and she doesn't know what to say.

4 They have just finished running a race I think, so they probably feel very _____ .

5 It looks cold and wet. I don't think the family sitting on the beach are enjoying their day out. They all look really _____ .

3 Put the words in order to make phrases. Then complete the descriptions.

shows / a / This / classroom / photo
This photo shows a classroom. The children are young and it looks noisy.

1 of / photo, / can / I / this / In / see / lots / photographers

_____.
They are all trying to take a picture of this lady.

2 in / I / so / think / he's
There are books everywhere, _____
_____ a library, or maybe a bookshop.

3 nurse / middle / the / in / The
_____ looks very friendly.

4 so / looks / He / perhaps / smart, / very
_____ it is a job interview.

5 my / In / opinion
_____ , shopping is a boring way to spend your time.

REMEMBER THIS

+ _I think he's in a bookshop._

– _I don't think he's in a library._

~~I think he isn't in a library.~~

4 Complete the description of the photo with the words and phrases from the box. There are two extra items.

> happy   I imagine   In the middle   looks
> next to   On the left   Personally   so I think
> They are   ~~This photo shows~~

This photo shows people watching a film at the cinema. There are children in the audience, ¹_____ it's a family film. In the foreground, there is a family. ²_____ , there is a man holding a drink. He's probably the dad. ³_____ , is a little boy. He ⁴_____ about six or seven years old. His mum is sitting ⁵_____ him. They all look really ⁶_____ . They are laughing, so ⁷_____ they're watching a comedy.

1   In pairs, ask and answer the questions.

PART 1

Talk about science.
1   Which scientific invention is the most important in your life? Why?
2   In your science studies, do you prefer doing experiments in the lab or doing research in the library? Why?
3   Would you prefer to be a marine biologist or a linguist? Why?
4   Does technology have any bad influence on our lives? Why?/Why not?
5   How do you think science will change the world in the next fifty years?

PART 2

Talk about the arts.
1   What book have you read recently? Who can you recommend it to and why?
2   What's your favourite type of TV programme? Why?
3   Would you prefer to read a crime novel or historical fiction? Why?
4   Do you enjoy superhero films? Why?/Why not?
5   What's more important in a film: the acting, the script or the special effects?

2   Look at the photos of art exhibitions.

PART 1

Take turns to describe the photos.

A

B

PART 2

In pairs, ask and answer the questions about the photos.

Student A's photo
1   What place does the photo show?
2   What form of art can you see in the photo?
3   What can you see in the background of the photo?
4   What do you personally think of this work of art?
5   Why do you think the work of art is located in this place?

Student B's photo
1   What place can you see in this photo?
2   What form of art does the photo show?
3   What can you see on the right of the photo?
4   What is there on the left of the photo?
5   What's your opinion of the art in the photo?

3   Read the instructions on your card. In pairs, take turns to role-play the conversation.

Student A

You are doing a survey about the forms of art that students enjoy. Ask Student B the questions.

*   Ask Student B if he/she can help you with your art survey.
*   Ask if he/she thinks that cooking programmes are more entertaining than talent shows.
*   Ask what he/she thinks is the best type of TV programme.
*   Ask what book he/she has just finished and how he/she can describe it.
*   Ask what is the most gripping film he/she has watched recently.
*   Ask which form of art he/she finds most engaging.
*   Thank him/her and end conversation.

Student B

Student A is doing a survey about the forms of art that students enjoy. Answer his/her questions.

*   Say yes, you're happy to help.
*   Tell Student B your opinion about cooking programmes and talent shows.
*   Answer the question about TV programmes.
*   Tell Student B about a book you have just finished.
*   Answer the question about a film you have seen recently.
*   Tell Student B your opinion about art forms.

3.10 SELF-CHECK

VOCABULARY AND GRAMMAR

1 Complete the sentences with the correct words. The first and last letters are given.

Paul loves art. I think he should become a p<u>ainte</u>r.

1 Matt says **m**_____**s** like *La La Land* are silly because people in the real world don't sing and dance when they speak.

2 Oh no! There's been another earthquake in Mexico. It's on all the **n**_____**s b**_____**s** at the moment.

3 My favourite **c**_____**g p**_____**e** was on TV this morning. It showed us how to make Polish doughnuts with rose marmalade.

4 At the art gallery, Ben liked the paintings of nature best, but I liked the **p**_____**s**. I love paintings of real people.

5 Stephen King's books are usually so **g**_____**g** that they are hard to stop reading once you start them.

/5

2 Choose the correct answers.

The Da Vinci Code is just one of many of Dan Brown's excellent (thrillers)/ *biographies* / *classic novels*.

1 Jackson Pollock's *classic oil paintings* / *modern abstract paintings* / *street art* were very controversial and many people said his art looked like pictures by children.

2 I wouldn't like to be a(n) *A-list* / *genre* / *blockbuster* actor. You have no private life.

3 Some fairy *programmes* / *tales* / *novels* are really scary. In fact, quite a lot of the famous ones have witches or monsters in them.

4 Gavin thought the *plot* / *script* / *setting* of the film was very original – especially the end which was a complete surprise for him.

5 Johnny Depp is my favourite actor. His new film comes *on* / *up* / *out* soon and I'm really excited.

/5

3 Complete the sentences with words from the box. There are two extra items.

> box office   comic books   costumes   documentary
> horrors   photographer   sculpture   ~~special effects~~

The *special effects* in this science fiction film are amazing.

1 Fiona's uncle was a _____ . He took pictures of some of the biggest stars in the 60s.

2 My grandpa has had a very interesting life. He worked as a fashion designer for some years and then he got a job making _____ for films.

3 Peter will collect the cinema tickets from the _____ this afternoon.

4 Bob has a large collection of _____ . He has some with Superman and Batman from the 1960s.

5 There's an interesting _____ on telly tomorrow. It's about the life of the artist Claude Monet.

/5

4 Choose the correct words.

Tomorrow will be as cold *than* /(as)/ *with* today.

1 Hollywood is *bit* / *far* / *just* hotter than London at this time of year.

2 Ella is not *fit* / *fitter* / *fittest* than Sandra. They both finished the marathon.

3 The *far* / *further* / *furthest* Leo has ever swum is 2.5 kilometres.

4 I think a hot bath is *most* / *more* / *as* relaxing than watching TV.

5 That was *as* / *the* / *than* most entertaining film I've seen in ages.

/5

5 Complete the sentences with the Present Perfect form of the verbs in brackets. Choose one of the time expressions and put it in the correct place in the sentence.

I*'ve already found* (find) a suitable birthday present for Emily _____ . (already/yet)

1 I _____ (finish) a new poem. Would you like to be the first person to hear it _____ ? (just/yet)

2 Eileen _____ (see) the new James Bond film _____ . (already/yet)

3 _____ Rosa _____ (look) at a travel guide for Spain _____ ? (already/yet)

4 Mum _____ (pay) for the theatre tickets. I gave her the money back last week _____ . (already/just)

5 We _____ (not/meet) any of the other guests _____ . We only arrived at the party two minutes ago. (just/yet)

/5

6 Complete each pair of sentences with the same answer A–C.

My favourite types of books are historical ____ .
Blade Runner is a classic science ____ film.
A books   B stories   (C) fiction

1 This new ____ is much better than my last one.
Too many films are all just ____ generated images nowadays.
A photo   B computer   C animation

2 Tony gave ____ his job in a supermarket to play in a band.
Don't let Adam tell you what to do. Stand ____ for yourself.
A out   B in   C up

3 We ____ just come back from a very loud concert and I still can't hear very well.
Does he ____ any books about the history of football?
A had   B have   C has

4 The exhibition is ____ next week, so we should go this weekend.
You'll never guess the ____ to this thriller.
A ending   B finishing   C setting

5 Chris is the same age ____ me.
History is not as difficult ____ Maths.
A than   B like   C as

/5

Total   /30

44

7 Choose the correct answers A–C.

Ealing Film Studios

Ealing Studios is a _A_ and television production company in west London. It may not be as well-known ¹__ Hollywood, but it started making films in 1902. In fact, it is the ²__ working film studio in the world.

The studio became famous for making a series of films called the Ealing ³__ and they made people laugh in cinemas around the world. They ⁴__ seventeen of these highly successful films between 1947 and 1958.

From 1955 to 1995 the BBC owned the company. Although the studio is now not theirs, they have continued to make TV shows at Ealing. In fact, they ⁵__ making the final season of the very popular period drama _Downtown Abbey_ there.

	(A) film	B show	C setting
1	A as	B than	C like
2	A old	B older	C oldest
3	A comedies	B horrors	C thrillers
4	A made	B have made	C were making
5	A just finished	B have just finished	C just finish

/5

8 Complete the sentences with the correct form of the word in brackets.

Have you seen the weather _forecast_ (CAST) today? Is it going to rain?

1 I've just seen the _____ (TRAIL) for the new film by Oliver Stone. It looks excellent!

2 Amy wants to be a _____ (SCULPT) when she finishes art school.

3 My mum bought me the CD of the _____ (TRACK) of the _La La Land_ musical. How embarrassing!

4 Lewis can't paint _____ (LAND), so he only does portraits of people.

5 I could never be an artist. I'm not _____ (IMAGINE) enough.

/5

9 Complete the sentences with the words in brackets in the correct form. Do not change the order of the words. You may need to add words. Use no more than six words in each gap.

Don't tell me how the film ends! I _haven't seen the film_ (not / see / film) yet.

1 _Now You See Me 2_ is _____ (far / bad) than the first film.

2 We are _____ (much / early) we need to be. Let's buy a drink and some popcorn.

3 Karen is _____ (just / excite / as) I am about the Adele concert.

4 Harry _____ (just / finish) season 2 of _Game of Thrones_.

5 Brad Pitt is _____ (much / good / actor) Tom Cruise!

/5

10 Choose the correct answers A–C to replace the underlined part of the sentence.

This film is <u>not as funny as it should be</u> to be a called a romantic 'comedy'.
A not much fun
B not too funny
(C) not funny enough

1 I like British sitcoms best because I can <u>relate to</u> the characters.
A understand
B feel like
C follow

2 There are <u>not enough</u> travel shows on TV in my opinion.
A not any
B not many
C too many

3 There are not <u>too many</u> tickets left. We should buy them now.
A any
B many
C enough

4 Game shows are <u>much more entertaining than</u> reality TV shows.
A not as entertaining as
B a bit more entertaining than
C far more entertaining than

5 Thrillers are <u>far more complex than</u> horror films.
A much more complex than
B more complex than
C a bit more complex than

/5

Total	/20

4 Home sweet home

VOCABULARY

4.1

Describing houses • inside a house
• *make or do*

SHOW WHAT YOU KNOW

1 Choose the odd one out in each group of four words.

	table	oven	dishwasher	~~desk~~
1	shower	coffee table	armchair	sofa
2	lamp	rug	microwave	bed
3	bath	dining table	washbasin	toilet
4	kitchen	living room	plant	bedroom
5	chair	bathroom	study	hall

WORD STORE 4A | Describing houses

2 Match the words from the box to pictures B–L.

> bungalow ~~concrete~~ cottage glass
> housing estate semi-detached house
> stone suburbs terraced house
> the countryside wood village

Material	Houses	Location
concrete		

---

3 Complete the information on the website. The first and last letters are given.

HouseProperties

| Home | Search | Hot | Contact |

This week's Hot Homes
See our list of the top five houses/flats for sale

22 Greenways Road – This is a lovely s<u>emi</u>-d<u>etache</u>d house, with neighbours on the south side only. Greenways Road is in the quiet ¹**s**_____**s** of the city, and good transport links get you to the historic centre in only 15 minutes. **More →**

78 Darrington Avenue – This small ²**t**_____**d** house (quiet neighbours on both sides) is made of red ³**b**_____**k** and has a private garden at the back and a real fire in the living room – very ⁴**c**_____**y** on cold winter nights! **More →**

8 Denholme Street – This 300-year-old stone ⁵**c**_____**e** is very near the ⁶**s**_____**a** and has wonderful views across the water. It also comes with a few nice surprises: there's a study downstairs in the ⁷**b**_____**t** and a small guest bedroom on the second ⁸**f**_____**r**. **More →**

Oak House, Long Lane – A large and very ⁹**s**_____**s** home (8 big rooms!) in a small, friendly ¹⁰**v**_____**e** only 30 miles from London. This ¹¹**d**_____**d** house has large gardens all round. Built in the 1800s, this is a very ¹²**t**_____**l** English home. **More →**

128/14 Ivy Close – These new ¹³**f**_____**s** (seven in each building) are very ¹⁴**m**_____**n** and have hi-tech kitchens and bathrooms. The kitchen, living room and dining room are ¹⁵**o**_____**n** plan, so there's one very big living space. Ivy Close is right in the city ¹⁶**c**_____**e**, close to shops and offices, so it's perfect for young professionals. **More →**

WORD STORE 4B | Inside a house

4 Match the numbers in the picture to the words in the box. There are three extra items.

- [7] bedside table
- [ ] bookcase
- [ ] carpet
- [ ] chest of drawers
- [ ] cooker
- [ ] cupboard
- [ ] desk
- [ ] fridge
- [ ] front door
- [ ] kitchen sink
- [ ] ladder
- [ ] radiator
- [ ] shelves
- [ ] stairs
- [ ] wardrobe
- [ ] wooden floor

In which room do the three extra items go?
The _____

WORD STORE 4C | make or do

5 Choose *make* or *do* to complete the sentences.

1. Gordon's food is delicious, but he always ᵃ*does* / *makes* a mess in the kitchen when he ᵇ*does* / *makes* the cooking.
2. When Mum and Dad ᵃ*do* / *make* the housework, they ᵇ*do* / *make* a lot of noise, and I can't concentrate on my homework.
3. Helen never ᵃ*does* / *makes* the shopping on Saturdays. She prefers to ᵇ*do* / *make* the gardening if the weather is nice.
4. I would like to *do* / *make* a complaint about this meal. My burger is cold and my cola is warm.
5. Katy, I want you to ᵃ*do* / *make* your bed while I ᵇ*do* / *make* dinner.
6. Which would you prefer – ᵃ*doing* / *making* the ironing or ᵇ*doing* / *making* the washing-up?
7. Right! I've ᵃ*done* / *made* a decision. I'm going to ᵇ*do* / *make* my homework now and then clean my room.
8. Do you *do* / *make* your own washing? My mum still washes all of my clothes.

REMEMBER THIS

stay at home = don't leave your house/flat
leave home = leave your house/flat
go home = go back to your house/flat
get home = arrive at your house/flat

---

6 Read REMEMBER THIS. Complete the sentences with the phrases in bold.

> Tomorrow, I need to *leave* home at 6 a.m. My flight is at 8:15 a.m. and it takes about half an hour to get to the airport.

1. Kim doesn't feel like going out, so we are going to _____ at home and watch a film.
2. It's 11:00 p.m. and you have to be up early tomorrow – I think you should _____ home and get some sleep.
3. I'm hungry, Alex. When we _____ home, I'll start cooking dinner straight away, OK?

REMEMBER BETTER

To remember the collocations with *home* in Exercise 6, write sentences about a typical day or weekend in your life.

Complete the sentences with personal information.

> On school days, I leave home at *7.30 a.m.* (time).

1. After school, I usually go home by _____ (means of transport).
2. On weekdays, I usually get home at _____ (time).
3. Sometimes I go out at the weekend, but sometimes I just enjoy staying at home and _____ (activity).

SHOW WHAT YOU'VE LEARNT

7 Choose the correct words.

1. My grandma chose a *terraced house* / *bungalow* / *detached house* because this type of house is all on the ground floor and doesn't have stairs.
2. Diana keeps all of her clothes in an antique *cupboard* / *desk* / *wardrobe* next to her bed.
3. Grandad built his own house out of *wood* / *concrete* / *stone* from trees in the local forest.
4. A greenhouse is a building where you grow plants. It is made of *metal* / *brick* / *glass* so that the light and heat from the sun can get in easily.
5. Sue has a flat *on the top floor* / *on the ground floor* / *in the basement* of her building. You can see the whole town from her living room window.
6. I wonder how long it will take to build this red *concrete* / *brick* / *stone* wall – probably a couple of months.
7. Kevin, the washing is dry and it's your turn to *do the shopping* / *do the cooking* / *do the ironing*. Dad needs a shirt and a pair of trousers for work tomorrow.
8. No, leave the plates, please! You made dinner, so I'll *do the gardening* / *do the washing* / *do the washing-up*.
9. Sssh. Don't *make a complaint* / *make a mess* / *make a noise*. The baby is sleeping.
10. Thomas's flat is always cold because the *ladders* / *radiators* / *fridges* don't work.

/10

SHOW WHAT YOU KNOW

1 Decide if the underlined part of each sentence describes a *point in time* or *period of time*.

I was born in <u>1997</u>.	(point)/period
The film was <u>two hours</u> long.	point /(period)
1 I like living in the city, so <u>a week</u> in the country is long enough.	point /period
2 Sasha moved into her flat in <u>2017</u>.	point /period
3 It took us <u>3 days</u> to paint the walls in my bedroom.	point /period
4 Zara finished her homework at <u>6:00 p.m.</u>	point /period
5 The village is <u>375 years</u> old.	point /period
6 My parents bought the house <u>when they got married.</u>	point /period

2 ★ Choose the correct words.

1 Luke has lived in this cottage *for / since* he was three years old.

2 I haven't done the washing *for / since* two weeks. I have no clean clothes.

3 We have wanted to live in a village near the sea *for / since* so many years!

4 Annie has been in bed *for / since* yesterday morning. She's really sick.

5 People have built houses in this area *for / since* thousands of years.

6 My brother hasn't had a bath *for / since* at least six months. He prefers the shower.

7 They've had a wood-burner *for / since* about three years but now they want to change it because it's not good for their health.

8 The pasta has been in the cupboard *for / since* we moved into this flat four years ago.

9 Dad hasn't cut the grass *for / since* he lost the key to the shed.

3 ★ ★ Complete the sentences with the Present Perfect form of the verbs in brackets and *for* or *since*.

Kevin's in his room, but he *hasn't made* (not/make) a noise *since* one o'clock. Do you think he's OK?

1 We ᵃ_____ (have) this pizza in our fridge ᵇ_____ two weeks.

2 Harry ᵃ_____ (write) lots of miserable poems ᵇ_____ he stopped seeing Ellen.

3 Chloe ᵃ_____ (not/make) her bed ᵇ_____ three days.

4 Lewis and Oliver ᵃ_____ (play) for the school football team ᵇ_____ two years.

5 ᵃ_____ last month, there ᵇ_____ (be) a market in the city centre.

4 ★ ★ ★ Use the words in brackets to complete the questions and answers in the Present Perfect. Add *for* or *since*.

Q: How long *have you lived* (you/live) in London?

A: We*'ve lived in London for* 5 years.

1 Q: How long ᵃ_____ (Olivia/want) to be an architect?
   A: Oh, Olivia ᵇ_____ she visited Barcelona.

2 Q: How long ᵃ_____ (your parents/be) married?
   A: I don't really know, but they ᵇ_____ a long time.

3 Q: How long ᵃ_____ (Alice/know) Samuel?
   A: She ᵇ_____ they started school together.

4 Q: How long ᵃ_____ (your sister/have) long hair?
   A: She ᵇ_____ at least six months.

SHOW WHAT YOU'VE LEARNT

5 Use the information in brackets to write Present Perfect sentences. Use *for* or *since* if necessary.

I've been passionate about poetry for (be/ passionate about poetry) three years.

1 I _____ (not/be/ to school) two weeks.

2 Molly _____ (not/read/a good book) last year.

3 How long _____ (Polly/be busy) in the kitchen?

4 The World Wide Web _____ _____ (exist) 1989.

5 Lauren _____ (not/see/Oliver) four days.

6 How long _____ (your grandparents/live) in a bungalow?

/6

GRAMMAR: Train and Try Again page 147

Verb-noun collocations
• phrasal verbs

1 Read what Speaker 1 says about his/her family. Choose the correct verbs to complete the collocations.

Extract from Students' Book recording 🔊 **2.7**

S1: I ¹*have / am / do* a big family – there are seven of us in this house, and we're all very noisy people. It's okay when you're feeling sociable, but sometimes I want to ²*have / be / spend* on my own and have some quiet time. So I ³*shut / open / enter* my bedroom door, ⁴*do / listen / put* my headphones on and listen to music or ⁵*chat / see / spend* with my friends. I have a sign on the door that says 'Keep Out' and it's not just for my parents. My brothers and sisters ⁶*do / are / have* not welcome either. My room is a calm place for me to get away from other people.

2 Complete what Speaker 3 says about his/her room with the verbs from the box. There are two extra verbs.

~~decorate~~ have make painted
played showed write

Extract from Students' Book recording 🔊 **2.7**

S3: I think my room reflects my personality. My parents let me *decorate* it in my favourite colour, so I ¹_____ the walls black and put different coloured lights everywhere. I love making things – I use my room as a kind of studio. I paint and ²_____ music lyrics. On my computer, I ³_____ music mixes and create light shows to go with them. It's awesome. When my friends ⁴_____ a party, they always ask me to do the music.

3 Complete gaps 1–4 on the word maps with the verbs from the box. There are two extra verbs. Then complete gaps a–d with underlined words from the recording extracts.

chat listen ~~paint~~ play put shut write

paint ·········· *the walls*
··········· a picture

1 _____ ·········· a _____
··········· a blog

2 _____ ·········· b _____
··········· the window

3 _____ ·········· c _____
··········· a sign on your door

4 _____ ·········· d _____
··········· about school

Use diagrams to record verb noun collocations. Write them on Post-it notes and stick them on your computer. Look at them and revise whenever you can!

Add three more items to the word maps for *play* and *listen to*.

1 play ················ together
··········· computer games
·········· *music*
······ a _____
······ b _____
······ c _____

2 listen to ·········· my MP3 player
··········· your parents
··········· music
······ d _____
······ e _____
······ f _____

WORD STORE 4D | Phrasal verbs

4 Complete the sentences with the correct prepositions.

from in x2 out ~~on~~ round

Caleb has taken <u>on</u> a job near the sea, so we won't see him so often now.

1 That's Sarah at the door. Can you let her _____ ? I'm busy cooking in the kitchen.

2 Matt always comes _____ on Fridays and we play computer games.

3 My mum wants to move to the countryside to get away _____ the noise of the big city.

4 Adam has decided to stay _____ tonight and watch the match on telly.

5 James's father has replaced the front door on their shop with a big metal one. He hopes it will keep _____ criminals.

1 Read the text quickly and choose the best title.

1 England's Shyest Man
2 England's Most Unusual Duke
3 England's Strangest House

W. J. Cavendish-Scott-Bentinck, the fifth Duke* of Portland, was a very wealthy and very odd Englishman. He was born in 1800 and lived to be nearly 80 years old. The Duke was a successful businessman with lots of money and an amazing home, but he was not an average aristocrat.

The first unusual thing about him was his choice of clothes. ¹_____ He also liked wearing wigs*, and pieces of material tied around his ankles (nobody knows why!).

Another unusual thing about him was his incredible shyness. He lived in a huge house called Welbeck Abbey, but spent most of his time in just one or two of the rooms. He had many servants*, but he was too shy to talk to them. ²_____ If servants did meet him anywhere in the house or garden,

they had to stand completely still, say nothing, and look down at the ground until he was gone. Inside Welbeck Abbey, there was a mini-railway and, to avoid any face-to-face contact, the servants from the kitchen used to send meals to his room on the mini-train.

As well as this unusual form of transport, there were many other amazing things in the Duke's house. ³_____ Also underground*, he built many tunnels and used them to move around his giant house and garden without seeing anyone. One of the tunnels went all the way from Welbeck Abbey to the nearby town of Worksop – almost 3 km away! Welbeck Abbey wasn't the Duke's only home. ⁴_____ He didn't build this one though; the Duke's grandfather

won it in a game of cards! In total, nearly 1,500 people worked for W.J. Cavendish-Scott-Bentinck. Sometimes he was a moody and unusual boss, but at other times he was very kind. ⁵_____ He also built a boating lake, an area for ice-skating and a horse-riding school for his servants to use. The horse-riding school had a glass roof over 100 metres long!

When the Duke died in 1879, his relatives found that most of the rooms in his house had no furniture and the walls were all pink. In one room, there was only a toilet – nothing else at all! In another room were hundreds of green boxes, and in each one there was a dark brown wig. Nobody knows how many of them he actually wore.

GLOSSARY

duke (n) – a very important English aristocrat
wig (n) – false hair worn on the head
servant (n) – in the past, people paid servants to cook and clean, etc. for them

underground (adj, adv) – below the ground, e.g. you can leave your car in the underground car park; rabbits live underground

2 Read the text again. Complete gaps 1–5 with sentences A–F. There is one extra sentence.

A Instead, he communicated with them by ringing a bell and leaving notes in special boxes.

B He had another beautiful house in London and sometimes stayed there.

C A third unusual thing about him was that he hated all kinds of dancing.

D For example, he gave each servant an umbrella and bought horses for them to ride through the gardens and in the tunnels under his house.

E He often wore two or more coats at the same time and a very strange hat – it was nearly a metre tall.

F For instance, he built an underground ballroom with space for 2,000 guests, but he never used it because he was too shy to invite anyone.

3 Read the questions and underline the parts of the text with the answers.

1 What was unusual about the Duke's hat?
2 Why did he write notes to his servants?
3 How did his servants deliver his food?
4 Why was the underground ballroom never used?
5 How did the Duke's grandfather get the house in London?
6 How long was the roof of the riding school?
7 What was in the room with the toilet?

VOCABULARY PRACTICE | Landscape features

4 Look at the vocabulary in lesson 4.4 in the Students' Book. Complete the sentences with the correct word or phrase from the box.

cave crater island rainforest ruins rock
stilts treehouse turquoise oceans volcano

Aitken Basin is the largest _crater_ on the moon. It's 2,500 km wide and 12 km deep.

1 I fell out of a _____ in my garden when I was younger and broke my arm.
2 In some countries, they build houses on _____ to protect them from floods and help keep dangerous snakes out of the home.
3 Europe's largest _____ is actually in South America in French-owned Guiana! It is home to over 1,000 animal species and 5,625 types of plant.
4 Mauna Loa, Hawaii, is the world's largest _____ – it's also one of the most active. There have been 33 eruptions since 1843.
5 The _____ of Machu Picchu are one of the most famous historical places in the world.
6 If you like _____ , you should visit the Maldives where you can swim in some of the clearest waters on Earth.
7 Postojna is a famous _____ in Slovenia. Actually, it's a 24,340-metre long system of underground rooms full of stalactites and stalagmites.
8 If we say Australia is a continent, Greenland is actually the biggest _____ in the world.
9 Aphrodite _____ , located near the coast of Cyprus, marks the place where Aphrodite, the goddess of love, beauty, procreation, and pleasure, was born.

VOCABULARY PRACTICE | Describing places

5 Look at the vocabulary in lesson 4.4 in the Students' Book. Match the sentence halves. There is one extra ending.

Calico in California is an old mining [h]
1 I really don't like such hot ☐
2 There are a lot of traffic ☐
3 Good bars and restaurants attract ☐
4 Guangzhou is one of the main trading ☐
5 There are plenty of historic ☐
6 The main terrace in Parc Güell offers some of the most breathtaking ☐

a and humid weather.
b monuments worth seeing in Venice, not just Saint Mark's Square.
c visitors to the city centre.
d village next to the sea.
e jams in my city.
f views in the whole of Barcelona.
g centres in China.
h and ghost town where some buildings come from the 1880s.

WORD STORE 4E | Collocations

6 Look at the vocabulary in lesson 4.4 in the Students' Book. Complete the collocations in the sentences. The first and last letters are given.

The a_ncien_t city of Troy, once a great and beautiful place, is now just a load of old stones.

1 The Daintree is a d_____e rainforest in the north-east of Australia. Some experts believe it is 180 million years old, so much older than the Amazon rainforest.
2 There are plenty of h_____t s_____s in Europe, but the most famous is probably the Blue Lagoon in Iceland. The water temperature there is 37–39°C.
3 Cantabria in northern Spain is famous for its l_____h vegetation. It has a very wet climate and is part of a larger area that people call 'Green Spain'.
4 Mount Tambora in Indonesia is the world's largest volcanic c_____r. It is 4.36 miles wide and 1 mile deep.
5 The Lut Desert in Iran is the hottest place on Earth. Because of the s_____g temperatures, there is very little life in the area.
6 A n_____c t_____e is a group of people that are always moving. Examples are the Bedouin in the Middle East and the Cherokee Native Americans.

GRAMMAR

4.5

Future forms: Present Continuous, *be going to* and *will*

SHOW WHAT YOU KNOW

1 Complete the sentences with the Present Continuous form of the verbs in brackets.

Charles! Your fish and chips *are getting* (get) cold now. Hurry up!

1 I _____ (not/lie) now. Really! I promise it's true.

2 Hello? _____ (you/come)? I'm waiting here but I can't see you.

3 Lisa can't come to the phone now. She _____ (run) in the park.

4 Ian and Emma _____ (not/talk) at the moment. They disagree about the bathroom.

5 _____ (Mum and Dad/sleep)? I want to practise playing my drums.

2 ★ Choose the correct future forms.

Conversation 1: Adrian and Bradley

A: I hear your parents have just bought a new house. When ᵃ*are you moving / will you move* in?

B: Oh, we ᵇ*won't move / aren't moving* in until next month. The 28th I think it is.

Conversation 2: Alice, Ben and Caroline

A: Are you coming to class? It's almost 9:00.

B: Yes. *I'm seeing / I'll see* you later Caroline, OK?

C: OK, bye.

Conversation 3: Anna and Brian

A: Oh no! That man has just stolen my bag!

B: *I'm calling / I'll call* the police.

Conversation 4: Amanda and Mum

A: Mum, what ᵃ*will we have / are we having* for dinner today?

M: Oh, I don't know. ᵇ*We'll see / We're seeing* what's in the fridge.

3 ★ ★ Complete each pair of sentences. Look at the context and choose *be going to* + verb or the Present Continuous.

1 a *We're going to eat* (eat) in a restaurant, but we haven't decided which one.

   b We _____ (eat) in a restaurant tonight. The table is booked for 7:00.

2 a Nathan _____ (visit) his friend in the UK next week. He reserved a seat yesterday.

   b Nathan _____ (visit) his friend in the UK if he can find a cheap flight.

3 a Penny and Jill _____ (play) tennis if it stops raining.

   b Penny and Jill _____ (play) tennis at 4:30 at the sports centre.

4 ★ ★ ★ Complete the messages with the most suitable future form of the verbs in brackets.

A: Hi Lily. Got any plans for today?

B: Hi Alex. I *'m meeting* (meet) Fran at 4 p.m. We ¹_____ (see) the new James Bond movie if there are any seats left. Wanna come?

A: Love to :) Do you need a lift to town? I ²_____ (pick) you up, if you want.

B: Cool. Katie's here now – we ³_____ (do) some homework after lunch (at least that's the plan!). I think we ⁴_____ (be) free by 3 p.m. though.

A: OK. By the way, Pete ⁵_____ (have) a party tonight. We can all go after the film.

B: Fantastic. Fran loves parties.

SHOW WHAT YOU'VE LEARNT

5 Choose the correct answers A–C.

1 There's someone at the front door. __ it?
   A Are you going to get
   B Will you get
   C Are you getting

2 Jasmine and William __ house tomorrow.
   A are going to move
   B will move
   C are moving

3 I think I __ a ham and mushroom pizza ... no, actually ... salami and pepper.
   A 'm going to have
   B 'll have
   C 'm having

4 Becky __ a bookcase when she has time.
   A 's going to buy
   B 'll buy
   C 's buying

5 We __ on Saturday night anymore. The airline moved the flight to Sunday morning.
   A aren't going to fly
   B won't fly
   C aren't flying

6 I'm afraid your sister __ . She called to say she's sick.
   A isn't going to come
   B won't come
   C isn't coming

/6

GRAMMAR: Train and Try Again page 147

1 ★ **Complete the sentences with the correct words in capitals.**

1 COMPLETE / COMPLETELY
   a The heavy rain ruined the picnic _____ .
   b The meal I cooked was a _____ disaster.

2 EASY / EASILY
   a It wasn't _____ to move those heavy cupboards upstairs.
   b We can make bookshelves _____ with some bricks and pieces of wood.

3 HEALTHY / HEALTHILY
   a I really need to start eating more _____ .
   b Sofia is in the kitchen cooking us all a _____ meal.

4 REAL / REALLY
   a Is that a _____ Picasso on your wall?
   b That painting is _____ beautiful. Did you do it?

5 WISE / WISELY
   a Jonathan has _____ decided not to travel alone to Jordan.
   b Amanda made the _____ decision to buy a flat in the city centre.

6 BEAUTIFUL / BEAUTIFULLY
   a You live in a _____ part of the country, Patrick.
   b Stan has painted the room _____ , hasn't he?

2 ★ **Complete the sentences with the correct form of the words in bold.**

Jack is always **careful**. He does his homework _carefully_.

1 Mandy is always **fast**. She rides her bike _____ .

2 Dean is always **early**. He arrived at my house _____ .

3 My brother Luke is always **slow**. He walks _____ .

4 Margaret is **good** at everything. She sings _____ .

5 Alan is always **late**. He gets to school _____ .

3 ★ ★ **Complete the sentences with the correct forms of the words in brackets.**

Amy writes _more clearly_ (more/clear) than Richard and I prefer her style too.

1 Arthur does the ironing _____ (pretty/bad). I usually have to do it again.

2 I'm _____ (slight/worry) about moving from the city to the countryside.

3 Tabby makes her bed _____ (really/careful). What's the point when you are only going to make it messy again?

4 Mike's dad drives _____ (quite/quick). I don't feel safe in his car.

5 Sarah was _____ (little/embarrassed) when she realised she was still wearing her pyjamas.

6 David works _____ (much/hard) than me but we get the same results.

7 Joanna looked _____ (bit/sad) when I saw her this morning. Do you know what's wrong?

4 ★ ★ ★ **Find and correct the mistakes. One sentence is correct.**

I went to bed really ~~lately~~ last night. _late_

1 James always works extremely hardly compared to how I normally work. _____

2 I always do the washing-up rather bad, so you should probably do it yourself. _____

3 Do you really think that Oliver speaks more polite than his little brother? _____

4 If you want my opinion, I actually think Eva drives a little too fast. _____

5 Hannah's mother cooks pretty good. Her pizzas are the best thing ever! _____

5 ★ ★ ★ **Complete the second sentence so that it has a similar meaning to the first. Use no more than six words, including the word in capitals.**

It's amazing that James is a really quick learner of everything. **EXTREMELY**

It's amazing that James learns everything _extremely quickly_.

1 Marta speaks quite good French, don't you think? **PRETTY**

Marta speaks French _____ , don't you think?

2 I really don't like the fact that Jennifer is slightly lazy. **LITTLE**

I really don't like the fact that Jennifer does everything _____ .

3 It's absolutely great news that Jake's house is quite near mine. **RATHER**

It's absolutely great news that Jake lives _____ .

4 Everybody in school knows that Stephen is a very fast runner. **REALLY**

Everybody in school knows that Stephen runs _____ .

5 Actually, I am a little better at gardening than Paul. **BIT**

Actually, Paul is _____ me.

WRITING

4.7

A blog entry

VOCABULARY PRACTICE | Sightseeing

1 Look at the vocabulary in lesson 4.7 in the Students' Book. Read the blog about Manchester and choose the correct words a–e.

BLOG

¹Last month, I spent a day in Manchester with my friend, Emily. Today, I'm blogging about it.

Manchester ²is the UK's third largest city and is a very popular ªspeciality / destination, especially for fans of fashion and music.

I met Emily on Saturday morning and we went shopping. The city has a wide ᵇattraction / selection of shops, and ³most people tend to visit one of the large shopping centres. But if you are looking for experimental fashions, then go to Affleck's Palace. It's ᶜa historic site / a must – a building in the centre with lots of really cool shops.

After shopping, we were hungry, so we went to Chinatown. For Asian food, Chinatown is a ᵈmust / local speciality. ⁴We had a delicious lunch.

Old Trafford football ground is one of the most popular ᵉattractions / specialities in the city, but we went on a musical tour. Oasis and The Stone Roses come from Manchester, and if you like 90s music, ⁵I would recommend doing the tour.

Manchester is a great city. Visit it if you have the chance! ☺

2 Put the words in order to make phrases. Then match them with similar phrases 1–5 in the blog.

seem / people / to ... / Most
Most people seem to ...   ③

visitors, / For / must / tour / is / the / a
1 _____   ◯

was / Lunch / fantastic!
2 _____   ◯

Last / went / month, / to ... / I
3 _____   ◯

very / a / ... is / city / big
4 _____   ◯

3 Match the sentence halves. There is one extra ending.

The Cartoon Art Museum is   ⑨
1 It's one of   ◯
2 Most tourists tend   ◯
3 I would definitely   ◯
4 One of the local   ◯
5 Paris is a popular tourist   ◯

a destination of all the people in love.
b recommend seeing the city centre by night.
c shopping for traditional food.
d the busiest capital cities in Europe.
e to stay in smaller, cheaper hotels.
f specialities of Iceland is shark meat.
g a must for all comic lovers.

4 Add seven commas to the text about Hampstead Heath.

blog

Hampstead Heath

I've never been to Manchester but it sounds great! But I know England's capital city so I'll write about that. If you are in London you must visit Hampstead Heath Camden. Each year over 10 million visitors come to this beautiful part of England's most famous city. This ancient park is famous for its summer concerts but you can also enjoy the restaurants lakes wildlife and outdoor art gallery which make the area so special. Take a relaxing walk through nature and then climb Parliament Hill to see the spectacular panoramic view of London.

5 Read the task below. Then read the first paragraph of the blog entry and in 1–3 choose the correct word, *for* or *since*.

> You are on holiday in a country you are visiting for the first time. Write a blog entry. Include and develop these points:
>
> • Introduce the country and say how long you have been there.
> • Write about what you have done so far and what you plan to do on your trip.
> • Give your opinion of the country as a place for a holiday.
> • Write about ideas you have for a future trip or trips.

I've been in Ireland ¹*for / since* 10 days now and ²*for / since* I've been here I've met some wonderful people and have had great fun. I've enjoyed the city centre of Dublin and the wild nature in the countryside because the weather has been good ³*for / since* I came to this magical island.

Tomorrow I ⁴_____ (travel) to Belfast and I think I ⁵_____ (stay) there for three days. Then I ⁶_____ (visit) my sister who lives in Cork. She's expecting me. I ⁷_____ (fly) home next Friday, so hopefully I ⁸_____ (see) a lot more before then.

Ireland is a beautiful place that you must see. For my next trip I ⁹_____ (go) to Spain. Or maybe Italy.

6 Read the rest of the blog entry. Complete it using verbs 4–9 in the correct future forms.

SHOW WHAT YOU'VE LEARNT

7 Imagine you visited York recently. Give your impressions in a blog entry. Use the information from the advert below and go online to find out more. Include and develop these points:

• Introduce the place and say when you visited.
• Write about what you did and saw while you were there.
• Give your opinion of the town.
• Make recommendations about attractions and interesting places.

The beautiful city of **York**

✔ In the north of England – 2 hours from London by train.

✔ Popular tourist destination – famous for its historic sights, architecture, shops and restaurants.

✔ Visitor attractions – York Minster (cathedral), York river cruise, National Railway Museum, JORVIK Viking Centre.

✔ Local speciality – York Ham.

Find out more at **www.visityork.org**

SHOW THAT YOU'VE CHECKED

Finished? Always check your writing. Can you tick √ everything on this list?

In my blog:

• I have introduced the place and said when and/or why I visited.	☐
• I have written about what I did and saw while I was there.	☐
• I have used phrases such as *I thought it was great* or *It is an interesting place* to give my opinion of the city.	☐
• I have used appropriate vocabulary for describing a destination, e.g. *historic sites, local specialities.*	☐
• I have made recommendations.	
• I have perhaps used some emoticons ☺ and abbreviations (*info / CU / gr8*) – but not too many!	☐
• I have checked my spelling and punctuation.	☐
• My text is neat and clear.	☐

1 Translate the phrases into your own language.

SPEAKING BANK

Making suggestions

Do you fancy (going) …? _____

Let's (go) … _____

How about (going) …? _____

We could (go) … _____

(I think) we should (go) … _____

_____

What about (going) …? _____

Why don't we (go) …? _____

Agreeing with suggestions

(That's a) good/great idea! _____

(That) sounds good/great! _____

Why not! _____

Disagreeing with suggestions

(I'm sorry) I'm not keen on … _____

_____

I don't really like … _____

I'd rather (go) … _____

_____

I'm not sure about that. _____

_____

Let's (go) … instead. _____

2 Choose the correct responses.

1 I think we should stop for a break. We've already walked for hours.

I'd rather keep going. / That sounds good. My feet hurt and I'm thirsty.

2 Let's go ice skating. I haven't done it for years.

Why not! / I'm sorry, I'm not keen on ice skating. Can we get the bus there?

3 What about visiting Grandma this weekend?

I'm not sure about that. / Good idea! I've got lots of homework to do and I'm going to a party.

4 Do you fancy having a BBQ in the garden?

Let's get a Chinese takeaway instead. / Sounds great. Have we got any sausages?

5 Why don't we invite Naomi to the party?

I don't really like Naomi. / That's a great idea. She's so arrogant.

6 How about going to the school disco with me?

Great idea! / I'd rather go on my own. Sorry.

3 Complete the suggestions with the infinitive or -ing form of the verbs in brackets. Then match the suggestions with replies a–f.

Why don't we _go_ (go) out for dinner tonight? ⬜g

1 Let's _____ (fly) to Spain and have a few days in the sun. There are cheap flights at the moment. ⬜

2 How about _____ (sit) down for ten minutes? I need a rest. ⬜

3 We could _____ (do) our homework together. You could help me. ⬜

4 I think we should _____ (camp). It's cheaper than staying in a hotel. ⬜

5 Do you fancy _____ (cook) fish tonight? We should have something healthy. ⬜

6 What about _____ (buy) Dan a book for his birthday? ⬜

a To be honest, I'd rather have steak.

b That's a good idea. I am better at Maths than you.

c Why not! Has he read the new J.K. Rowling novel?

d That sounds great. There are some seats over there. Do you want a coffee?

e I'm sorry, I'm not keen on sleeping outside. We could look for a cheap hostel.

f We went there last year. Let's go to Croatia instead.

g I'm not sure about that. We've already eaten out twice this week.

4 Complete the dialogue. The first letters are given.

Lydia: I can't believe I didn't win the swimming, Sophie. All that training and I was only fifth!

Sophie: Don't worry, Lydia. There'll be other races. W*hy* d*on't* we do something fun to cheer you up? ¹W_____ a_____ going for ice cream?

Lydia: ²I don't r_____ like ice cream. I'd ³r_____ go shopping.

Sophie: ⁴T_____ a good i_____ . I need something new to wear for the party on Saturday.

Lydia: ⁵D_____ you f_____ going to the new shopping centre? There are sales at the moment, I think.

Sophie: ⁶W_____ n_____ ? – and then we ⁷c_____ go for a pizza or something.

Lydia: ⁸T_____ s_____ great. Thanks, Sophie.

Sophie: My pleasure. Really! Let's get going then.

1 In pairs, ask and answer the questions.

PART 1

Talk about the arts.
1 Do you think it's better to binge watch a TV series or wait each week for a new episode? Why?
2 Who's your favourite character in a film? Why?
3 What's the best concert you've ever been to? Why?
4 Would you prefer to be a great photographer, a great sculptor or a great painter? Why?
5 What are your two favourite types of book? Why?

PART 2

Talk about homes.
1 What does your home look like?
2 Do you like modern architecture? Why?/Why not?
3 Where do you want to live in the future: in the city, in a small town or in a village? Why?
4 Can you describe your ideal bedroom?
5 Would you prefer to live in a treehouse near the ocean or in a house on stilts in the rainforest? Why?

2 Look at the pictures that show different locations for homes.

PART 1

Which of these locations do you like? Discuss in pairs.

PART 2

In pairs, ask and answer the questions.
1 What are the most attractive things about living in a village?
2 Why do you think so many people live in the city?
3 What are the good things about living on a lake?
4 What are the good things about living in the suburbs of a city instead of the centre of the city?
5 What are the health benefits of living near the sea?
6 Would you prefer to live in a small flat in a city or a big house in the country? Why?
7 Which of these locations do you like best for your future home? Why?

3 Discuss this question together. 'Is it better to live in the countryside or the city?' What do you think?

For the countryside:

Living in the countryside …
• is quieter, healthier and more relaxing.
• means you're closer to nature.
• is usually cheaper.
• means you usually have more space.

For the city:

Living in a city …
• is more interesting (restaurants, exhibitions, cafés, shows, etc).
• can help you to find a job.
• gives you the opportunity to meet more people.
• means that you are closer to airports, stations, etc, so it's easier to travel.

VOCABULARY AND GRAMMAR

1 Choose the correct words.

We live in a *terraced house* /*detached house*/ *tree house*, so we don't have any problems with neighbours.

1 Poor Susan burned her hand on the *ladder* / *cupboard* / *cooker* yesterday evening.

2 The *fridge* / *wardrobe* / *chest of drawers* is empty. We need to go shopping for food.

3 When I was a kid, I lived in a house on *craters* / *stilts* / *rocks*. I used to play under our home sometimes because it was nice and cool there.

4 Rome is most famous for the ancient *caves* / *volcanoes* / *ruins* of the Roman Empire.

5 Anastasia loves reading. The *shelves* / *bookcase* / *cupboard* in her bedroom is full.

/5

2 Complete the sentences with the correct words. The first and last letters are given.

Sem**i**-detached houses are often quieter because there are no neighbours on one side.

1 I wouldn't like to live in Egypt because of the s_____g t_____s they have there most of the year. It's too hot for me!

2 Do you want to visit them or not? Please make a **d**_____**n** so we can plan our weekend.

3 If you haven't seen Venice, a beautiful sinking town in Italy, it's a **m**_____**t**!

4 There are some amazing **h**_____**c s**_____**s** in London. My favourite is the statue of Nelson in Trafalgar Square.

5 Now I live with my family in the **s**_____**s**, but when I'm older, I want to live in the city centre.

/5

3 Complete the sentences with words from the box. There are two extra words.

breathtaking   cosy   drawers   humid
ironing   ladder   ~~ancient~~   wood

Juan and Miguel were born near the *ancient* city of Chichen Itza in Mexico.

1 My mum loves old furniture. She's just bought an antique chest of _____ for her bedroom.

2 We skied all morning, then stopped for lunch in a warm and _____ little restaurant at the top of the mountain.

3 There are some _____ views from our new flat on the ninth floor.

4 The books on the shelf are too high. I need a small _____ to get them.

5 When I was a little girl, I tried to do the _____ , but I burned my mum's favourite dress.

/5

4 Write sentences from the prompts. Use the Present Perfect and *for* or *since*.

Rick / work as a builder / 2010
Rick has worked as a builder since 2010.

1 The statue of the King / be / in the square / 1754
_____

2 The river / not have / fish in it / two years
_____

3 We / know about / the problem / this morning
_____

4 Nina / live / in a flat / ten years
_____

5 I / not feel well / last weekend
_____

/5

5 Choose the correct answers A–C.

What shall we have for dinner? Perhaps I __ pizza. Does that sound OK?
A 'm making   B going to make
C 'll make

1 Hannah and I __ to a concert on Friday night. Hannah's uncle bought us tickets.
A are going   B going to go
C will go

2 Oliver has a plan for next weekend. He __ to the campsite near the sea.
A 's cycling   B 's going to cycle
C 'll cycle

3 Your temperature is very high and you look terrible. I think I __ the doctor.
A 'm calling   B 'm going to call
C 'll call

4 Ryan __ dinner tonight because he's broken his arm.
A isn't making   B is going to make
C will make

5 We __ to visit Auntie Joan on Thursday and Granddad on Friday.
A 're planning   B 're going to plan
C 'll plan

/5

6 Choose the correct answers A–C.

We *C* in this old **1**__ on the 9th floor of a block in the city centre since I was born, but tonight is our very last night here. Tomorrow morning at 8 a.m. we **2**__ to a new house in a small **3**__ 25 miles from the city. I'm looking forward to living there, but I'll miss this old place. I **4**__ to the same school for the last five years and I'm worried because I **5**__ at a new school next Monday morning.

	A live	B lived	C have lived
1	A cottage	B flat	C bungalow
2	A 're moving	B 're going to move	C 'll move
3	A village	B suburbs	C island
4	A go	B went	C 've gone
5	A 'm starting	B 'm going to start	C 'll start

/5

Total   /30

7 Complete each pair of sentences with the same answer A–C.

One day I'd like to live ___ a tropical island all by myself.

James's flat is ___ the fifth floor of an old building, so there are a lot of stairs to climb every day.

A in   (B) on   C at

1 Please don't ___ a mess in the kitchen. I've just cleaned it.

Can you ___ dinner, please? I'm working till 9 p.m.

A do   B make   C have

2 Let's meet in the city ___ for a coffee and a chat tomorrow. At 2 p.m.?

The Grand Bazaar in Istanbul is perhaps the oldest trading ___ in the world.

A estate   B centre   C block

3 Andy is coming ___ later and we're going to watch a film.

Ships and boats have ___ windows because they are stronger.

A round   B around   C over

4 I think I'd ___ go to the theatre than the rock concert.

Your room is ___ large. You're lucky – mine is really small.

A better   B much   C rather

5 I'm too tired to go to the concert, so I've decided to stay ___ tonight.

Why is your washing machine downstairs ___ the basement?

A at   B on   C in

/5

8 Complete the sentences with the words in brackets in the correct form. Do not change the order of the words. You may need to add words. Use no more than six words.

Anne: That must be Sandra at the front door.

Meg: Don't worry, *I'll let* (I / let) her in.

1 Laura: Eliza _____ (come / dinner / eight) tonight.

Phil: Great! I haven't seen her for months.

2 Mum: Jimmy _____ (do / shop / real / quick).

Grandma: Yes, but he forgot to buy chocolate for me.

3 Estate agent: It _____ (be / tradition / build), but the flat is quite modern.

Customer: I think it looks really nice.

4 Tom: Is Janet _____ (go / make / complain) about the service in that café?

Ed: I'm not sure. I think she should.

5 Dad: Where's Bob?

Mum: In his bedroom. He _____ (be / make) his bed.

/5

9 Complete the second sentence so that it has a similar meaning to the first. Use between two and five words, including the word in capitals.

Jonathan and Tina moved to Rome in 2014. **LIVED**

Jonathan and Tina *have lived in Rome since* 2014.

1 Sarah last visited us in March. **NOT**

Sarah _____ March.

2 Margaret wakes up really early compared to me. **FAR**

Margaret wakes up _____ I do.

3 Joy is an extremely good cook. She could be famous one day. **WELL**

Joy _____ . She could be famous one day.

4 Kazuo wants to live outside of the city because it's too noisy. **GET**

Kazuo wants to _____ because it's too noisy.

5 Dennis is planning to buy a flat close to where I live. **GOING**

Dennis _____ a flat close to where I live.

/5

10 Complete the text with the correct form of the words in brackets.

Grandma's dream home

After living most of her *life* (LIVE) in the city, my grandmother finally decided to sell her flat on a large ¹_____ (HOUSE) estate. She lived there for fifty-five years but last week she moved into her dream cottage in the ²_____ (COUNTRY). The place where she lives now is really quiet and there is very little traffic. Nothing like her old place. I've never seen her so happy!

Her new home is lovely. It looks like a traditional cottage from the outside, but it has beautiful ³_____ (WOOD) floors in every room and is quite modern inside. It's also pretty large, so it is much more ⁴_____ (SPACE) than her previous home. And because it's not a flat, she can spend time at the weekends doing the ⁵_____ (GARDEN). She's always loved flowers, and now she can grow her own!

/5

Total /20

5 Time to learn

VOCABULARY

5.1

Places in school • education • phrasal verbs • collocations

SHOW WHAT YOU KNOW

1 Complete the names of places in school. The first letters are given.

All parents coming for Parents' Evening should go first to **r**eception to register.

1 The **s**_____ **r**_____ is the place where teachers go to escape from their students.

2 Our school's really modern. There's an interactive whiteboard, a laptop and a projector in every **c**_____ .

3 The school **l**_____ has over 3,000 books and five desktop computers for doing research.

4 We have an assembly meeting once a week in the **s**_____ **h**_____ . This is where the headmaster tells us the latest news about the school.

5 I was late for class and got into trouble for running in the **c**_____ .

6 Adrian hurt his leg in the **p**_____ when he was chasing Barbara.

7 Have you seen Mrs Burke, the Physics teacher? I looked in the **S**_____ **l**_____ but she wasn't there.

8 There's a lot of administration involved in running a school. Just go to the **s**_____ **o**_____ and you'll see how busy everybody is.

9 Our school has a large **s**_____ **f**_____ where we can play football, rugby and cricket.

10 Sam's school has excellent sports facilities. There's a swimming pool, two tennis courts, a football pitch and a fully-equipped **g**_____ .

11 There's a new menu this term in the **c**_____ . You can now order fish and chips.

WORD STORE 5A | Education

2 Complete the sentences with the correct word or phrase from the box.

> academic subjects   ~~after-school activities~~
> classmate   compulsory   curriculum   graduate
> learn by heart   mixed ability   term   timetable

Diego's school offers lots of *after-school activities* in the late afternoon such as Music lessons as well as Chess and Photography classes.

1 Teachers can find _____ classes challenging because they need to teach students of different levels equally well.

2 Languages are _____ in my school. That means everybody has to study Spanish or English.

3 What is your _____ like on Fridays? Will you still have time to play on the basketball team in the afternoon?

4 I've got a _____ who never arrives on time to classes and usually forgets to bring his books.

5 Hugh's sister, Laura, is a university _____ , so she often helps him with his homework. Would you like to study Maths at university like Laura?

6 There are a lot of important dates and other facts that you need to _____ when you study History.

7 I've decided to study a lot harder this _____ to get better grades.

8 My favourite _____ are Geography and Physics. What are yours?

9 Every school in the country now has Physical Education on the _____ .

WORD STORE 5B | Phrasal verbs

3 Choose the correct answers A–C.

1 Everybody, please line ___ by the door and we will go together calmly to the gym.
   A up   B out   C into

2 I'm really sorry, Mr Smith, but can I please hand ___ my History homework tomorrow?
   A out   B in   C on

3 This term Sandra is having trouble keeping ___ with all of her schoolwork.
   A in   B on   C up

4 I don't think my test results are good enough for me to move ___ a level in my English class.
   A out   B on   C up

5 What will you do if you don't get ___ university next year?
   A in   B into   C to

6 Andrew isn't coping very well ___ his schoolwork and his after-school activities. He's doing too many things at the same time.
   A with   B at   C for

7 As soon as school breaks ___ for summer, I'm going to Greece on holiday for three weeks.
   A up   B down   C out

4 Choose the verb which does <u>not</u> collocate.

1 *pass / get / revise for* an exam
2 *skip / miss / pay* lessons
3 *set / make / mark* homework
4 *drop / take / leave* a subject
5 *drop / finish / attend* school
6 *get / make / have* a degree
7 *learn from / make / do* mistakes
8 *charge / pay / do* tuition fees

5 Complete the sentences with the collocations from Exercise 4 in the correct form.

I don't know why, but Arakan is worried that he won't *pass* his exam tomorrow.

1 My father has _____ a degree in Physics, but he works as a journalist.
2 Joseph's sister doesn't _____ school for another three years. She's still sixteen.
3 Janice wants to _____ another subject next term. She's thinking of learning Spanish.
4 People that never _____ their mistakes will continue to make the same mistakes.
5 James _____ the Chemistry lesson yesterday because he had to go to the dentist.
6 I'd hate to be a teacher. Can you imagine going home after work to _____ homework?

6 Complete the text with the missing verbs in the correct form.

```
○○○
```

teen talk 🗨 [   ] [ask]

Welcome to Teentalk online advice for teenagers. You can ask anything you like and you don't have to give your name. We will try to answer your question in the next 24 hours.

My older sister isn't doing well at school this year. She often gets into trouble because she doesn't *pay* attention in lessons or ¹_____ lessons and goes to meet her boyfriend at the shopping centre. She never does any homework and she doesn't ²_____ for any of her tests or exams. Most students ³_____ eight subjects in their final year, but my sister wants to ⁴_____ Science because it's too difficult and she doesn't think she will ⁵_____ the exam. She's going to ⁶_____ her final exams at the end of this year and Mum is afraid she'll ⁷_____ all of them. It's difficult for a younger sister to give advice to an older sister. How can I help her?

REMEMBER THIS

sit/take a test or exam = do a test/exam
pass a test or exam = get a good score or grade on a test/exam

7 Read REMEMBER THIS. Complete the sentences with the correct form of *sit/take* or *pass*.

I'm *taking/sitting* my driving test tomorrow. Wish me good luck!

1 Guess what! I _____ the History test that I was so worried about last week.
2 How often do you have to _____ tests at your English school?
3 I need to _____ all of my tests to get into the university that I want to go to.
4 Mum promised to buy me a new smartphone if I _____ my Maths test.

SHOW WHAT YOU'VE LEARNT

8 Complete the second sentence so that it has a similar meaning to the first. Use between two and five words, including the word in capitals.

How much do the extra classes cost? **TUITION**
What are the *tuition fees* for the extra classes?

1 You should listen more carefully to what your teachers tell you. **ATTENTION**
You _____ what your teachers tell you.
2 When did you give your Geography homework to Ms Burke? **HAND**
When _____ Geography homework to Ms Burke?
3 It's not easy to pass the driving test first time. **FAIL**
It's _____ the driving test first time.
4 Roger is finding it rather difficult to work part time and study. **COPING**
Roger _____ working part time and studying very well.
5 I must stop making the same mistakes. **LEARN**
I must _____ more.
6 Everybody in John's class is better than him at French now. **UP**
John isn't _____ everybody in his French class.
7 I'd like everyone to stand in a line in front of the whiteboard. **UP**
I'd like everyone _____ in front of the whiteboard.
8 I think classes with students at different levels can be hard for both teachers and students. **ABILITY**
I think _____ can be hard for both teachers and students.
9 We have to memorise all of these dates for the History exam next week. **HEART**
We have to _____ all of these dates for the History exam next week.
10 Did Dan and Lucy use to be in the same class at school? **CLASSMATES**
Were _____ at school?

/10

GRAMMAR

5.2

First Conditional

1 Change the underlined verbs to make negative sentences. Use short forms.

They're classmates. They are in the same class.
They aren't classmates, but they meet after school.

1 My sister has Maths classes on Mondays.
My sister _____ have Maths classes on Tuesdays.

2 We'll live together next year. We are going to university in the same town.
We _____ live together next year. We are going to university in different towns.

3 She's a very good student. She likes studying.
She _____ a very good student. She hates studying.

2 ★ Put the words in order to complete the First Conditional sentences.

you / pass / you'll / study / hard, / your / final
If you study hard, you'll pass your final exams.

1 write / forget / number / if / my / he / it / doesn't
He'll _____ down.

2 hurry up, / she'll / her / miss / doesn't / Samantha
If _____ train.

3 how / you / he'll / sure / understand / him / tell / if / you
I'm _____ feel.

4 listen / don't / know / you / carefully, / what / to / you / won't
If _____ do.

5 with / dance / ask / you / you / won't / don't / if
Anzu _____ her.

6 go / he / will / feels / if / tomorrow / back / school / to
Sam _____ better.

3 ★ ★ Complete the First Conditional sentences and questions with the correct form of the verbs in brackets.

If Stacey *does* (do) well at school this year, she *'ll get* (get) into university next year.

1 What ᵃ_____ (Ella/do) if she ᵇ_____ (fail) her exams?

2 We ᵃ_____ (be) in trouble if we ᵇ_____ (skip) another lesson.

3 If Julia and Toby ᵃ_____ (not/have) extra lessons at a private academy, they ᵇ_____ (not/pass) their exams.

4 If you ᵃ_____ (not/look) at the timetable, you ᵇ_____ (not/know) what classes you have.

4 ★ ★ ★ Complete the Internet forum with the correct form of the verbs from the box. There are two extra words.

> be   learn   not enjoy   not like   not pass
> pay   pass   stop   take   ~~want~~

ASK ANYTHING

jayne17 asks …

What will I have to do if I want to learn to drive? I'm 17 years old. Can anyone help?

MOST HELPFUL ANSWERS

carfanbrendan answers …

Hi Jayne. Before you learn to drive, you'll need to choose a driving instructor (or teacher). It's important to choose carefully because if you ¹_____ your instructor, you ²_____ the lessons. My instructor was great and I really enjoyed learning to drive. Good luck ☺

philthechill answers …

You will probably feel nervous the first time you drive, but if your instructor ³_____ you to a quiet place to practise, it ⁴_____ much less stressful.

agablueeyes answers …

My brother is learning to drive and he's worried about the theory test (the one you do on a computer). I think that he ⁵_____ the test without any problems if he ⁶_____ the rules of the road.

jayne17 asks …

Thanks for the advice. One more question. If I ⁷_____ the test, will I have to pay again?

There are no answers to your question yet.

5 Match 1–6 with information a–f and write First Conditional sentences. Change the verb form if necessary.

visit Brazil ⬜g

1 see kangaroos and koalas ⬜
2 drive to school every day ⬜
3 study at a private academy ⬜
4 buy a laptop ⬜
5 have to make sandwiches every morning ⬜
6 want to learn to snowboard ⬜

a need to have strong legs
b pass the driving test
c have to pay tuition fees
d not eat in the school canteen
e do a gap year in Australia
f not have to borrow mine
g learn some basic Portuguese

If Mark *visits Brazil*, he *'ll learn some basic Portuguese*.

1 She _____ if she _____.
2 I _____ if I _____.
3 If Sarah and Ken _____, they _____.
4 If Katie _____, she _____.
5 You _____ if you _____.
6 If your friend _____, he _____.

/6

GRAMMAR: Train and Try Again page 148

62

5.3

Expressions with prepositions
• synonyms • *get*

1 Read the dialogue between Grace and Tom. Choose the correct prepositions.

Extract from Students' Book recording 🔊 **2.29**

G: Hi Tom. Are you coming out ¹*with / by / for* us tonight?

T: Oh no, I can't. I'm revising ²*to / about / for* exams. I need to learn fifty French verbs ³*on / by / with* heart tonight.

G: But the exams don't <u>start</u> until next month.

T: I know, but I get really nervous ⁴*on / about / for* exams. If I don't <u>revise</u> every night, I'll get stressed.

G: I don't know why you're so worried. You always get good marks in class.

T: I know, but that's different. In exams, I panic. And I really want to get good grades for my A levels. I want to get ⁵*into / with / in* a good university.

G: Listen, you need to take it easy. If you continue like this, you'll get <u>ill</u>.

T: Well, what can I do?

G: Okay, first you need to make a revision timetable. If you make a timetable, you'll see that you have <u>plenty of</u> time to do everything.

T: Um, yeah, that's quite a good idea.

G: And I think you spend too much time alone – sometimes it's good to study ⁶*about / by / with* other people.

T: Is it? I'm not so sure. They might know more than I do!

G: You're so <u>negative</u>.

T: Well, it's okay for you, you don't get nervous.

G: Of course I get nervous. But I try to be <u>positive</u>. For example, ⁷*before / in / on* an exam, I imagine myself ⁸*to / in / on* the exam – I know all the answers, and I pass the exam ⁹*on / by / with* the best marks.

T: Hm. It's true, I'm not very confident.

2 Complete the sentences with a preposition in each gap.

1 I am getting nervous ᵃ*about* tomorrow. Jake asked me to study ᵇ_____ him. He's so handsome. I don't think I'll learn anything!

2 Vince stayed up too late revising and then he actually fell asleep _____ the English exam.

3 Our exams don't start until May, so we've still got three months to revise ᵃ_____ them. I'm going to study hard because I want to pass ᵇ_____ the best marks and get ᶜ_____ university to study Medicine.

4 We have to learn 15 words ᵃ_____ heart for a test tomorrow. I'll come out ᵇ_____ you another time.

3 Match the words below to underlined words in Exercise 1 with similar meanings.

sick = *ill*
1 more than enough = _____
2 optimistic = _____
3 study for exams = _____
4 begin = _____
5 pessimistic = _____

REMEMBER BETTER

Synonyms are different words with the same or similar meanings. When you learn a new word and you have time, check in the dictionary and see if you can also learn a synonym. Knowledge of synonyms will help you understand more when you read and listen, especially more advanced texts.

Replace the underlined words in the sentences with synonyms. The first letters are given.

Today Naomi and Leon had their final exams, so tonight they are going to go out and <u>enjoy themselves.</u> (h___ a g___ t___)

1 The teacher said we should try to <u>relax</u> (t_____ it e_____) the night before the exam.

2 I don't like studying with other people. I work best <u>alone</u> (o_____ m_____ o_____).

WORD STORE 5D | *get*

4 Complete the mini-dialogues with the phrases from the box. Change the form of *get* if necessary.

get a job   get exhausted   get good grades
get ill   get into trouble   get nervous   ~~get rid of~~

A: Did you *get rid of* those horrible old slippers?
B: Yes, I got a new pair for my birthday. Not the most exciting present, but useful.

1 A: Were you sick after the school field trip?
B: Yes, I was cold and wet all day. I think that was when I _____ . I still feel pretty bad.

2 A: How is your nephew doing at school?
B: Not very well. He often _____ with his teachers. They say he talks too much during lessons.

3 A: Are you prepared for your presentation tomorrow?
B: Well, yes, I am. But I'm already _____ thinking about talking in front of such a large group of people.

4 A: You can't work all night. You'll _____ and won't be able to focus in school tomorrow.
B: I know. But I have to finish this project for tomorrow morning.

5 A: It's not fair. I always work hard, but I never _____ .
B: I wouldn't worry too much about that. What's really important is that you're trying!

6 A: Are you free at the weekend?
B: Not during the day. Last week, I _____ in a bookshop near my house and Saturday is my first day at work.

1 Read the text quickly and decide why it was written.

1 To explain how to get a job you love ☐
2 To give advice on where to study the subject you love ☐
3 To present the benefits of studying a subject you love ☐

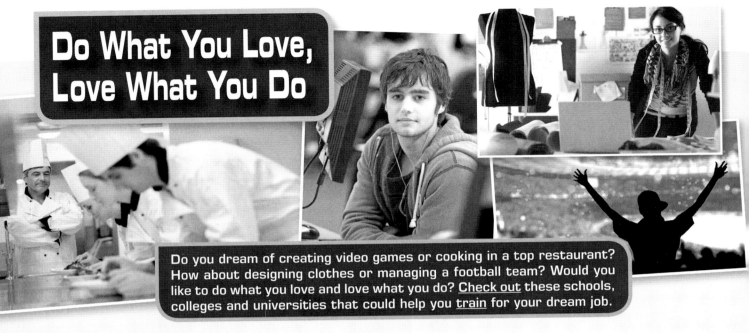

Do What You Love, Love What You Do

Do you dream of creating video games or cooking in a top restaurant? How about designing clothes or managing a football team? Would you like to do what you love and love what you do? Check out these schools, colleges and universities that could help you train for your dream job.

A So you love … video games?

A new course at the University of Derby in the UK could be ideal for you if you dream of a job in the video game industry. The School of Computing and Mathematics offers a degree in Computer Games Modelling and Animation. Students on the course develop their artistic skills and learn how to create game characters and digital worlds using the university's powerful computers and software. Lecturers on the course have years of industry experience and the company that created Lara Croft from the famous *Tomb Raider* games helped to design the course. Students can choose to take their third year as a work placement* year and get some experience of what it's really like to work in the video games industry. If you want to apply for a place on the course, you will need a good grade in A level Art and Design, and of course you will need to love computers and video games!

B So you love … cooking?

If you are happier in the kitchen than in front of a computer screen, you might be interested in a course organised by the London School of Hospitality and Tourism. Many students on the Culinary Arts and Professional Cookery course go on to work in top restaurants after they graduate. The school has its own award-winning training restaurant called 'Pillars'. 'Pillars' is a real working restaurant, so you'll experience what it's like to work in the restaurant industry and customers will come and pay to eat your homework! On the course, you'll study French and Italian cooking, and if you decide on this course, you'll need to buy chef's whites, the traditional all-white uniform of professional chefs.

C So you love … clothes?

The UK's capital city is the place to study if you want to be the next Armani or Versace. London College of Fashion offers a wide range of degree courses for the fashion industry. If you love shoes then you could try the degree in Footwear* Design and Development. Perhaps you are more interested in designing clothing for sports – check out the course in Fashion Sportswear. There are design courses for menswear, womenswear and even for underwear! The course is popular with international students, so it's not unusual to hear lots of foreign languages at the college. Every year the college organises fashion shows and some of the biggest clothing companies and buyers with years of experience are there to look at students' designs.

D So you love … football?

Do you love football? Do you dream of managing Manchester United or Real Madrid? Southampton Solent University could help to make your dreams come true. Football is part of the history of Southampton and if you get a place to do the Football Studies degree, you'll go on field trips* to the most well-known stadiums and football clubs in the region. Famous managers and players from the world of football regularly give guest lectures at the university. Students have the opportunity to hear about their years of experience in the football industry. Many students find jobs with big international football clubs such as Chelsea FC or FC Spartak Moscow after they finish the course. For this reason, graduates who speak another language have a real advantage in the world of modern football.

GLOSSARY

work placement (n) – when students work for a short time as part of their studies

footwear (n) – a formal word for shoes and boots

field trip (n) – when students go somewhere (e.g. a museum or historic site) to learn about a particular subject

---

2 Read the text. Match the statements below to paragraphs A–D.

1 Large companies will be interested to see your work on this course. ☐

2 Some successful people in this industry helped to create this course. ☐

3 You can benefit from knowing a foreign language when you finish this course. ☐

4 You'll have to buy special clothes for this course. ☐

5 You'll probably meet someone famous on this course. ☐

6 A year of work experience is an option on this course. ☐

3 Read the text again. Are statements 1–6 true (T) or false (F)?

1 A lecturer from the University of Derby created the famous game character Lara Croft. ☐

2 Students need their own computer for the Computer Games Modelling and Animation course. ☐

3 'Pillars' training restaurant is open to the public. ☐

4 Foreign languages are part of the Culinary Arts and Professional Cookery course. ☐

5 You have to be good at sports if you want to study Fashion Sportswear. ☐

4 Use the underlined words and phrases from the text to replace the crossed out words in the sentences below.

I think Australia is the ~~perfect~~ *ideal* place for a gap year. There is so much to see and do there.

1 If you want to ~~learn the skills you need~~ _____ to be an actor, you'll have to go to drama school.

2 ~~Maybe~~ _____ it's not a good idea to go out tonight. I have a Maths test tomorrow and I need to revise.

3 You should ~~look at~~ _____ the school's new website. There are some funny pictures of all the teachers.

4 The French Alps are ~~famous~~ _____ for some of the best skiing and snowboarding in Europe.

5 I'm not planning to do a gap year. I want to ~~complete my studies~~ _____ first and then go travelling.

5 Match the beginnings with the correct endings to make sentences from the text.

Check out these schools, colleges and universities that could help you *train* ☐ f

1 A new course at the University of Derby, in the UK could be ideal for you if you *dream* ☐

2 If you want to *apply* ☐

3 If you *decide* ☐

4 Buyers with years of experience are there to *look* ☐

5 Students have the opportunity to *hear* ☐

a *for* a place on the course, you will need a good grade in A level Art and Design.

b *on* this course, you'll need to buy chef's whites.

c *about* their years of experience in the football industry.

d *of* a job in the video game industry.

e *at* students' designs.

f *for* your dream job.

REMEMBER THIS

After some verbs, we put a preposition before the object. Try to learn these verbs and prepositions together.

verb + **preposition** + **object**

I want to *apply* **for a place on the course**.

6 Read REMEMBER THIS. Complete the sentences with the correct prepositions. Use a dictionary if necessary.

Greg Mortenson didn't succeed *in* his plan to reach the summit of K2.

1 After he got lost, he stayed ____ a tiny village.

2 He thought ____ how he could help the villagers who looked after him.

3 His programme 'Pennies for Pakistan' helped to pay ____ a new school for girls in the village.

VOCABULARY PRACTICE | Nouns and verbs

7 Look at the vocabulary in lesson 5.4 in the Students' Book. Complete the sentences with the correct form of the words from the box.

bully ~~concentrate~~ encourage expert mentor misunderstand struggle visual thinker

Please don't talk to me at the moment. I'm *concentrating* on this difficult Maths problem.

1 If somebody _____ you at school, don't be afraid to stand up for yourself.

2 Plenty of _____ agree that reading fiction is really good for your imagination.

3 Mike's been having German lessons for two years, but he is still _____ with verbs.

4 I think Sophie _____ me. I said we can study together on Thursday, not Tuesday.

5 Aiko is so good at Biology that I'm hoping she'll be my _____ .

6 Brian keeps _____ me to study harder. That's why my grades are better this year.

7 The theory says that _____ learn better when there are more pictures and graphics.

FOCUS ON WORDS | of and for

8 Complete the sentences with the missing words. Some letters are given.

Sally **d r _e_ a _m_ s** of becoming a vet, so she's taking all the Maths, Chemistry, Biology and Physics classes she can.

1 Jamie got over the difficulty of failing to get into university with the **s _ p _ _ _ t** of his family and friends.

2 Terry's father is a **p r o _ _ _ _ _ o _** of Science at Cambridge University.

3 Rachel has always had a **p _ _ _ i _ _** for art. She goes to galleries at least twice a month.

4 You really shouldn't make **f _ _** of people who aren't as intelligent as you. It's not very nice and you can make them sad.

5 Gary made the **m _ _ _ _ k _** of not revising before his exam. He was too confident and now he has to take the exam again next week.

GRAMMAR

5.5
Defining relative clauses

SHOW WHAT YOU KNOW

1 Match the definitions with the words.

a classmate ☐   a bungalow ☐   a cooker ☐
a linguist ☐   a university ☐   ~~a village~~

This is a place where people in the countryside live.
1 This is a machine that you use to heat food.
2 This is a person who is in your class at school.
3 This is a house which has only one floor.
4 This is a place where you study for a degree.
5 This is a person that studies languages.

2 ★ Choose the correct relative pronoun.

1 Mr Jones is the teacher *which / who* broke his leg on the field trip. He still can't walk properly.
2 'Rose's Place' is the café *that / where* I worked during the summer holidays. I saved a lot of money.
3 Look! That's the guy *that / which* cheated in the exam. He still got bad marks though.
4 Here's the text book *where / that* you left at my house. Now you can do your homework.
5 Do you remember the number of the room *which / where* the exam is later on today? I'm so stressed I can't remember anything.
6 This is the computer *which / where* always goes wrong. Someone should fix it.

3 ★ ★ Complete the gaps with *which/that*, *who/that* or *where*.

- *Do you own a dog <u>that/which</u> you can't control?*
- *Do you have a postman [1]_____ worries every time he has to visit your house?*
- *Does your dog take you for a walk?*

*If the answer is '**yes**' then maybe we can help.*

'Good Dog Academy' is a school [2]_____ helps to train difficult dogs. We work with dog owners [3]_____ have big problems with their pets. Come and visit the 'Good Dog Academy', a place [4]_____ difficult dogs can become perfect pets in only two weeks!

Phone **0801 333 333** for details

66

---

4 ★ ★ Write sentences with relative clauses.

Sydney / the city / my father was born.
Sydney is the city where my father was born.

1 Football / a sport / is cheap and fun.
_____
_____

2 A pupil / a child / goes to primary school.
_____
_____

3 A tattoo / a picture under your skin / never disappears.
_____
_____

4 Mrs Kemp / the teacher / always gives us lots of homework.
_____
_____

5 Oxford / the city / has the oldest university in the UK.
_____
_____

6 The Japanese / the people / invented sushi.
_____
_____

5 ★ ★ ★ Cross out the relative pronoun if it's not necessary.

This is a photo of the girl ~~that~~ I met last weekend at Sasha's party.
1 If Mum can't pick me up from school, I get the bus which stops outside our house.
2 I've written down the phone number of the private tutor that my cousin recommended.
3 This is the hospital where I was born. It's much bigger now than it was in the past.
4 Can you buy some apples, some cheese, and the eggs that say 'organic' on the box?
5 This is the puppy which I chose. Don't you think he's cute?

SHOW WHAT YOU'VE LEARNT

6 Choose the correct answers A–C.

1 This is ____ I bought on Saturday. Do you like it?
   A a bag which   B the bag that   C a bag
2 Where is ____ lost his MP3 player?
   A the student who   B a student that
   C the student
3 Take me to ____ we had lunch last week.
   A the place which   B a place that
   C the place where
4 Can I see ____ you bought?
   A the phone that   B a phone which
   C a phone
5 This is ____ taught us last week.
   A the teacher   B the teacher that
   C a teacher who
6 That is ____ I have my English lessons.
   A the classroom   B the classroom where
   C a classroom that

/6

GRAMMAR: Train and Try Again page 148

USE OF ENGLISH

5.6

Future time and conditional clauses

1 ★ Choose the correct words.

1 Maarten's parents won't pay his tuition fees *if / before* he doesn't promise to work hard.
2 *Before / If* I leave the cafeteria, I'll finish my coffee.
3 *As soon as / Unless* Josie passes her driving test, she'll buy a motorbike.
4 *After / Before* I see my timetable, I'll tell you when I'm able to meet you.
5 *When / If* our music classes finish, we'll go shopping.
6 Sarah won't move up a class *if / unless* she studies hard.

2 ★ ★ Complete the sentences with the correct form of the verbs in brackets.

I'm sure I ᵃ*will get* (get) bored with basketball when I ᵇ*play* (play) it every day in P.E. next term.

1 If Ellen ᵃ_____ (lose) the next match, she ᵇ_____ (be) in the tennis final.
2 Lauren ᵃ_____ (make) herself ill unless she ᵇ_____ (stop) practising so much.
3 Alexei ᵃ_____ (earn) more as soon as he ᵇ_____ (sign) a new contract with the team.
4 After we ᵃ_____ (win) the league, we ᵇ_____ (go) on a tour around Australia.
5 Edgar and Allan ᵃ_____ (have) to agree to be friends again before they ᵇ_____ (start) training together.

3 ★ ★ ★ Complete the sentences with the words in brackets in the correct form. Do not change the order of the words. You may need to add words. Use no more than six words.

Mum: I'll cook you your favourite meal *when/ after Dad comes home* (Dad / come / home) with the shopping.

Jeremy: Thanks, Mum. You're the best!

1 Ms Jones: _____ (you / teacher / mark) your Chemistry projects, he'll give you your grades. He really can't do it earlier than that.

Colin and Brett: Thank you, Ms Jones.

2 Graeme: Mitsuko wants to travel for a year before she _____ (final / decide / go) to university.

Douglas: Where does she want to go?

3 Ben: Nora will get into trouble _____ (start / attend / class) more often.

Rosa: I think you're right. We should warn her.

4 Mum: _____ (soon / Peter / do) his homework, he'll call you, OK? He needs to revise Maths for his test tomorrow first.

Ashley: OK. Tell him I'll wait for him in the skate park.

5 Carl: So, I will finally see you play with Kevin _____ (he / not / forget) his racket, of course.

Robin: I hope he'll remember it this time. See you on the court at 5:00.

4 ★ ★ ★ Choose the correct answers A–C.

A sports education

A lot of people say that you won't get a good job ¹____ you get a university degree. But in fact, that's not true. Steve Jobs never finished his university education and Abraham Lincoln didn't even finish school! Nowadays, people who are interested in sport, like I am, have plenty of other options. A good education is important, however, and one thing is for sure: ²____ you study hard at school, you won't regret it.

I'm quite lucky because I know exactly what I want to do. ³____ I finish school with good grades in Physical Education, I'll go to a sports academy in Berlin and I'll train to become a basketball coach ⁴____ I get there. I won't need to get a degree, but I will need to study for a special diploma in Sports Science and Psychology ⁵____ I become qualified. What next? Well, ⁶____ I finish my training, I will get a job with a successful basketball team.

1	A unless	B when	C if
2	A before	B if	C as soon as
3	A After	B Before	C Unless
4	A before	B if	C when
5	A when	B before	C if
6	A before	B unless	C as soon as

WRITING

5.7 An email of enquiry

1 Put the words in order to make indirect questions.

Could you / my / tell me / have to / if / own books / bring / I / ?
Could you tell me if I have to bring my own books?

1 there is a library / tell me if / Could you / in the school / ?
_____
_____

2 I would / whether there is / in the city / a sports centre / like to know / .
_____
_____

3 sharing a room with somebody / like to know / I would also / if I will be / .
_____
_____

4 Could / whether I have to / for my meals / you tell me / pay extra / ?
_____
_____

5 I / if you could tell me / classes each day / would be grateful / when we finish / .
_____
_____

2 Complete the indirect questions.

Do I need to bring a laptop?
Could you tell me if *I need to bring a laptop?*

1 How many hours of English will we study each day?
I would like to know _____
_____

2 Is there a TV in the room?
Could you tell me if _____
_____

3 How much does an average meal cost in the canteen?
I would also like to know _____
_____

4 Will someone pick me up from the airport?
Could you also tell me if _____
_____

5 Do I need to buy insurance?
Finally, I would like to ask _____
_____

3 Put the words in order to make phrases.

Sir / Dear / Madam, / or
Dear Sir or Madam,

1 enquire / to / I / writing / am / about ...
_____

2 in ... / interested / am / particularly / I
_____

3 would / I / grateful / if ... / be
_____

4 look / to / you. / forward / I / hearing / from
_____

5 faithfully / Yours
_____

4 Use the phrases from Exercise 3 and indirect questions to make seven improvements to the student's email of enquiry.

Hello there,

[1]I'm a nineteen-year old Italian student, and [2]I want to know about your 'Surf & Study' course in the south of England this summer. [3]I want to do an international English exam, and if I can also get better at surfing at the same time, I'll be very happy. I have tried windsurfing before, but never surfing.
I would like to know how many hours of English we will study each day. [4]Will I be able to do the exam at the end of the course? I would also like to know if I need to bring my own surfboard. [5]Finally, is the sea warm in the summer?
[6]Please write back and answer my questions.

[7]Yours sincerely
Sandra Brunetti

Dear Sir or Madam

1 _____

2 _____

3 _____

4 Could you also tell me _____
_____

5 I would like to ask _____

6 _____

7 _____

5 Find and correct the mistakes.

Could you tell me does the hotel have a sauna?
Could you tell me if the hotel has a sauna?

1 I would also like to know you offer any sports classes.
_____

2 Could you tell me how old are my classmates?
_____

3 Dear Sir or Madame,
_____

4 I look forward to hear from you soon.
_____

5 Your faithfully,
_____

6 I would like to know how much does it cost.
_____

68

6 Read the task below. Then read the email and choose the correct answers A–C.

You have seen the advertisement below and are interested in attending the course.

THE INTERNATIONAL SCHOOL OF DRAMA

Spend a month studying drama in English in Barcelona.

For international students aged 17-23, small class sizes, all key drama skills practised.

On-campus accommodation provided.

For more information call
00 44 844 44 33 22

or visit us online at
study@isd.edu

Write your email of enquiry. Include and develop these points:

- Give information about yourself and say why you are writing the email.
- Ask for information about the nationality of students, the number of students in a class and what drama skills are practised on the course.
- Ask about accommodation.
- Say that you expect a reply.

Dear Sir or Madam,

I am a ¹___ Ukrainian student, and I am writing to enquire ^A*for / on / about* the one-month drama course ^B*at / on / by* your school.

I would like to know ²___ countries your students typically come ^C*by / out / from*. Also, if I ³___ your course, will there be other students from Ukraine? Could you also tell me what the size ^D*at / – / of* your classes ⁴___ and, if you accept me, which particular drama skills ⁵___ and whether I must ⁶___ an exam?

I would also like to know if you can provide single accommodation. If this ⁷___ possible, how much will it cost?

Finally, ⁸___ ^E*for / to / off* the course three months in advance, will the school offer me a discount?

I look forward to hearing ^F*by / – / from* you.

Yours faithfully,
Anton Romanyuk

1	A seventeen-years-old	B seventeen years
	C seventeen-year-old	
2	A where	B what	C that
3	A attend	B attended	C will attend
4	A is	B are	C be
5	A I will learn	B I learn	C will I learn
6	A make	B revise	C take
7	A is	B be	C will be
8	A do I pay	B if I pay	C will I pay

7 Read the email again. Choose the correct prepositions.

8 You have seen the advert below and want to study English at The Australian Centre. Write an email of enquiry to the school. Include and develop these points:

- Give information about yourself and say why you are writing.
- Ask for information about the length and cost of the course and about the social programme.
- Say what you would like the reader to do.
- Say that you expect a reply.

The Australian Centre

Study English in incredible Sydney. Experience one of the world's great cities and improve your English at the same time.

We offer experienced teachers, city-centre accommodation and a lively social programme. For information about courses, fees and availability, write to:

David Cochran at <u>davidc@tacs.edu</u>

Finished? Always check your writing. Can you tick √ everything on this list?

In my email of enquiry:

- the beginning matches the end (*Dear Mr Smith ⇨ Yours sincerely; Dear Sir or Madam ⇨ Yours faithfully*). ☐
- he first paragraph gives information about me and why I am writing. ☐
- the second paragraph asks polite questions about the information I need. ☐
- the third paragraph says what I would like the reader to do. ☐
- I have asked indirect questions, not direct questions. ☐
- I have not used contraction (e.g. *I'm / aren't / that's*) or abbreviations (*info / CU / v. good*). ☐
- I have checked my spelling and punctuation. ☐
- My text is neat and clear. ☐

1 Translate the phrases into your own language.

> **SPEAKING BANK**
>
> **Giving an opinion**
>
> I think he …   _____
>
> I don't think it's …   _____
>
> Personally, I think …   _____
>
> I really believe …   _____
>
> In my opinion, …   _____
>
> If you ask me, …   _____
>
>   _____
>
> **Agreeing**
>
> I couldn't agree more.   _____
>
>   _____
>
>   _____
>
> That's a good point.   _____
>
> **Disagreeing politely**
>
> I see what you mean, but … _____
>
>   _____
>
> That's true, but …   _____
>
> I'm not so sure.   _____
>
> **Disagreeing**
>
> I totally disagree!   _____
>
> Oh come on! That's   _____
> nonsense.   _____

2 Find and correct the mistakes.

    I'm not ~~to~~ sure.   *so*

1 I see that you mean, but …   _____
2 I am totally disagree.   _____
3 Oh come all! That's nonsense.   _____
4 That's good point.   _____
5 That's a true, but …   _____
6 I couldn't agree most.   _____

3 Complete the dialogue with the phrases for expressing opinions, agreeing and disagreeing. The first letters are given.

A: If y<u>ou</u> a<u>sk</u> m<u>e</u>, I <u>think</u> learning a language on your own without a teacher is really difficult.

B: Really? ¹I t_____ disagree. ²I_____ my o_____ , it's a good way to learn because you can choose what and when you study. If you have a busy day, you don't have to do a lesson. But if you have some free time, for example at the weekend, you can study then.

A: ³T_____ true, b_____ what if you need to ask a question? ⁴P_____ , I think that learning with a teacher is better. You can ask questions and the teacher can explain things and correct your mistakes. ⁵I t_____ private lessons are best. You get lots of attention from the teacher if you are the only student.

A: Well, ⁶I s_____ w_____ you m_____ , but I get stressed if it's just me and the teacher. I'd prefer to learn in a group. In a group, you can stay quiet. You don't have to speak if you don't want to.

B: ⁷O_____ c_____ on! That's n_____ . If you don't practise speaking in lessons, you will never pass your speaking exam.

A: Hmm. You sound like our teacher.

4 Put the words in order to make phrases and complete the conversations. There is one extra phrase for each dialogue.

1 I / believe … / really
    That's / come / Oh / on! / nonsense.
    agree / more. / couldn't / I

A: Students worry too much about fashion and not enough about studying. *I really believe* that wearing a uniform to school would help to improve exam results.

B: _____ . It is possible to be fashionable and hardworking, you know.

2 I / you / If / me, / ask / think …
    point. / a / That's / good
    so / not / I'm / sure.

A: ¹_____ doing a gap year is a great idea. Young people get a lot out of travel.

B: ²_____ . Isn't it better to get your qualifications first and then travel?

3 couldn't / more. / agree / I
    doesn't / think … / she
    true, / but … / That's

A: Well, I spoke to my sister and ¹_____ single-sex schools are a good idea at all. She thinks girls and boys should learn to live, study and work together from a young age.

B: ²_____ exam results are often better at single-sex schools. What is more important?

4 think … / Personally, / I
    totally / I / disagree.
    agree / I / more. / couldn't

A: ¹_____ doing sport at school is as important as learning to read and write.

B: ²_____ . If kids are going to do well at school, they need to be fit and healthy.

1 In pairs, ask and answer the questions.

PART 1

Talk about homes.
1 Describe your ideal home.
2 What jobs do you do around the house?
3 What is good about living in a very high block of flats? Why?
4 Would you like to live in a cave? Why?/Why not?
5 What's the most interesting building you've ever seen? Why?

PART 2

Talk about school.
1 What's your dream school like?
2 Do you think there shouldn't be Art classes in the school curriculum? Why?/Why not?
3 What's your favourite after-school activity? Why?
4 Do you think school should be compulsory until the age of 18? Why?/Why not?
5 Do you want to have a gap year before you start work? Why?/Why not?

2 Look at the photos of people doing voluntary work.

A

B

Take turns to talk about what you can see in the photos.
1 Talk about the people.
2 Talk about the places.
3 Talk about the other things in the photographs.

3 Read the instructions on your card. In pairs, take turns to role-play the conversation.

Student A

You and Student B are talking about your school. Share your ideas and say if you agree or disagree.

- Give your opinion about your school curriculum.
- Give your opinion about the food in the school canteen.
- Ask Student B if he/she has any ideas.
- Listen to his/her opinion about homework, then agree or disagree politely.
- Listen to his/her opinion about the after-school activities, then agree or disagree politely.
- Summarise the things you disagree about, then end the conversation.

Student B

You and Student A are talking about your school. Share your ideas and say if you agree or disagree.

- Listen to Student A's opinion about the curriculum, then agree or disagree politely.
- Listen to his/her opinion about the food in the canteen, then agree or disagree politely.
- Give your opinion about the amount/type of homework you get.
- Give your opinion about the after-school activities.
- Summarise the things you agree about.

VOCABULARY AND GRAMMAR

1 Complete the sentences with the words from the box. There are two extra words.

> bully ~~classmate~~ compulsory exhausted
> grades ill job nervous

Mum, this is my new _classmate_, Will. We're going to do our homework together.

1 Sam, you won't get good _____ if you don't study for the exam.

2 My brother has got a part-time _____ working in a shop.

3 Anthony always gets _____ when the teacher asks him a question in class.

4 If somebody starts to _____ you, tell a teacher immediately.

5 Maths is _____ , which means that everybody has to study it.

/5

2 Complete the second sentence so it has a similar meaning to the first. Use between two and five words, including the word in capitals.

How do you manage to learn three foreign languages at the same time? **COPE**
How do you _cope with learning_ three foreign languages at the same time?

1 I really want to visit Australia one day. **DREAMING**
I _____ to Australia one day.

2 Our school year finishes on the fifth of June this year. **BREAKS**
Our school _____ the fifth of June this year.

3 Dad wanted me to choose a teaching job like him. **ENCOURAGED**
Dad _____ a teacher like him.

4 Jack is going from level two to level four next term. **UP**
Jack is _____ level four from level two next term.

5 Did you laugh at your boyfriend's clothes? **FUN**
Did _____ the way your boyfriend was dressed?

/5

3 Complete the sentences with the correct words. The first letters are given.

I think you **m**_isunderstood_ me. That's not what I meant at all.

1 I'm a **v**_____ **t**_____ , so I remember things better when I can have a picture of them in my head.

2 What's your **t**_____ for the next term? Are you going to have lessons on Saturday?

3 I hope ancient history is on the school **c**_____ this year. I love reading about old cultures like the Romans and the Aztecs.

4 My **m**_____ at work is great. She's very experienced and has a lot of knowledge, so she can really advise me well.

5 Jake's father is an **e**_____ on Biology. Why not ask him for help with your project?

/5

4 Complete the dialogue between Ellie and Auntie Jean with the correct form of the verbs in brackets.

AJ: You look unhappy, Ellie. What's the matter?

E: Well, you know I'm starting university next year and I have some difficult choices to make. The first decision is where to study. If I _go_ (go) to university in my hometown, I'll stay with Mum and Dad. But if I decide to study in London, I ¹_____ (rent) a flat with my friend Lena. I'm sure I ²_____ (save) more money if I live at home with my parents, but Lena says we'll have more fun if we ³_____ (get) a flat together in London.

AJ: So you have to decide what is more important to you.

E: Well, another problem is, Lena is a good friend, but she's not a very good student and she ⁴_____ (not/pass) her exams if she doesn't revise a lot. If she ⁵_____ (fail) her exams, she won't go to university at all and then I'll be on my own in London. Why is life so complicated?

AJ: Hmm. Do you really want to go to university and live with someone who is not a good student?

/5

5 Find and correct the mistakes.

This is the park ~~that~~ I usually walk the dog. _where_

1 I'd like to try some Indian food who isn't too spicy. _____

2 This is the language school that my cousin studied Japanese. _____

3 That's the girl which took her exams a year early. _____

4 Is this the university where has the best medical courses? _____

5 I'd like a teacher what doesn't set us too much homework. _____

/5

6 Choose the correct answers A–C.

The life of a future ballerina

Anna goes to ballet school in Moscow. It's a private school, so her parents have to pay the _B_ fees. Every morning, she wakes up at 05:30 and travels across the city to the place ¹___ the school is. Anna has to work hard because there are a lot of classes on her ²___ . She studies normal subjects for five hours every day and then ballet for another four hours. She's a good student and she never ³___ any of her lessons. If she ⁴___ the exams at the end of the year, she'll stay in Moscow for another year. Anna has a true passion ⁵___ dancing and wants to be a professional ballerina in the future.

	A	B	C
	A subject	(B) tuition	C lesson
1	A where	B when	C who
2	A curriculum	B timetable	C degree
3	A misses	B drops	C does
4	A 'll pass	B passes	C 's passing
5	A with	B of	C for

/5

Total   /30

7 Complete each pair of sentences with the same answer A–C.

To begin the next dance, I'd like everyone to line __ in front of me.

I need to work all weekend to keep __ with my school work.

A at   B on   Ⓒ up

1 Could you tell me __ I can find Mr Jackson?

James, __ are you going when school finishes for the summer?

A who   B where   C when

2 I needed the love and support __ my family after the difficult time I had last year.

My mother is a professor __ Maths at Edinburgh University.

A of   B from   C in

3 __ I finish university, I'll be a graduate in Science.

I'll call you __ I get home, OK?

A when   B unless   C before

4 Ollie is going to __ a degree in Sports Science next year.

I usually __ my homework in my bedroom.

A get   B have   C do

5 Are you __ German next term?

Yves is __ the Maths exam again because he failed first time.

A passing   B skipping   C taking

            /5

8 Complete the dialogues with the correct answers A–C.

Aidan: You look really tired.

Jack: Yes, I __ after playing football all day.

A got nervous   Ⓑ am exhausted

C broke up

1 Ed: You seem to have a very good education.

Heida: Yes, I __ in both Maths and Physics.

A have got degrees   B passed exams

C finished school

2 Phil: I'm hoping to __ Brunel University in London to study Creative Writing.

Kyle: Why's that? Do you want to write a novel one day?

A be into   B go into

C get into

3 Harry: Will you keep all of the books that you bought after you finish university?

Ila: No, I __ .

A will miss them   B will get rid of them

C will hand them in

4 Pam: When will you give me back my book?

Emma: __ I finish reading it.

A If   B Unless

C As soon as

5 Sean: Could you tell me __ ?

Chris: Sure, the blue one with white stripes.

A who bought that T-shirt?

B where you bought that T-shirt?

C which T-shirt you bought?

            /5

9 Choose the correct answers A–C to replace the underlined part of the sentence.

Did Ms Jones <u>set</u> us any homework for the weekend?

Ⓐ give   B mark   C do

1 I can't <u>concentrate on</u> my homework with that loud music playing.

A focus on   B think about   C revise for

2 Jane <u>attended</u> a private school in Washington, D.C.

A left   B finished   C went to

3 You won't finish your degree <u>unless you study harder</u>.

A if you won't study harder

B if you don't study harder

C when you study so little

4 I'm positive Sarah will <u>drop music lessons</u> next year.

A stop studying music

B skip music lessons

C continue music lessons

5 I want to go to Liverpool University <u>when I finish school</u>.

A if I finish school

B before I finish school

C as soon as I finish school

            /5

10 Choose the correct answers A–D.

A practical education

Would you like to _C_ to a school which doesn't teach traditional subjects like Maths and Science in the classroom? How about a school **1**___ they don't set any exams for its students? Sounds great, right? Well, in fact, such schools exist.

There are a number of schools across Europe and America that follow a non-traditional curriculum. Students study subjects like Maths and Science through practical projects like building boats or making sculptures. This means no revising for exams and learning boring facts **2**___ heart!

Some of these schools began because they wanted to help children that used to get **3**___ trouble in a regular school. They behaved badly, didn't pay attention in class and struggled **4**___ learning in the classroom. Other students in these schools have parents who do not agree with traditional methods of teaching and testing.

Unfortunately, all these schools have something in common: they are expensive. Parents must pay high tuition fees for their children to attend. So, **5**___ you are the child of someone with plenty of money to spend, you'll have to be satisfied with doing most of your learning in the classroom.

	A	B	C	D
	A start	B attend	Ⓒ go	D leave
1	A which	B who	C that	D where
2	A on	B through	C by	D with
3	A in	B into	C on	D off
4	A with	B at	C on	D to
5	A when	B unless	C if	D as soon as

            /5

Total   /20

6 Just the job

VOCABULARY

6.1 Jobs • collocations • describing jobs • phrasal verbs

SHOW WHAT YOU KNOW

1 Complete the jobs. Some letters are given.

h*airdress*er

1 f_____r

2 d_____r

3 s_____p
  a_____nt

4 b_____er

5 s_____ist

6 r_____ist

7 p_____ian

8 e_____ian

9 p_____er

10 f_____t
  a_____ant

11 s_____
  i_____or

WORD STORE 6A | Collocations

2 Choose the correct words.

www.jobsa2z.com

Planning your future? ¹Applying *on / for / to* your first job? Thinking about ²resigning *from / off / down* your current job?
We tell you the truth about jobs: the pluses and minuses from A–Z!

You searched for three jobs. Here are the best results:

Tour Guide:

Pluses: Many tour guides ³*get / are* self-employed, so they can't ⁴*get / have* the sack. It's also easy to ⁵*take / do* days off when you choose, because you run your own company.

Minuses: Most tour guides ⁶*are / have* badly-paid. Because they ⁷*do / work* outdoors, tour guides often only have a ⁸*full-time job / part-time job* when the weather is not very good. In the summer, however, when there are lots of tourists, you can expect to work ⁹*nights shifts / long hours* every day.

Doctor:

Pluses: Experienced doctors are generally pretty ¹⁰*well-paid / badly-paid*. They can take between 20 and 30 days ¹¹*overtime / paid holiday* per year.

Minuses: Training is long and expensive. Junior doctors usually work ¹²*long hours / a job* which also often involves doing ¹³*night shifts / overtime* one day per week.

Office Manager:

Pluses: Office managers have a ¹⁴*part-time job / full-time job* and like other employees they ¹⁵*have / do* four weeks' paid holiday per year.

Minuses: Office managers rarely travel in their jobs and often have to work ¹⁶*overtime / indoors* after their regular 8-hour day. They are usually ¹⁷*responsible / fired* for keeping an office problem-free, so it can be very stressful work when things go wrong.

74

WORD STORE 6B| Describing jobs

3 Complete the sentences with the words from the box.

> challenging creative ~~demanding~~
> repetitive rewarding stressful tiring

Working as a flight attendant is extremely
demanding. You need to be focused and patient all
the time and you often spend a long time away from
home.

1 My work as a politician is difficult, but very
interesting and that's why I like it. I always wanted
a _____ job because I think I would get
bored if it wasn't.

2 Working as a builder can be _____
because it's a physical job. I work hard outdoors all
day and I sleep *very* well at night!

3 I like my job as a receptionist because I meet
lots of interesting people. However, it can be
rather _____ because I do the same things
all day, every day.

4 The best thing about being a teacher is that the job
is very _____ . I get a lot of satisfaction
from knowing that I'm helping young people learn.

5 I'm a doctor and my job is very _____ .
It can be hard to relax after a hard day at work in the
hospital.

6 I'm an artist and in my job it's important to be
_____ because I need to use original ideas
all the time.

WORD STORE 6C | Phrasal verbs

4 Complete the job advertisements with *on*, *up* or *off*.

HOME-WORK-FOR-ALL

**can find you the perfect job which you can do
from your own home. You don't have to put** _up_
**with annoying co-workers OR need to worry
about turning ¹____ late for work ever again!**

Call today: 0800 123 456

Don't let a negative experience of running your
own company put you ²_____ the idea of being
self-employed forever. At BeYourOwnBoss you
can get the best advice for making your business
a success.

Email: jonsmith@beyourownboss.org

TOPLOGO is taking ³____ intelligent and
imaginative young people to come ⁴____ with
creative and interesting logos for new companies.

Contact us today on 678 007 900

Job (countable noun) means 'the regular paid work
that you do to earn money':

Emma has a very well-paid job as a lawyer.

Work (uncountable noun) is often used to mean the
place where you do your job:

What time do you get to work (e.g. to your office)?

Work (uncountable noun) can also mean all the
activities connected with my job':

I start work at 9.00 a.m. and finish at 5.00 p.m.

5 Read REMEMBER THIS. Choose the correct words.

1 Sara applied for a *job* / *work* as a plumber.
2 Mum will be late home from *job* / *work* tonight.
3 What time will you finish *job* / *work* tonight?
4 Jenna is looking for a summer *job* / *work*.
5 I enjoy *work* / *job* because I have some lovely
colleagues.
6 Mike left his computer at *job* / *work*.
7 My uncle lost his *job* / *work* when the factory closed.
8 What do you do all day at *job* / *work*?

SHOW WHAT YOU'VE LEARNT

**6 Complete the sentences with the missing words.
The first letters are given.**

Studying full-time and working at weekends is
t_iring_. I've got no energy left to do the things
I really enjoy.

1 Money is very important to me, so I want a job
where I a_____ w_____-p_____ .
2 Jade wants to be her own boss. She wants to
b_____ s_____-e_____ .
3 Did Charlie t_____ u_____ late to work
again today? He'll get the sack if he's not careful.
4 My job is very d_____ . It's difficult and
requires a lot of both mental strength and physical
energy.
5 If you want more money, why don't you
d_____ o_____ ? The company is
always offering extra hours after work.
6 Erin loves the outdoors. She would hate to
w_____ i_____ in an office every day.
7 Alfie wants to h_____
a p_____-_____ j_____ because
he likes working for only four hours a day.
8 Natalie helped me c_____ u_____
w_____ an idea for the new magazine.
9 A: Why did John r_____ f_____ his job?
B: I think he didn't like his boss.
10 Kathy's brother has p_____ me o_____
the job of a swimming instructor because he says
it's really badly-paid.

/10

GRAMMAR

Second Conditional

SHOW WHAT YOU KNOW

1 Complete the First Conditional sentences with the correct forms of the verbs in brackets.

Zoe wants to go to the cinema with her friends tonight, but …

If she <u>goes</u> (go) to the cinema, she <u>'ll miss</u> (miss) the last bus home.

1 If she ᵃ_____ (not/catch) the last bus, she ᵇ_____ (have to take) a taxi.

2 It ᵃ_____ (cost) a lot of money if she ᵇ_____ (go home) by taxi.

3 She ᵃ_____ (not/have) any money for the weekend if she ᵇ_____ (spend) it all tonight.

4 If she ᵃ_____ (not/have) any money at the weekend, what ᵇ_____ (she/do)?

2 ★ Choose the correct verb forms.

decisionsdecisions.com
helping teens with tricky choices

To go or not to go – that is the question!

We asked some teenagers …

What ¹*would* / *did* you miss about home if you ²*went* / *'d go* to study in another country?

This is what they said …

Diego 15:
My mum's cooking. I ³*'d miss* / *missed* her food if I ⁴*'d live* / *lived* anywhere except home. Can you put empanadas in the post?

Elle and Anna (Twins) 17:
We ⁵*'d never see* / *never saw* our cats if we ⁶*'d study* / *studied* in another country. We really love them. If we ⁷*'d get* / *got* the chance to study in another country, we ⁸*wouldn't* / *didn't* leave without them.

Tom 16:
If I ⁹*'d do* / *did* a course in another country, I ¹⁰*wouldn't* / *didn't* miss anything except my family. One day, I want to live in the US or Canada for a few years.

Camilla 17:
If I ¹¹*went* / *'d go* to study in another country, I ¹²*'d feel* / *felt* lonely without my boyfriend. I can't imagine life on my own.

3 ★ ★ Complete the dialogue between Jason and Holly with Second Conditional sentences. Use the correct form of the verbs in brackets.

J: I really like her, Holly, but I don't think I should tell her.

H: Wrong! You should definitely tell her.

J: Really? But, if I <u>told</u> (tell) her, she ¹_____ (know).

H: Er … obviously! That's the idea.

J: But, if she ²_____ (know), I ³_____ (feel) totally embarrassed. I wouldn't even be able to look at her. Anyway, she probably doesn't even like me.

H: Look Jason, I'll tell you a secret. Listen. Let's just say I had a very similar conversation with her yesterday. If I ⁴_____ (be) you, I ⁵_____ (tell) her.

J: What? Really?

H: Jason, she feels the same way about you! Will you just go and find her NOW and ask her on a date?

J: Now? No way! What ⁶_____ (I/say) if I ⁷_____ (see) her now? I'm not ready.

H: Oh Jason! You're nearly eighteen. It's time to be a man!

4 ★ ★ ★ Rewrite the sentences. Use the Second Conditional.

Ben doesn't have a job in the mountains this winter, because he has exams soon.
Ben would have a job in the mountains this winter if he didn't have exams soon.

1 He doesn't have a job in the mountains, so he doesn't go snowboarding every week.
He _____
_____

2 He doesn't go snowboarding every week, so he's not good at it.
If _____
_____

3 He doesn't teach Charlotte to snowboard because he's not good at it.
He _____
_____

4 He doesn't teach Charlotte, so they don't spend time together.
If _____
_____

SHOW WHAT YOU'VE LEARNT

5 Find and correct the mistakes. One sentence is correct.

Jenny would get long holidays if she would be a teacher. <u>she was</u>

1 Adam wouldn't lived with his parents if he had a job in Milan. _____

2 If Pedro would be a plumber, he'd fix the pipes in the kitchen. _____

3 If you'd worked for your father, would you argue all the time? _____

4 If I were you, I'd put it on now because it's getting cold. _____

5 We moved out of our flat if houses weren't so expensive. _____

6 Would you be surprised if your country win the World Cup? _____

/6

GRAMMAR: Train and Try Again page 149

6.3

Countable and uncountable nouns related to work • collocations • jobs

1 Read the dialogue between Sophie and her aunt, Mary. Choose the correct words 1–6 to complete the extract.

Extract from Students' Book recording 🔊 **3.6**

S: I want to do your job.

M: Ah! Right. Well, why not? It's a great job. And we need more women in the ¹*profession / colleagues / qualification*. There aren't many female pilots. Did you know that only 5% of airline pilots are women?

S: That's terrible. Why is that?

M: I'm not sure. The ²*experience / overtime / training* is long and very expensive, but it's the same for men and women. Maybe women think it's a man's job, so they don't apply for the training.

S: If I wanted to be an airline pilot, would I find the training difficult?

M: No, I don't think so. In fact, I think you have the right ³*salary / qualities / colleagues*.

S: Really?

M: Yes, you're healthy and you have excellent eyesight. You're intelligent, you're good at Maths and Science, and you get on well with people. If you got your university ⁴*experience / overtime / degree* first, and then went to pilot school, you could be a great pilot.

S: Do you enjoy your job?

M: I love it. I work long hours, but there are lots of good things about my job. For instance, I can travel anywhere in the world for free. (…)

S: What about your ⁵*colleagues / salary / overtime*?

M: I work with some great people – we have a really good time together. (…)

S: Is it easy to become a captain and get a pay rise?

M: No, you need a lot of ⁶*bonuses / experience / salary*. I've only been doing this job for five years. I may become captain after another ten years.

2 Complete the sentences with the words from the box. There are two extra words.

> colleagues   degree   experience   overtime
> profession   qualities   salary   ~~training~~

Dog *training* helps your pet behave better and can be fun for the dog and its owner.

1 The new education minister has over twenty years of _____ in politics.

2 Pat has one _____ in History and another in Literature.

3 What are the _____ of a good teacher? Knowledge, patience, tact, sense of humour …

4 How was your first day at work? What about the other people? Do you have any nice _____ ?

5 You need a high level of education and training to work in the legal or medical _____ .

REMEMBER THIS

When you learn new nouns, use a dictionary or go online and check if they are countable or uncountable. Remember some nouns can be both countable and uncountable depending on the context:

You need lots of experience *to become a professional footballer.*

(uncountable – knowledge and skill learnt from the time spent doing something)

Working in the USA was a great experience.

(countable – something memorable that happened to you).

VOCABULARY PRACTICE | Collocations

3 Look at the vocabulary in lesson 6.3 in the Students' Book. Choose the correct words.

Conversation 1: Boris and Andriey

B: Andriey, are you good at Maths?

A: I think so. I *do / have / take* a university degree in Astrophysics.

Conversation 2: Sandy and Millie

S: Do you like your new job, Millie?

M: I do. And I *do / spend / take* training quite often, so I'm learning lots.

Conversation 3: Amy and Barbara

A: Do you *take / spend / get* on well with your new boss?

B: Yes, I do. She's lovely.

Conversation 4: Sharon and Trevor

S: Are you sure you *have / get / do* excellent eyesight?

T: Yes, I can see very well, thank you.

Conversation 5: Morris and Colin

M: Why do you *take / get / spend* so much time away from home?

C: I go away on a lot of business trips.

Conversation 6: Gloria and Michael

G: I haven't seen you at work recently, Michael.

M: No, I *took / spent / did* time off to go travelling.

WORD STORE 6D | Jobs

4 Complete the jobs.

Who can help you …

	find what you are looking for in a shop?	shop a*ssistant*
1	learn to drive?	d_____ instructor
2	get home on public transport?	b_____ driver
3	book a holiday?	t_____ agent
4	with paperwork and photocopying?	o_____ assistant
5	learn a winter sport?	s_____ instructor
6	get home late at night?	t_____ driver
7	buy a house or a flat?	e_____ agent

Sylvie ①

I'm adaptable, sensitive and good at listening to people of all ages. I don't get stressed about unexpected things. I can put up with working long hours, but I don't like water sports.

②

ALEXANDER

I live close to the ocean and am dedicated to water sports. I'd like a demanding job because I find repetitive jobs boring. I'm not keen on children and I have a dog.

Mia ③

I'd like a job where I can be active. I love water sports and am good at problem-solving. I get on well with children, but I'm scared of dogs. Free accommodation would be great.

④

Felix

I'd like to live somewhere new, but I don't have money for a flat. I'm active, spend lots of time outdoors and love water sports. I enjoy being alone and jobs which aren't too challenging. I haven't worked with kids.

Looking for a summer *job*?

Read on to find out about the most popular summer work for teenagers.

Ⓐ LIFEGUARD

Being a lifeguard is the perfect way to spend time on the beach and learn new skills like first aid* and water rescue*. You must be a strong swimmer to cope with big waves, and a reliable person. It's a serious job and you don't know what's going to happen each day. It's only for those who have a passion for water. You also need to live near the coast.

Ⓑ CAMP COUNSELLOR*

Are you a good leader? Do you find it easy to make decisions? The camp counsellor job involves organising activities as well as helping children with any problems, so it's essential you are caring. This job is well-paid and accommodation is included, but you have to be ready for anything. You must be hard-working and be ready to work with adults and children.

Ⓒ WINDSURFING INSTRUCTOR

If you already have some skills, then take a course and become a windsurfing instructor. You need to be patient as most people you teach will be beginners. You also have to be sociable because you are going to work with adults and kids all day long. If you live near a lake or sea then this is a good job for you.

Ⓓ PET SITTER

Taking care of people's pets when they go on holiday is a great summer job for animal lovers. You need to be active as the job can include walking dogs and cleaning animal cages*. The pay isn't great, but sometimes you can live for free in the same house as the animals you are looking after, so it is possible to save some money.

Ⓔ GARDENER

Another option for nature-lovers is looking after people's gardens when they go on holiday, or helping them if they are too busy at work. It's important that you know about different plants and trees and how to care for them. There's plenty of alone-time in this job, so it's good for quiet people.

Ⓕ ACTIVITY LEADER

You have to love kids to do this job. You also need to be good at a wide variety of different sports and activities such as volleyball and painting. This job is for active and adventurous people only. So, if swimming in a river is not your favourite activity, then this is not the job for you. The money isn't great, but accommodation is usually free.

GLOSSARY

first aid (n) – simple medical treatment given straight after an accident
to rescue (v) – to save someone or something from danger

counsellor (n) – a job where someone gives advice and helps people with their problems
cage (n) – a box with thin metal bars for keeping small animals or birds

1 Four teenagers are looking for summer jobs. Read the texts and match each person 1–4 to a suitable job A–F. There are two extra jobs.

1 ◯
2 ◯
3 ◯
4 ◯

2 Read the texts again. Are statements 1–8 true (T) or false (F)?

1 Pet sitters have to sleep with the animals they look after. ◯
2 Camp counsellors work with kids, but older people too. ◯
3 Working as a gardener is a good job for introverted people. ◯
4 You learn how to deal with accidents when you work as a lifeguard. ◯
5 Lifeguards follow the same routine every day. ◯
6 Teaching people how to windsurf is a repetitive job. ◯
7 Activity leaders have to pay for a place to stay. ◯
8 Camp counsellors can make quite a lot of money. ◯

3 Read the clues and complete the crossword. Use the underlined words in the texts to help.

```
1
O
C
E   3
2 A
N
        4
   5         6
       7
   8
```

Across

2 an area of sand or small stones at the edge of the sea or a lake

5 bigger than a lake; smaller than an ocean

7 a large area of water surrounded by land

8 e.g. the Nile, the Amazon

Down

1 e.g. the Pacific, the Atlantic

3 the area where the land meets the sea

4 H$_2$O

6 movements of water that surfers can surf on across the sea

REMEMBER BETTER

You can record some groups of words on lines to show their relationship in terms of an increasing/decreasing quality or chronological order.

Put the words from the box in the right place on the line.

ocean   lake   sea   ~~swimming pool~~

small – _swimming pool_ – _____ – _____ – _____ **big**

VOCABULARY PRACTICE | Compound nouns

4 Look at the vocabulary in lesson 6.4 in the Students' Book. Complete the sentences with compound nouns. Use the words in brackets to help you.

I think being a _fire-fighter_ (FIGHT) is one of the most dangerous jobs. They don't only rescue cats from trees, you know.

1 We are making no progress with this project. Who is the _____ (DECISION) in this group?

2 Greg's a _____ (SOCIAL). He helps care for people with mental illness.

3 I love computers and computer programming and one day I hope to work as a _____ (SOFTWARE).

4 Adam's a real _____ (NATURE). He really enjoys being outdoors in forests and climbing mountains.

5 Why don't you ask Mandy for advice? She's the best _____ (PROBLEM) I know.

WORD STORE 6E | Word families

5 Complete each pair of sentences with the correct form of the word from the box. There is one extra word.

charm   competition   determination
logic   ~~peace~~   reliance

a It's so _peaceful_ here during the nightshift. Much quieter than in the daytime.
b Isabella loves the _peace_ in the countryside. She's thinking of leaving London.

1 a John is extremely _____ and can get angry if he doesn't win.
  b Mandy Ferris wants to _____ in this year's Best Boss Competition. Do you think she can win?

2 a I met this really _____ guy yesterday. He's so polite and friendly. You'll love him!
  b Marius has so much _____ that I usually do anything he asks me to do.

3 a Last week Matt was _____ to learn Hungarian. But after three lessons all his enthusiasm disappeared.
  b To succeed in business you need a lot of _____ and good luck.

4 a You can't _____ on Adam. I asked him to meet me an hour ago and where is he?
  b Patrick isn't very _____ , so I wouldn't ask him to give you a job.

SHOW WHAT YOU KNOW

1 Complete the sentences with *must* or *mustn't*.

I _must_ try to do more exercise. I want to be fit and healthy.

1 We are lucky to have enough food and a warm house. We _____ complain about unimportant things.

2 I feel exhausted all the time. I _____ try to get more sleep.

3 We _____ be late again. We don't want the others to think we are unreliable.

4 I _____ stop biting my nails. They look terrible.

2 Complete the sentences with the correct form of *have to* or *don't have to* and the words in brackets.

The gallery is free if you have a student card, so _students don't have to pay_ (students/pay).

1 _____ (Emma/miss) school today because she's going to the hospital.

2 It's unfair._____ (Alec/clean) his own bedroom, so why should I?

3 I can't concentrate on my homework. _____ (you/sing) so loudly?

4 (Nina/go)_____ to school on Monday because it's a national holiday.

3 ★ Complete the gaps with the modal verbs in capitals. One verb in each group is not needed.

NEEDN'T / HAVE TO / CAN'T

1 A You _____ walk – why not save your energy? I'll take you in the car.

B You _____ walk – it's freezing cold and you don't have a coat.

HAS TO / DOESN'T HAVE TO / CAN

2 A Beth _____ bring food to the party, but it's not really necessary.

B Beth _____ bring food to the party – we've already got plenty.

HAVE TO / MUSTN'T / DON'T HAVE TO

3 A The students _____ revise – the exams are in three weeks.

B The students _____ revise – the exams finished last week.

HAS TO / CAN / MUSTN'T

4 A Katy _____ wear formal clothes – the wedding invitation says 'formal dress'.

B Katy _____ wear formal clothes, but not everyone is going to be smart.

4 ★ ★ Think about rules and arrangements and choose the most suitable modal verb.

1 Sarah *must / has to* be there at four o'clock. The others will be waiting for her.

2 I *must / have to* stop staying up so late. I fell asleep at school yesterday!

3 The sign says you *can't / mustn't* park here.

4 I *can't / mustn't* forget to speak to Dad tonight. I need to ask him for some money.

5 Police officers and soldiers *must / have to* wear uniforms.

6 You *can't / mustn't* go on this rollercoaster if you are less than 1.4 metres tall.

5 ★ ★ ★ It's Julia's first day of work experience. Complete the dialogue with the most suitable modal verbs. Sometimes more than one answer is possible.

W: So, Julia, welcome to the chocolate factory. I'm William. Nice to meet you.

J: Hi. Nice to meet you too.

W: OK. Let's have a look round first of all. There are a few rules in the factory – you _need to/have to_ wear these special plastic shoes at all times and I'm afraid you ¹_____ wear any jewellery … oh, actually if you are married, you ²_____ take off your wedding ring, but no other jewellery, please.

J: OK, that's fine. I'm not married, so no problem.

W: OK. Follow me then please …This is where we make the chocolate. We tell our workers that it's OK to eat as much chocolate as they like and of course, they ³_____ pay – it's free.

J: Really? ⁴_____ I try some?

W: Of course, but you ⁵_____ use your fingers. Here, put this glove on.

J: Thanks. Mmmm, it's delicious. Oh dear, I ⁶_____ eat too much though.

W: Don't worry. We usually find that after a few days, people have had enough.

J: Hmm. I'm not sure about that.

SHOW WHAT YOU'VE LEARNT

6 Choose the correct words.

1 You ___ be 17 to drive a car in the UK.
   A have to   B mustn't   C can't

2 Architects ___ be good at drawing.
   A mustn't   B need to   C needn't

3 I ___ remember to say thanks to Jenny.
   A must   B have to   C mustn't

4 You ___ be female to be a nurse.
   A need to   B mustn't   C don't need to

5 Students ___ make a lot of noise in the library.
   A can   B can't   C needn't

6 Women ___ become police officers if they want to.
   A can   B must   C needn't

/6

GRAMMAR: Train and Try Again page 149

1 ⭐ Choose the correct words.

Ann: How was your first day at work?

Max: Hmm. It was OK, but I found a lot of things really ¹*confused / confusing*.

Ann: Well, that's not ²*surprised / surprising*. It was your first day.

Max: I know. But I made lots of mistakes, so it was also quite ³*embarrassed / embarrassing*. To be honest, I feel a little ⁴*depressed / depressing*.

Ann: Oh, Max. Don't be silly! Tomorrow will be better. What about the work? Is it ⁵*interested / interesting*?

Max: It is, yes. I admit that I was a little ⁶*frustrated / frustrating*, but my day certainly wasn't ⁷*bored / boring*. And I think the job will be very ⁸*rewarded / rewarding*.

Ann: Well, then. So don't be ⁹*annoyed / annoying* with yourself. Give it a little more time and everything will be perfect! Let's have an ice cream to celebrate finishing your first day!

REMEMBER THIS

*Everybody was **interested** in the exhibition.*
*What an **interesting** exhibition!*

Sometimes instead of the -ing form of the adjective, a different form is used:

*I was **scared** to death while I was watching the film.*
*What a **scary** film!*

*Tom was too **stressed** to say anything.*
*An exam is an example of a very **stressful** situation.*

2 ⭐⭐ Complete the sentences with the correct form of the word in capitals.

The food in our canteen at work is *disgusting*.
Everything tastes horrible! **DISGUST**

1 My first day at work was really _____ .
I learnt lots of new things and met some great people. **EXCITE**

2 James works as a skiing instructor. It's physical work, so that's why he's always so _____ all of the time. **EXHAUST**

3 Amy's job is quite badly paid. She finds this _____ because she works very hard and earlier studied for six years. **DISAPPOINT**

4 Sarah read on the Internet about a charity organisation in Africa. Now she's feeling _____ and wants to apply for a job with them. **INSPIRE**

5 I get five weeks' paid holiday in my new job. It's _____ . I only had two in my last company. **AMAZE**

6 One of the most _____ things about my job is that it's very stressful. **WORRY**

3 ⭐⭐⭐ Complete the sentences with missing adjectives. The first letters are given.

My boss is always very **e**ncouraging. He says very positive things about my work.

1 Working outdoors all day in this heat is very **t**_____ . I think I'll go to bed early tonight.

2 Guess what? Viviana got the shop assistant job that she really wanted. She's absolutely **d**_____ , so she's having a party to celebrate!

3 I was so **s**_____ of making a mistake on my first day in the office that I didn't manage to do very much work at all.

4 Karl thought he was going to get the sack yesterday. He was very **r**_____ when his boss only gave him a warning.

5 Janice was **a**_____ when they fired her. It was a complete surprise.

6 I saw something so **m**_____ this morning that I nearly cried. A big punk guy was stopping the traffic to help a little old lady cross the road.

4 ⭐⭐⭐ Complete the sentences with the words in brackets in the correct form. Do not change the order of the words. You may need to add words. Use no more than six words

Mrs Bennet: The new tour guide *is a charming man* (be / charm / man). I'm sure you'll like him.

Mr Bennet: I can't wait to meet him.

1 **Don:** I'm a firefighter.
Mrs Price: Are you? That _____ (be / such / demand) job!

2 **Kim:** What are your colleagues at work like?
Jon: To be honest, I _____ (be / real / irritate) by what they think about our company.

3 **Ella:** What _____ (be / stressful) thing in your work you've ever done?
Jill: Giving a presentation to a big audience.

4 **Petra:** How did your first lesson with class B go?
Greg: Don't even ask. I _____ (be / extremely / embarrass) when I entered the classroom 13 minutes late and saw all those eyes looking up at me.

5 **Journalist:** Do you like being a farmer?
Farmer: Yes, I do. I think work on a farm _____ (be / very / relax) for me.

1 Replace the informal phrases in the sentences with the formal words from the box.

> a suitable candidate   at present   available
> confident   experience of working
> many opportunities   obtained   possess
> succeed   requires

I've got all the skills needed to be an office assistant.
possess

1 At the moment I'm working as a travel agent.
_____

2 I am free to begin work from Monday 6th June.
_____

3 I have worked on over twelve fruit farms in Europe.
_____

4 I believe that I am the right person for the position of shop assistant. _____

5 I am sure you will be satisfied with my work.
_____

6 I work hard and I have the right attitude to do well.
_____

7 This job will provide me with plenty of chances to develop myself. _____

8 I got a certificate in teaching from Cambridge University. _____

9 I truly believe I have the talent the position needs.
_____

2 Put the words in order to make phrases for a job application.

1 reference / With / your / advertisement / in ... / to
With reference to your advertisement in ...

2 position / the / writing / I / am / express / my / to / in / interest / of ...
_____
_____

3 advertisement / very / found / because ... / I / your / interesting
_____
_____

4 would / suitable / because ... / I / be / a / candidate / the / job / for
_____
_____

5 experience / My / includes ...
_____

6 enclose / CV / my / for / information. / I / your
_____

7 any / at / available / I / be / can / interview / for / time.
_____
_____

8 am ... / Currently, / I
_____

3 Match the beginnings and the correct endings to make sentences for a job application.

I am writing in response to your advertisement ☐ f
1 I would like to apply for the position of ☐
2 At the moment, ☐
3 I am particularly interested in your company because ☐
4 As you will see ☐
5 I would be a suitable candidate for the job because ☐

a I am in my final year at senior school.
b I volunteered for a charity last summer.
c I am responsible and creative.
d part-time sales assistant.
e I would like to work for an international organisation.
f in the _Student Times_.

4 Replace the underlined phrases a–e in the job application with similar phrases from Exercise 2.

Dear Sir or Madam,

_1_ I am writing in response to your advertisement in _Work and Travel Magazine_. ᵃ___ I would like to apply for the position of children's activity organiser at the Grand Hotel this summer. ᵇ___ At the moment, I am preparing for my final exams, and I will be available to start work from July 5th.

ᶜ___ I am particularly interested in your company because I plan to do Hotel Management at university. I enclose my CV for your information. As you will see,ᵈ___ I spent last summer working as a summer camp supervisor at a local primary school.

ᵉ___ I would be a good candidate for the job because I get on well with children and am a responsible, creative and organised person.

I have provided my contact details on my CV and can be available for interview at any time.

I look forward to hearing from you.

Yours faithfully,
Mia Read

5 Read the task below. Then read the email and complete the gaps with the correct forms of the verbs from the box.

> You have seen the advertisement below in the *International Student Times* and want to apply for one of the jobs. Write a letter of application to Barry Winston.

WINSTON CAMPSITES ARE LOOKING FOR STAFF

Do you want to spend the summer living and working in Ireland?

We need friendly, outgoing young people with a good knowledge of English for the following posts:

- Reception staff
- Promoting tours and trips
- Tour guide
- Snack bar staff

Experience preferred but not necessary
To apply or to receive an information pack write to

Barry Winston at
bwinston@winstoncampsites.com

> Write your letter of application in about 80–130 words. Include and develop these points:
>
> - Say where you saw the advertisement.
> - Say what you are doing now, which post you are applying for and why you are interested in the job.
> - Mention your CV and any relevant work experience.
> - Say when you could have a telephone interview.

> advertise   apply   attach   could
> gain   hear   work   would

Dear Mr Winston,

With reference ^A^to / by your advertisement in the *International Student Times*, I would like to ¹_____ for the position ^B^to / of tour guide. I am currently ^C^in / on my final year at school but would like to ²_____ more work experience before studying Tourism ^D^on / at university next year.
I have ³_____ my CV ^E^with / for your information.
As you will see, I have some experience as a tour guide ^F^in / to Poland and enjoy ⁴_____ with people ^G^in / of all ages. For these reasons, I feel I ⁵_____ be a suitable candidate for the job you are ⁶_____ .
I would be grateful if you ⁷_____ send me an information pack.
I can be available for interview at any time.
I look forward to ⁸_____ from you.

Yours sincerely,
Richard Marsh

6 Read the email again and choose the correct prepositions.

SHOW WHAT YOU'VE LEARNT

7 You have seen the advertisement below in the *Metro* newspaper and you want to apply for the job. Write a letter of application. Include and develop these points:

- Say where you saw the advertisement.
- Say what you are doing now and give reasons why you are interested the job.
- Mention your CV and any relevant work experience.
- Say when you are available for interview.

BIG MIKE'S BURGERS REQUIRE SUMMER STAFF

- ✔ Are you a teenager looking for valuable work experience in the summer holidays?
- ✔ Can you cook, clean and take orders?

We are looking for punctual, easy-going and trustworthy young people to join our team for the summer. Experience in customer service and kitchen work is an advantage.

Contact Mike Pickles:
bigmikepickles@bmb.net

SHOW THAT YOU'VE CHECKED

Finished? Always check your writing.
Can you tick √ everything on this list?

In my letter of application:

• the beginning matches the end (*Dear Mr Smith* ⇨ *Yours sincerely; Dear Sir or Madam* ⇨ *Yours faithfully*).	☐
• I have said where I saw the job advert and why I am writing.	☐
• I have said what I am doing now and given reasons why I am interested in the job.	☐
• I have mentioned my CV and any relevant work experience.	☐
• I have given reasons why I am suitable for the job and said when I will be available for interview.	☐
• I have not used contractions	
• I have not used emoticons ☺, or abbreviations (*info / CU / gr8*).	☐
• I have checked my spelling and punctuation.	☐
• My text is neat and clear.	☐

SPEAKING

Asking for and giving advice

1 Translate the phrases into your own language.

SPEAKING BANK

Asking for advice

What do you think I should do? _____

Do you have any tips on what/ ideas about how to …? _____

Giving advice

You should … _____

I think you should … _____
_____

I don't think you should … _____
_____

Why don't you (go) …? _____
_____

My best advice would be to … _____
_____

It's a good idea to … _____

If I were you, I'd … _____

Accepting advice

Thanks, that's really helpful. _____

That's great advice. Thanks! _____

That's a good idea! _____

Rejecting advice

I'm not sure that's a good idea. _____
_____

2 Complete the dialogue between Henry and Samantha with the phrases from the box. There are two extra phrases.

> Do you have any tips on how to
> I'm not sure that's a good idea
> It's a good idea   ~~What do you think I should wear?~~
> Thanks! That's really helpful   You should

H: Tomorrow is my first day of work experience, Samantha. *What do you think I should wear?*

S: ¹_____ definitely wear a suit, Henry. Iron a shirt and clean your shoes. ²_____ to look smart on your first day.

H: ³_____ , Samantha.

S: Why not?

H: I'm going to work on a farm.

S: Oh.

3 Put the words in order and complete the mini-dialogues. There is one extra phrase in each dialogue.

A really / Thanks, / helpful / that's
should / think / I / you
do / think / should / do? / What / you / I
~~have / tips / on / Do / how / a / you / any / to~~

Amy: *Do you have any tips on how to* become a model?

Mia: ¹_____ keep yourself fit and look after your skin.

Amy: ²_____ .

B helpful / really / that's / Thanks,
that's / good / a / sure / I'm / not / idea
about / any / you / how / Do / have / to / ideas
you / Why / don't

Tim: ¹_____ get a summer job during the school holidays?

Dan: ²_____ come and work on my cousin's farm?

Tim: ³_____ . I have lots of allergies.

C should / you / What / think / do / I / do?
great / That's / Thanks! / advice
Do / to / you / have / tips / any / how / on
were / I / you / If / I / 'd

Rosie: I can't believe I forgot his birthday.
¹_____

Melissa: ²_____ call him and say sorry then buy him a nice gift.

Rosie: ³_____ What should I buy?

4 Complete the dialogue with the missing phrases. The first letters are given.

A local vet has just finished talking to Olivia and Toby's class about her job …

V: So, does anyone have any questions?

O: Yes, I do. I'd really like to become a vet. What **d**o you **t**hink I **s**hould do?

V: Well, ¹**m**_____ best **a**_____ **w**_____ be to work really hard in your Science classes! You'll need very good grades to get a place at a university veterinary school. ²**W**_____ **d**_____ you have a look at some of the university websites?

O: ³**T**_____ , that's really **h**_____ .

V: Anyone else?

T: Hi. Yeah, I have a question. Do you ⁴**h**_____ **a**_____ idea about **h**_____ to get some work experience as a vet?

V: Good question. Most universities expect you to have some experience, so it's a ⁵**g**_____ **i**_____ to try and work in a veterinary clinic, or perhaps a zoo during your school holidays. ⁶**I**_____ I **w**_____ you , I'd email all the local ones and ask if they can help you. But, I don't ⁷**t**_____ you **s**_____ expect them to pay you, unfortunately!

T: OK, well that's ⁸**g**_____ **a**_____ . Thanks.

1 In pairs, ask and answer the questions.

PART 1

Talk about school.
1 Do you think teachers should set their students homework? Why?/Why not?
2 Do you prefer academic subjects to Art, Music or PE? Why?/Why not?
3 Do you like your timetable at school? Why?/Why not?
4 What are the advantages and disadvantages of going to a university abroad?
5 What support is there in your school for students with learning disorders?

PART 2

Talk about work.
1 Have you ever had a part-time job during the school holidays? Would you like to?
2 Which jobs are male-dominated at the moment? How can we change this?
3 What kind of person do you have to be to be a politician?
4 What are the advantages and disadvantages of being a pilot?
5 Would you like to be the managing director responsible for running a big corporation? Why?/Why not?

2 Some students are going to do work experience over the summer holidays. Here are some of the jobs that they can try.

PART 1

Talk together about the different jobs and say which would be the most interesting.

PART 2

Talk about work experience.
• Would you like to do work experience? What job would you like to try?
• How do you think you would feel on your first day of work experience?
• What do you think you should wear when you do work experience?
• What skills can you learn by doing work experience?
• How is work experience useful when you apply for a job or university?

3 Discuss this question together. 'It's better to be self-employed than work for a company.' What do you think?

For self-employed work:

Self-employed people …
• are free to do what they want to in their careers.
• can decide on their own working hours.
• can work where they want to.
• choose who they want to work with.

Against self-employed work:

Self-employed people …
• don't earn money when they're sick or on holiday.
• don't get benefits, such as a pension or insurance.
• could be unemployed for periods of time.
• sometimes get lonely if they work on their own.

6.10 SELF-CHECK

VOCABULARY AND GRAMMAR

1 Match the beginnings and endings to form sentences.

I am self- _[f]_

1 Most shop assistants are
2 Actors spend a lot of
3 Ethan would like a job where he doesn't
4 I am contacting you to
5 I love my job because I get

a time away from home.
b work long hours.
c apply for a job.
d badly-paid.
e ten weeks' paid holiday.
f employed and work as a freelance photographer.

/5

2 Choose the correct words.

Lena's dad is a driving guide /(instructor)/ trainer, but he refuses to teach her to drive.

1 Carly's mum is a society / social / sociable worker and helps homeless people.
2 Dad has been unemployed / employed / fired for a year, so we can't afford to go on holiday.
3 Molly got paid holiday / the sack / a day off for being impolite to customers.
4 I'd like to be a teacher, but the low pay puts / gets / takes me off this career choice.
5 Susie is a great problem maker / developer / solver, so she's the best person to ask for help.

/5

3 Find and correct the mistakes.

Leon is a very ambition person. _ambitious_

1 I work a full-time job. _____
2 Doctors are responsible to their patients. _____
3 Artists have to be creating people. _____
4 My job is boring because it's so repeating. _____
5 Nelly's total rely on her mother is worrying. _____

/5

4 Put the words in order to form sentences and questions. Add a comma where necessary.

go surfing / I'd / lived / I / in Australia
If _I lived in Australia, I'd go surfing_ every weekend.

1 went / exhausted all the time / wouldn't / if / feel / she
Rosie _____ to bed earlier.
2 invited / come / you / would / I / you
If _____ to the party?
3 would / Laura and Kath / miss / worked from home / they
If _____ their colleagues in the office.
4 wouldn't / if / were / I / go out with him again
I _____ you.
5 give / if / you / won / some money / me / you
Would _____ the lottery?

/5

5 Choose the correct words.

You (don't need to)/ mustn't / need to be attractive to be a DJ.

1 Fire-fighters need to / mustn't / needn't be fit and healthy.
2 Hotel guests must / can / needn't use the swimming pool for free.
3 Young children needn't / can't / can watch horror movies at the cinema.
4 I have to / mustn't / must remember to send Grandma a birthday card.
5 Students in our school needn't / mustn't / need to have uniforms on in the classroom, but they usually wear dark clothes.

/5

6 Complete each pair of sentences with the same answers A–C.

Has the taxi driver turned __ yet?
I won't put __ with your rude behaviour any more.
A in
(B) up
C on

1 I'm an office __ , so I help people with their administration work.
Mum works as a shop __ in a toy shop.
A worker
B agent
C assistant
2 William's father is a(n) __ agent.
Roxy and Dave have just bought a house on a large housing __ .
A travel
B estate
C secret
3 I'm going away __ a business trip next week.
Can we rely __ you to do a good job?
A on
B at
C for
4 Carlos prefers __ night shifts because he hates waking up in the mornings.
My brother is __ long hours at the moment because he has a lot of work.
A taking
B being
C working
5 What time did you __ to work this morning?
Can you help me __ up with a new company logo?
A get
B come
C make

/5

Total /30

86

7 Complete the text with the correct forms of the words in brackets.

First job advice

Starting any new job can be scary, but perhaps nothing is more _frightening_ (FRIGHTEN) than starting your first job ever. Here's some advice for you at the very beginning of your career.

Firstly, what you need to remember is that you are likely to start your working life at the very bottom. You can expect to be doing rather repetitive and less ¹_____ (CHALLENGE) work initially, but it's important to show a high level of ²_____ (DETERMINE) to do the job well and learn as much as you can. Your colleagues will notice if you have a bad attitude.

Secondly, your new career will probably be nothing like school or university. You will need to prove that you are ³_____ (RELY) and can be trusted to turn up on time and cope with ⁴_____ (DEMAND) amounts of work. You don't want to get fired after the first week because you can't organise your new life.

Thirdly, it's a good idea to ask questions and be open to learning from colleagues with more experience than you. Also, don't be too ⁵_____ (COMPETE) and be sure to pay attention to the things that people tell you.

/5

8 Complete the sentences with the words in brackets in the correct form. Do not change the order of the words. You may need to add words. Use no more than six words in each gap.

Russell _was not successful_ (be / not / success) in his attempt to find a job as a swimming instructor.

1 If Amanda and David didn't work at the weekend, _____ (come / the festival) with us on Sunday.

2 Jim _____ _____ (need / have) a university degree if he wanted to work for this company.

3 Aaron _____ (not / have / bring) his laptop tomorrow because he can use mine.

4 Where would you go if _____ _____ (you / take / time) from work for a month?

5 If Leonard _____ _____ (get / on / good) the boss, he'd have more chance of earning more money.

/5

9 Choose the correct answers A–C.

I've never had to work with a person as ___ as Paul. He can really get on people's nerves!
(A) annoying
B annoyed
C annoy

1 You ___ if you don't want to.
A don't have to work overtime
B can't work overtime
C wouldn't work overtime

2 If I had a few days off, I ___ to the countryside.
A will go
B would go
C go

3 Tom finds his work as a nurse ___
A extremely rewarding.
B extremely rewarded.
C very well rewarded.

4 Sarah ___ work on Saturday because her boss asked her.
A needs
B must
C has to

5 If Feng ___ , he would be happier.
A has a good job
B 'd worked better
C had a better job

/5

10 Complete the second sentence so that it has a similar meaning to the first. Use between four and six words, including the word in capitals.

The film was very scary, so Michael kept his eyes closed most of the time. **SO**
Michael was _so scared during the film that_ he kept his eyes closed most of the time.

1 Amanda can perfectly see things such as bus numbers from a distance. **PERFECT**
Amanda _____ , so she can see things such as bus numbers from a distance.

2 In our company, a short training on how to prepare reports is compulsory. **DO**
In our company, we _____ on how to prepare reports.

3 My good friend, Matt, is thinking of studying abroad, but it's impossible. He doesn't speak English. **IF**
My good friend, Matt, _____ English.

4 I'm really surprised Amy decided to stop working at this moment. **FROM**
I found Amy's decision _____ job at this moment really surprising.

5 My younger sister loves observing plants and animals in their natural habitat so much that she should live in the countryside. **LOVER**
My younger sister is _____ that she should live in the countryside.

/5

Total /20

VOCABULARY

7.1

Shops and services • clothes and appearance • collocations

SHOW WHAT YOU KNOW

1 Complete the names of the clothes. Some letters are given.

 t _i_ _e_

 1 _ k _ _ t

 2 s _ i _ _

 3 _ r _ _ s

 4 t _ _ c _ _ _ _ t

 5 _ o _ t _

 6 t _ _ i _ _ _ _

 7 _ l _ _ s _

 8 j _ c _ _ _

 9 _ u _ p _ _

 10 _ o _ d _ _

 11 _ i _ h _ _

 12 _ _ c _ s

 13 _ e _ t

 14 _ _ t

WORD STORE 7A | Shops and services

2 Complete the sentences with the words from the box. There are two extra items.

> bank   clothes shop   department store
> DIY store   estate agent's   florist's   health centre
> high street store   jeweller's   optician's
> pet shop   sports shop   ~~vintage shop~~

Max looked for some boots like those that the Beatles used to wear. He bought them in the _vintage shop_ on Carnaby Street.

1 Gabriel is going with his father to the _____ to buy a hammer and some paintbrushes.

2 I can't see anything in these glasses. I need to go to the _____ and buy a new pair.

3 Oh no! I've forgotten it's Mother's Day. I'll have to go to the _____ and buy some flowers.

4 Where can I buy new shoes, a book, and a board game for my little sister? Oh, I know. At the _____ . They sell everything there.

5 Anotonia bought those beautiful gold earrings in the _____ on Merton Road.

6 Most people buy clothes from a _____ now because they have a lot of choice and low prices.

7 I saw a lovely flat for rent in the _____ in town yesterday. I must see it.

8 Jack's mum is a doctor and she works in the _____ on Windsor Avenue.

9 Have you been to the new _____ next to the station? They've got some really nice looking jackets and skirts in the window.

10 We haven't got much cat food. I'll get some in the _____ on the way home tonight.

3 Choose the correct words.

1 There's a great *charity shop / greengrocer's / post office* near me that has some nice second-hand clothes.

2 I need to go to the *stationer's / computer shop / toy shop* to buy some paper for the laser printer.

3 Amanda and Ian are going to the *greengrocer's / butcher's / chemist's* to get some headache tablets.

4 Clara has gone to the *baker's / newsagent's / estate agent's* to buy a fashion magazine.

5 My sandals are broken. I need to take them back to the *toy shop / shoe shop / hairdresser's* where I bought them.

6 Jenna's gone to the *toy shop / post office / greengrocer's* to buy some stamps. She'll be back in 10 minutes.

7 I'd like to work in a *baker's / hairdresser's / butcher's –* the smell of fresh bread is wonderful!

8 These apples are tasty. I bought them in the *butcher's / greengrocer's / computer shop* next to my flat.

9 My sister's now a hair stylist for a film company but she started her career by cleaning the floor in a local *hairdresser's / computer shop / supermarket*.

10 Dad's in the *baker's / toy shop / butcher's* buying some bones for our dog, Muffin.

11 The *toy shop / stationer's / surgery* near my house has a big collection of jigsaws and board games.

12 You can buy cheap printers from a good Internet *computer shop / stationer's / post office*.

13 Mum does all the family shopping in a large *greengrocer's / newsagent's / supermarket* because she can buy everything in one place.

4 Complete the missing words. The first two letters are given.

Teen-advice.com

Jerry93: Hi guys. I've got my first ever job interview on Saturday morning. Any good advice on what I should wear to lo*ok* good? I'm not very ¹fa_____, so I need your help.

Mango14: You need to look ²sm_____ ! That means a suit and tie. Good luck!

Alice-cool: Well, it depends on the job. Sometimes you might want to look ³or_____ – something like nobody else so that they will remember you better. If it's an artistic or creative job, you could even look ⁴sc_____ – but then you'd need to wear ⁵de_____ cl_____ which are expensive.

Joe99: My advice is to wear something that ⁶su_____ you and ⁷fi_____ you well. You need to feel comfortable. Then you will be able to focus on the interview and be yourself.

SharonHeart: I always look ⁸go_____ when I wear pink. Try that! ☺

Trevor_R: You don't need to wear expensive ⁹br_____ , but you should wear ¹⁰go_____ qu_____ clothes. This tells the company that you are professional.

5 Complete the sentences with the words from the box.

cashmere cotton denim leather silk ~~wool~~

Jack Russell is wearing a lovely suit made of _wool_. It looks nice and warm and he looks so good in it!

1 My father bought me my first tie. It's _____ and was very expensive.
2 I only wear _____ shirts because they are light and stay nice and cool even in the summer.
3 Are black jeans also made of _____ ?
4 Alison wants to buy a _____ jacket which she can wear on her motorbike.
5 My grandma says that at her age there's nothing nicer than putting a soft warm _____ shawl round her shoulders and sitting by the fireplace with a good book.

6 Choose the correct words.

Conversation 1: Shop assistant and customer

SA: That's £29.99, please.
C: Erm ... excuse me. This is a gift for my sister. Can I bring it back if she doesn't like it?
SA: Certainly. Please keep your ¹*refund / bargain / receipt* and show it to the assistant if you bring the jumper back. You can exchange it for something else, or get a ²*refund / sale / offer* if you prefer to get your money back.

Conversation 2: Gina and Mia

G: How about going shopping this afternoon, Mia? Do you need anything?
M: Well, I want a new watch. There's a beautiful one in the jeweller's in town but it's too expensive. Maybe we can just go ³*a refund / on special offer / window shopping*? It doesn't cost anything to look!
G: That's true, but it's January. We might be able to pick up a(n) ⁴*offer / sale / bargain* for you in the sales.
M: Good idea. Let's go!

Conversation 3: Stacey and Dad

S: Dad, we need a new vacuum cleaner, remember? The old one broke.
D: That's right, we do. Shall we go to the electrical goods store? I saw a sign saying they are having ⁵*a sale / a bargain / a refund* at the moment. Perhaps they have vacuum cleaners on special ⁶*bargain / offer / receipt*.
S: Did you say 'we'? I can't go. I'm meeting my ... I mean ... I've got too much homework.

Conversation 4: Mum and Tracy

M: That's a lovely dress. When did you buy it? And how much was it?
T: I bought it yesterday. It was £50 but I think it's ⁷*worth / last / keep* it.
M: £50! Well, it should ⁸*keep / pick / last* for ages for that price.

7 Choose the correct words.

1 I'll never understand why people *pick up a bargain / are worth it / go window shopping*. Why look at things you can't buy?
2 Sara's little brother cried at the *shoe shop / post office / hairdresser's* because he was scared of sitting in that big chair that they have.
3 I need some new *silk / denim / leather* boots. The old ones have got holes and my feet get wet when it rains.
4 We need some fruit. Can you go to the *butcher's / greengrocer's / High Street store* and buy some?
5 My grandma used to run a *stationer's / pet shop / florist's*. She's always loved animals.
6 These jeans are much too big. They don't *fit / suit / go* me.
7 Paula never *goes / picks / keeps* her receipts. What will she do if she wants to take something back to the shop?
8 I'm not happy with these shoes. I don't want a new pair, I'd like to get a *refund / bargain / sale*, please.
9 Adam looks very *scruffy / smart / gorgeous* today. He hasn't shaved his face, brushed his hair or changed his clothes. Do you know why?
10 Martin bought wedding rings online but I think it's much safer to buy them from a well-known *post office / supermarket / jeweller's*.

/10

89

GRAMMAR

7.2

The Passive

---

1 Complete the sentences with the correct form of the verb be.

My dad _isn't_ keen on shopping, but my mum loves it.

1 We haven't _____ to the new pet shop yet.

2 Joel went to the newsagent's at 7 a.m., but it _____ open.

3 Trainers _____ so expensive these days. Some of them cost over £100.

4 My sister and I used to love playing 'shop' when we _____ little.

2 ★ Choose the correct forms, active or passive.

We love turkey!

Turkey Facts. Did you know ...

1 Archaeologists _have found / have been found_ evidence of turkeys that lived 10 million years ago.

2 The first turkeys _brought / were brought_ to England in 1526.

3 Turkey _has been eaten / has eaten_ by ordinary UK families since the 1950s (before that it was too expensive!).

4 Around 10 million turkeys _sell / are sold_ in the UK every Christmas.

5 About 20% of people in the UK _don't cook / aren't cooked_ turkey for Christmas dinner. However, over 80% do!

6 Neil Armstrong and Buzz Aldrin _ate / were eaten_ cold roast turkey when they landed on the moon.

3 ★ ★ Make the active sentences and questions passive.

What language do people speak in the Netherlands?
What language _is spoken_ in the Netherlands?

1 Special software protects the computer from viruses.
_____ by special software.

2 Who wrote _The Hobbit_?
Who _____ by?

3 A few people have seen the Loch Ness Monster since that moment.
The Loch Ness Monster _____

4 A famous chef has just opened a new restaurant.
_____ by a famous chef.

5 We don't sell used books here.
Used books _____

6 Did the sports teacher ask you to play in the school football team? _____
_____ by the sports teacher?

4 ★ ★ ★ Complete the article with the correct passive form of the verbs in brackets. One sentence does _not_ need the passive form.

This month's fact file is all about Scotforth Senior School Student Snack Shop (or 6S as we call it!)

- 6S _was opened_ (open) by students three years ago.
- 6S ¹_____ (not/start) to make money.
- Every year, the profits from 6S ²_____ (give) to a different charity.
- 6S ³_____ (make) over £2,000 for charity since it began.
- Unsold food from 6S ⁴_____ (not/throw) away; it's given to the local homeless shelter.
- Next year's charity ⁵_____ (not/choose) yet, so please put ideas in the 6S suggestion box.

We hope that 6S will continue to be '6Sful' next year! ☺

5 ★ ★ ★ Complete the text with the active or passive form of the verbs in brackets.

Today in the UK and the US over 50% of shopping _is paid_ (pay) for with plastic cards. The idea started in the US in the 1920s. The first cards ¹_____ (make) of paper and could only be used in a few shops and hotels. Then, in the 1950s, an American businessman called Frank McNamara had dinner at a restaurant one day, but ²_____ (not/have) enough cash to pay for his meal. This ³_____ (give) him the idea for the 'Diner's Club Card' and the first plastic credit card ⁴_____ (invent). Since the 1950s, plastic ⁵_____ (use) to make all credit cards. Today, there are over 1.5 billion credit cards in the US.

6 Choose the correct answers A–C.

1 Cigarette smoking ___ in public places in the UK since 2007.
A isn't permitted B hasn't permitted
C hasn't been permitted

2 On busy days, over 100,000 people ___ Harrods of London.
A visited B visit C is visited

3 In 2003 a lottery win of $28.5 million ___ by anyone. The money went to the State of California.
A wasn't collected B isn't collected
C hasn't been collected

4 Last year, millions of unsold sandwiches from shops and cafés ___ to homeless people across the UK.
A are given B were given
C have been given

5 The Walton family ___ the world's largest group of shops since it started in 1962.
A is owned B was owned C has owned

6 ___ in bookshops?
A Are e-books sold B Do e-books sell
C Have e-books sold

/6

GRAMMAR: Train and Try Again page 150

Synonyms • collocations • word families

1 Read the radio presenter's interview with Amy. Put the words in phrases 1–5 in the right order.

Extract from Students' Book recording 🔊 **3.21**

RP: Hello and welcome to *Ask the Expert*. The <u>topic</u> of today's <u>programme</u> is buying presents, and our expert is psychologist Amy Black. Thanks for joining us this afternoon Amy.

Amy: You're welcome. I'm <u>pleased</u> to be here.

RP: Amy, can you tell us *presents / at / good / person / sort of / what / is / choosing* <u>what sort of person is good at choosing presents</u>?

Amy: Well, it's true that ¹*buying / really / presents / some / are / people / good at* _____

_____

and some people are really bad, but I don't think it's a <u>question</u> of personality. I think anybody can buy a good present but they have to do some research … ²*presents / are / The best / after / a lot of / chosen / thinking.* _____

_____

_____ .

RP: Do you think women are better than men at buying presents?

Amy: Well, I <u>suppose</u> women like shopping more than men and this means they don't mind spending <u>hours</u> in shopping centres or online. But as I said, ³*buy / present / can / a good / anybody*

_____

_____ .

RP: Okay, let's read our first question. This was sent by Isabelle, 17 years old, from Bristol. She says 'My mum is going to be 40 … and ⁴*want / special / get / I / to / her / something* _____

_____

to cheer her up.' What do you think Amy?

Amy: Well, Isabelle, it's great that you want to get your mum something special. If you want to cheer her up, ⁵*idea / good / toiletries / a / are / always* _____

_____

but be careful. Your mum doesn't want to feel old. So don't buy face cream for the older woman.

2 Replace the underlined words in these sentences with an underlined word from the text in Exercise 1.

Can we go home now please? We've been in the shopping centre for <u>ages</u> / *hours*.

1 'Shopping Live' on the shopping channel is not a real TV <u>show</u> / _____ . It's more like one long advert.

2 The <u>subject</u> / _____ of the first chapter of the book is the oldest toy shop in the UK.

3 I don't really want to go shopping, but I <u>guess</u> / _____ we have to buy Lola a birthday present.

4 Which is nicer – modern furniture or antique furniture? Well, that's a <u>matter</u> / _____ of taste.

5 We're <u>happy</u> / _____ to say that we've already done all the Christmas shopping and it's only November.

REMEMBER THIS

Buy/get/give <u>somebody</u> a present

My parents bought/got/gave <u>me</u> a present when I passed my exams.

Get a present **(from someone)** = receive a present:

*I got a present **(from my parents)** after I passed my exams.*

---

3 Read REMEMBER THIS. Complete the second sentence so it has a similar meaning to the first. Use the word in capitals. Change the form if necessary.

My sister gave me a pair of socks for my birthday. **GET**
I got a pair of socks from my sister for my birthday.

1 I got a puppy from my parents for Christmas. **BUY**
My parents _____ for Christmas.

2 David gave Louise a gold necklace for her graduation. **FROM**
For her graduation, Louise _____ _____ David.

3 Vincent got a smartphone from Claire for his 18th birthday. **GIVE**
Claire _____ for his 18th birthday.

WORD STORE 7D | Word families

4 Complete the sentences with the correct forms of the words in capitals.

There's a *sale* today, so everything is 20% cheaper. **SELL**

1 Jason spends most of his _____ on his hobby – snowboarding. **EARN**

2 I refuse to borrow money from a bank because I don't like having _____ . **DEBT**

3 This unique _____ opportunity promises to make you rich in a year! **INVEST**

4 Did you know that the first cola was _____ in 1886? **PRODUCE**

5 You can make online _____ much more quickly and safely today than ten years ago. **PAY**

6 Sarah is a successful _____ on an Internet shopping website. **TRADE**

A

B

C

D

Globalholidays.com Home | Search | Contact

you searched for 'Boxing Day'

In Britain, Canada, New Zealand and parts of Australia, the 26th of December is **Boxing Day**. Originally, this was the day when rich people gave their servants small Christmas gifts, but these days **Boxing Day** is all about shopping. There are big sales with reductions on everything, and customers <u>spend</u> huge amounts of money. Shops and shopping centres open very early (some of them as early as 5 a.m.) and shoppers often <u>start</u> queuing* for bargains in the middle of the night, hours before the sales actually begin.

1

Saveourcitycentre.net   **discussion forum**

share your opinion and help save our city centre

Safari _23 says: For the last ten years, I have owned a clothes shop called 'Safari' on the main street of our town. About six months ago, a big shopping centre opened just outside the town and since then business has been bad. Every month fewer customers come into the shop and it is getting harder to make a living. I used to love my job, but standing there all day with hardly any customers is really <u>boring</u>. The little café opposite had to close down* last month. I know that other <u>small</u> businesses on the street are having big problems too. Some of them have actually moved to the shopping centre recently. I am not sure what the solution is, but I feel sad and angry, and I'm afraid that I will have to close down my shop too.

2

The shopping centre opened at half past nine. They met by the entrance at twenty-five past. There was no one else around. They waited next to the sign that showed the centre rules – no smoking; no dogs; no radios; no skateboards. They looked at each other nervously. At half past, the cleaner unlocked the doors. They were still the only people waiting. It looked <u>safe</u>. It was time. Through the doors, boards ready and then suddenly, full speed! They flew through the shopping centre, the wheels of their skateboards speeding silently on the perfectly flat floor. The feeling was fantastic, amazing; just as they imagined. And then ... they saw the security guard.

3

We are looking for

'secret shoppers'

to work for our large chain*
of clothing shops

Our secret shoppers travel around the UK, visit different stores* and pretend to be real customers. On a typical visit, they go into one of our stores and ask questions about our clothes and shoes. Their main job is to check that our in-store sales assistants are friendly, and know a lot about our products. Secret shoppers have to listen carefully, remember all the details and then send a report to our London office to describe their visit. If you are offered a job as a secret shopper, you will have to keep your job and your identity secret.

For an application form,
email <u>targetstores.gm@css.net</u>.
Interviews start in October.

4

GLOSSARY

to queue *(v)* – to stand in a line of people waiting to do something, e.g. pay in a shop
to close down *(phr. v)* – if a business closes down, it stops operating permanently

chain (of shops) *(n)* – a number of shops (also hotels, cinemas, restaurants, etc.) owned by the same company or person
store *(n)* – a large shop that sells many different things

1 **Read the texts. Match pictures A–D with texts 1–4.**

A ◯
B ◯
C ◯
D ◯

2 **Read the texts. For questions 1–4, choose the correct answer A–C.**

Text 1

The author of the text
- A discourages readers from going shopping on Boxing Day.
- B describes the origins and customs connected with Boxing Day.
- C shares his/her experience in shopping on Boxing Day.

Text 2

The owner of 'Safari'
- A is worried about her business.
- B wants to close down her business.
- C has moved her business recently.

Text 3

The boys 'looked at each other nervously' because
- A there was no one else around.
- B they saw the security guards.
- C they were planning to break the rules.

Text 4

The advert says that secret shoppers work
- A in one store.
- B in stores all over the country.
- C in the company's London office.

3 **Read the texts again. Are statements 1–8 true (T) or false (F)?**

1 Boxing Day is celebrated all over the world. ◯
2 Shops are open all night on Boxing Day. ◯
3 'Safari' hasn't closed down. ◯
4 'Safari' is located in a shopping centre. ◯
5 The shopping centre was closed when the boys met. ◯
6 There was no else inside the shopping centre that morning. ◯
7 To do their job, secret shoppers need to travel. ◯
8 The advert asks you to send a CV to apply for the job. ◯

4 **Complete the gaps with underlined opposites from the text.**

large	≠	_small_
1 finish	≠	_____
2 dangerous	≠	_____
3 save	≠	_____
4 interesting	≠	_____

REMEMBER BETTER

Some words have more than one antonym.
Use diagrams to help you remember these.

Complete the diagrams with words from the box. There are two extra words.

~~big~~ clear earn end exciting watch unsafe

small ········· large
                big

1 start ········· finish
                _____

2 safe ········· dangerous
                _____

3 spend ········· save

4 boring ········· interesting
                _____

WORD STORE 7E | Shopping

5 **Complete the sentences with the missing words. The first and last letters are given.**

Because of a change in tax regulations, there has been a **r** _i s_ **e** of 2% on the price of all items.

1 How much will it cost to **s** _ _ **p** these CDs to Australia?

2 Wow! Look at the length of the **q** _ _ _ **e**. Let's come back in half an hour.

3 Marvin has just placed an **o** _ _ _ **r** for a new laptop. It's fifty pounds cheaper online.

4 Excuse me, I'd like to pay for these trousers. Where's the **c** _ _ _ _ _ _ **t d** _ _ **k**?

5 I'm sorry, madam. This skirt is no longer **a** _ _ _ _ _ _ _ **e** in green. Would you like to try the blue one?

6 James, can you find this shoe in size 8 for the **c** _ _ _ _ _ _ **r** over there in the white dress?

GRAMMAR

7.5

Quantifiers

1 Is the underlined noun countable C or uncountable U in these sentences?

The teacher gave us <u>homework</u> to do over the holidays. It's so unfair. `[U]`

1 It will take <u>time</u> to find the right pair of shoes for the wedding. ☐

2 Our city has a major problem with traffic and the air <u>pollution</u> it causes. ☐

3 Helen caught a very serious <u>disease</u> on holiday. Luckily, she's much better now. ☐

4 Ian goes to the most expensive <u>school</u> in the city. His grades are not good though. ☐

5 I love Thai <u>food</u> because it's hot, tasty and usually very healthy. ☐

6 We don't get on with the <u>people</u> who live next door. They aren't very friendly. ☐

2 ★ Choose the correct quantifiers to complete the dialogue between a researcher and Lynn.

R: Excuse me, may I ask you a few quick questions about your experience in the shopping centre today?

L: Er ... will it take long?

R: No, not at all. Just ¹*a few / a little* minutes.

L: OK then.

R: Thank you. ²*How much / How many* shops did you visit today?

L: Oh, I'm not sure exactly. Certainly ³*too much / too many*. My feet hurt!

R: Oh dear. Poor you. I'll write more than 10 on the form then. ⁴*How much / How many* time did you spend in the food zone today?

L: Oh, ⁵*very few / very little*. I stopped for a cup of coffee, but only for ten minutes.

R: OK, thanks. Just one more question, if you don't mind. ⁶*How much / How many* money did you spend today?

L: Only ⁷*a few / a little*. Most of the time I was window shopping.

3 ★★ Use *not much* or *not many* to make the sentences negative.

Frieda has a lot of friends.
Frieda *doesn't have many* friends.

1 Peter goes to a lot of parties.
Peter _____ parties.

2 Nick and Nancy watch a lot of news.
Nick and Nancy _____ news.

3 Jenny drinks a lot of juice.
Jenny _____ juice.

4 Edward and Eve write a lot of emails.
Edward and Eve _____ emails.

5 Francis eats a lot of fruit.
Francis _____ fruit.

4 ★★ Add *a* before *little* and *few* if necessary.

There is <u>a</u> little milk left, so you don't have to have black coffee.

1 I have _____ little interest in shopping. I prefer playing football, to be honest.

2 Leah wasn't going to celebrate her birthday, but then _____ few friends organised a party for her.

3 There are _____ few shops in the village, so most people travel to the city to do their shopping.

4 With _____ little luck, we'll find a bargain in the sales.

5 ★★★ Choose the correct answers A–C.

1 I don't have __ time. Can we be very quick in the shop?
   A much   B some   C a little

2 Adam doesn't have __ male friends that like shopping.
   A some   B many   C much

3 On Fridays, Lauren always buys __ chocolate on the way home from school.
   A much   B any   C some

4 There are __ snowboards to choose from. I don't know which one to buy.
   A too much   B too many   C not much

5 __ people do their shopping online these days.
   A Lots of   B A little   C Any

6 Excuse me, do you have __ blue T-shirts?
   A a little   B much   C any

7 Jo has __ birthday money left, but she hasn't decided what to spend it on yet.
   A little   B a little   C a few

8 __ of my friends actually buy CDs now. I think Lewis is the only one.
   A Few   B Little   C A few

6 Complete the sentences with one word in each gap. In one sentence you don't need to add a word. Use each word only once.

We don't have *many* customers in the shop on Sundays.

1 How _____ time do we have before the shopping centre closes?

2 On our way back, we saw _____ ots of people queuing in front of the shopping centre.

3 There are definitely _____ many cars in the city centre on week days.

4 Excuse me, are there _____ black jeans in a size 32?

5 _____ people do their shopping in the local shops these days. Most of them prefer to go to hypermarkets.

6 We bought _____ nice clothes in the winter sales.

`/6`

GRAMMAR: Train and Try Again page 150

1 ★ **Choose the correct words.**

1 I know my wallet is *anywhere / somewhere / nowhere* here. I'm sure it is.
2 The robbery was frightening, but luckily *anyone / no one / someone* was hurt.
3 Hanna hasn't been *anywhere / somewhere / everywhere* interesting, but she hopes to visit Thailand one day soon.
4 There isn't *nothing / anything / something* in this box – it's completely empty. Has Tom taken his books and notes yet?
5 If you are rich, you can go *everywhere / somewhere / nowhere* in the world. If I had lots of money, I'd go to the Maldives.
6 Monica has bought you *anything / nothing / something* really nice for your birthday. So, when's the party?
7 I need to study a little longer because I haven't revised *everything / anything / something* for the exam tomorrow.
8 Listen! I thought I heard *somebody / anybody / everybody* talking in our garden.
9 I told you already. *Nobody / no one / none* of my family are rich. We have ordinary jobs and we don't live in fancy houses.
10 Has *anybody / somebody / everybody* bought a souvenir? Good, then we can leave now. The bus is waiting for us round the corner.

2 ★ **Choose the correct answers A–C.**

1 **Mum:** The fridge is empty. Have you eaten __ ?
  Emma: Yes, because I was really hungry.
  A anything
  B something
  C everything

2 **Anna:** Would you like __ to eat?
  Jane: Yes, please.
  A anything
  B everything
  C something

3 **Aiden:** I was quite bored at the party.
  Geoff: Why? Didn't you meet __ you know?
  A somebody
  B anybody
  C everybody

4 **Theresa:** I met __ knows you this morning.
  Patrick: Oh yeah? Who was that then?
  A something that
  B someone who
  C anyone that

5 **Damian:** Don't we need to go shopping?
  Jay: You're right. We need to buy __ for dinner tonight.
  A something to eat
  B nothing to eat
  C somewhere to eat

6 **Gloria:** Am I the first person to arrive?
  Jim: Yes, you are. __ of the other people are here yet.
  A No one
  B None
  C Anyone

7 **Dad:** Ah, there you are. I looked __ for you.
  Julian: Sorry, I was in the department store with Sam.
  A anywhere
  B somewhere
  C everywhere

3 ★ ★ **Complete the sentences with the words from the box.**

> anybody anything everybody everywhere
> nobody nothing ~~something~~ somewhere

Would you like *something* to drink?
1 The shop was so expensive I didn't buy
  _____ .
2 Now I have a car we can, go _____ we want to.
3 Does _____ live in that big house?
4 I'm bored because there's _____ to do.
5 It looks like the restaurant is closed and _____ has gone home.
6 The guidebook says there's a cheap hotel _____ close to the train station.
7 I didn't go to the concert because _____ gave me the address.

4 ★ ★ ★ **Complete the second sentence so it has a similar meaning to the first. Use between two and five words, including the word starting with *some-*, *any-*, *every-* or *no-*.**

I did nothing interesting at the weekend.
I *didn't do anything interesting* at the weekend.
1 Nobody I know likes spending money.
  I don't _____ likes spending money.
2 There's a nice place to eat lunch next to the cinema.
  There's _____ next to the cinema.
3 Jamie invited all of the people that are here.
  Jamie _____ here.
4 I didn't see a famous person at the party.
  I saw _____ at the party.
5 In fact, not one of my friends offered to pay for me.
  In fact, _____ offered to pay for me.
6 James gave me an inexpensive present.
  James _____ expensive as a present.
7 I think all of these places look nice to visit.
  I think _____ nice to visit.

WRITING

7.7 A formal written complaint

Complaints

1 Match the information to make customer problems.

I bought a watch from your website on 15th June.

1 I ordered a pair of skis from your company 5 days ago.

2 On 24/11, I booked tickets for the *Monster Truck Show* on your website.

3 Last month, I downloaded your 'free' app *Friendtracker*.

A I paid for them on the same day, but when I tried to print them, …

B When I checked my phone bill for this month, …

C You promised to send them to me the next day, but …

D It arrived two days later, but …

a … I am still waiting for them to be delivered.

b … the system said 'You have not paid yet'.

c … I noticed a payment of 3 euros for this 'free' app.

d … when I opened it, it was the wrong colour.

2 Complete the model email with the words from the box. There are two extra words.

> bought   complain   disappointed   faithfully
> grateful   refund   sincerely   ~~Sir or Madam~~   wrong

Dear *Sir or Madam*,

I am writing to ¹＿＿＿＿＿＿ about the service provided by your restaurant.

I recently organised my seventeenth birthday party at 'JW's All-American Diner'. I booked a table for ten, but when we arrived, the waitress said there was no reservation. We waited half an hour for a table. When we finally sat down, we were told that the chef was sick that day and we would have to wait at least an hour for our meal. The food arrived after 75 minutes and four out of ten orders were ²＿＿＿＿＿＿ . My vegetarian friend was given a steak!

I am very ³＿＿＿＿＿＿ with your service and feel sorry that I chose your restaurant for my birthday party. I would be ⁴＿＿＿＿＿＿ if you could send me a ⁵＿＿＿＿＿＿ for the cost of the meal, or invite my friends and me to one of your other restaurants for a free meal.

Yours ⁶＿＿＿＿＿＿ ,
Kay Jones

3 Tick the more formal version in each pair of sentences.

- a I didn't expect a pink smartphone.
- b I did not order a yellow laptop. ✓
1 a I got a jigsaw puzzle for my mother.
- b I bought a cashmere sweater for my sister.
2 a I returned the broken watch to you.
- b I sent the broken watch back to you.
3 a I swapped the jeans for a skirt.
- b I exchanged the phone for a tablet.
4 a I got the wrong colour.
- b I received the wrong size.
5 a I am disappointed with your staff.
- b I'm angry with your customer service.
6 a I want all of my money back from you.
- b I would be grateful if you could send me a full refund.

4 Put the words into the correct order to make sentences. Decide which sentences are formal *F* and which informal *I*.

buy / did / want / I / to / not / shirt / extra large / an
I did not want to buy an extra large shirt. Ⓕ

1 I / ring / to / gold / buy / wanted / a / wedding
＿＿＿＿＿＿＿＿＿＿＿＿＿＿＿＿ ◯

2 returned / I / the / to / you / bag
＿＿＿＿＿＿＿＿＿＿＿＿＿＿＿＿ ◯

3 work / I / got / when / the / it / didn't / TV
＿＿＿＿＿＿＿＿＿＿＿＿＿＿＿＿ ◯

4 sent / I / back / to / trousers / you / the
＿＿＿＿＿＿＿＿＿＿＿＿＿＿＿＿ ◯

5 I / phone / model / the / for / newer / exchanged / a
＿＿＿＿＿＿＿＿＿＿＿＿＿＿＿＿ ◯

6 another / want / I / to / the / swap / jeans / for / pair
＿＿＿＿＿＿＿＿＿＿＿＿＿＿＿＿ ◯

7 wallet / I / a / blue / instead / received
＿＿＿＿＿＿＿＿＿＿＿＿＿＿＿＿ ◯

8 am / I / with / service / of / disappointed / the / quality / your
＿＿＿＿＿＿＿＿＿＿＿＿＿＿＿＿ ◯

9 I / grateful / would / if / you / be / refund / could / me / send / a
＿＿＿＿＿＿＿＿＿＿＿＿＿＿＿＿ ◯

10 give / my / money / me / back
＿＿＿＿＿＿＿＿＿＿＿＿＿＿＿＿ ◯

5 Imagine you have received poor service or had a problem with a product you have bought. Tick the fair requests.

I would like a full refund of the money I paid. ✓
1 I would like an apology.
2 I would like to eat for free at your restaurant forever.
3 I would like you to close your business.
4 I would like you to send me a new one that works.
5 I would like you to send me the colour I ordered.
6 I would like the waitress to lose her job.
7 I would like to take you and your company to court.

6 Read the task below. Then choose the correct answers A–D to complete the email.

> You have recently bought an item of clothing from an online clothes store. Unfortunately, there are a few problems with the order.
>
> - The item of clothing isn't blue but green.
> - It's not the size you wanted.
> - You think it's dirty and somebody has used it.
>
> **Write your formal complaint. Include and develop these points:**
>
> - Give your reason for writing.
> - Say what you bought and when.
> - Explain the problem and give appropriate details.
> - Tell the reader what you expect the company to do.

Dear ¹__ ,

I am writing to ²__ about a ᴬ*recent / last* order which I ³__ . I bought a blue jacket from your website on 7th May. ᴮ*When / While* I opened it I ᶜ*noticed / looked* that the colour was wrong. I ⁴__ blue, not green. The jacket ⁵__ to you and it ⁶__ for the correct colour. ᴰ*Unfortunately / Fortunately*, this time the jacket was the wrong size. I ordered M not XL, and it ⁷__ large for me. ᴱ*First / Furthermore*, it looks like it ⁸__ and it is dirty on the back.

I am very ⁹__ with your service. I would be ᶠ*delighted / grateful* if you ¹⁰__ me a full ¹¹__ for the item and the ᴳ*cost / price* of sending it back to you.

Yours faithfully,
John Banks

1	A Sir or Madame	B Sir or Madam	
	C Sir and Madam	D Sirs or Madams	
2	A complaint	B complain	
	C argue	D argument	
3	A placed	B was placed	
	C did	D was done	
4	A ordered	B shopped	
	C liked	D put	
5	A returned	B was returned	
	C did return	D was returning	
6	A exchanged	B was exchanging	
	C did exchange	D was exchanged	
7	A is a lot	B is lots of	
	C is far too	D is too much	
8	A was wearing	B is worn	
	C has been worn	D wore	
9	A angry	B mad	
	C miserable	D disappointed	
10	A could send	B will send	
	C would be sent	D must send	
11	A return	B refund	
	C guarantee	D money	

7 Read the email again and choose the correct words A–G.

8 Look at the customer feedback form a gym and fitness centre. Use the information and write an email to make a polite complaint. Include and develop these points:

- Give your reason for writing.
- Explain when you joined and how much you paid.
- Explain the problem and give appropriate details.
- Tell the reader what you expect the company to do.

 Sunshine Gym & Fitness

Feedback and Suggestions
We are always keen to hear from our customers.
Tell us about your experience at Sunshine Gym & Fitness.
I want to complain about your service. On 18/11, I paid 200 euros to join your gym for a year, but I am not happy. Half of the machines in the gym are broken or dangerous, the changing rooms are always smelly and dirty and the staff are rude. When I complained about the broken running machine last week, the man at the desk told me I should run home instead! I'm not going to come to your gym anymore and I want all my money back.

Finished? Always check your writing.
Can you tick ✓ everything on this list?

In my written complaint:

- the beginning matches the end (*Dear Mr Smith ⇨ Yours sincerely; Dear Sir or Madam ⇨ Yours faithfully*). ☐
- I have given my reason for writing. ☐
- I have explained the problem giving details (what? where? when?). ☐
- I have told the recipient what I expect them to do (and asked for something fair). ☐
- I have used polite language. ☐
- I have not used emoticons ☺ abbreviations (*info / CU / gr8*), or contractions (*I'm / isn't*). ☐
- I have checked my spelling and punctuation. ☐
- My text is neat and clear. ☐

SPEAKING

Shopping

1 Translate the phrases into your own language.

SPEAKING BANK

Shopping for clothes

Shop assistant

Can I help you? _____

Would you like to try it on? _____
_____

The changing rooms are over there. _____

How would you like to pay? _____
_____

Make sure you keep your receipt. _____
_____

Customer

Excuse me, I'm looking for a top. _____
_____

I'm a size 10. _____

Do you have this in a size 12, please? _____
_____

I'll take it. _____

Cash, please./By credit card. _____

If it doesn't fit, can we get a refund? _____
_____
_____

Making complaints

Shop assistant

What's wrong with it? _____

Do you have your receipt? _____

We can exchange it for a new one. _____
_____

Customer

I bought this dress last week but the zip doesn't work. _____
_____

I think it's faulty./It shrank./There's a hole in it./The colour ran. _____
_____

I'd like a refund, please. _____

2 Complete the dialogue in a shop with the missing phrases. The first and last letters are given.

Harry: **E**xcus**e** me, I'm looking for a pair of dark blue jeans.

SA: Sure, we have several different brands. What [1]**s**_____**e** are you?

Harry: I don't really know. I think 32.

SA: OK … I'll give you a few different ones to try. [2]The **c**_____**g** **r**_____**s** are over there.

Five minutes later …

SA: Do you like any of those?

Harry: I like these, but they're a bit too big. Do you have them [3]**i**_____ **a** **s**_____**e** 30, please?

SA: Yes, we do. Just a moment … OK, here they are.

Harry: Thanks …

SA: … Are they better?

Harry: Yeah, I think [4]I'll **t**_____**e** them. You know what? If I buy them and my girlfriend doesn't like them, [5]can I get a **r**_____**d** ?

SA: Yes, for 28 days you can. Make sure you keep your [6]**r**_____**t**.

Harry: Great. How much are they?

SA: They're £ 99.99. [7]**H**_____**w** would you like to **p**_____**y** ?

Harry: What?! A hundred pounds for a pair of jeans?! Er … look I'm sorry, I have to go now. Maybe I'll … er … come back for them later, OK?

3 Choose the correct words.

1 What's wrong *to / for / with* it?
2 Do you *have / get / keep* your receipt?
3 We can exchange it *to / for / with* a new one.
4 I bought this last week but it *doesn't / isn't / hasn't* work.
5 I think it's *fault / faulting / faulty*.
6 *I'd / I'm / I* like a refund, please.

4 Complete the dialogue in a shop with the phrases in Exercise 2.

In the pet shop …

SA: Good morning, sir. Can I help you?

Harold: Yes, I hope so. <u>4</u>

SA: It doesn't work? But sir, it's a cat. [1]___

Harold: Well, I've had it for a week and it hasn't caught one mouse. Not one. It just sleeps in front of the fire all day. [2]___

SA: Faulty? But sir, it's a perfectly normal, healthy animal.

Harold: Well, I'm not satisfied with it and [3]___.

SA: A refund? For a cat? Er … well we don't normally … er … listen, I have an idea. Some new cats were delivered this morning. Perhaps [4]___

Harold: I don't want a new one, I want my money back.

SA: Well, I … er … well, I suppose … [5]___.

Harold: Yes, I do. Here you are. Thank you.

1 In pairs, ask and answer the questions.

PART 1

Talk about work.
1 Do you want a job where you can work indoors or outdoors?
2 What kind of skills do social workers need?
3 Would you like to be a journalist? Why?/Why not?
4 What kind of job do you think your best friend would like to do in the future? Why?
5 Do you want to do a job where you have to spend a lot of time away from home? Why?/Why not?

PART 2

Talk about shopping.
1 Do you ever shop in charity shops? Why?/Why not?
2 When was the last time you bought an item on special offer? What did you buy?
3 In what situations is window shopping useful? Why?
4 Why do you need to keep your receipts?
5 What's your favourite shop? Why?

2 Look at the photos of people shopping.

A

B

Take turns to talk about what you can see in the photos.
1 Talk about the people.
2 Talk about the places.
3 Talk about the other things in the photographs.

3 Read the instructions on your card. In pairs, take turns to role-play the conversation.

Student A

You are a shop assistant in a clothes shop. A customer, Student B, comes to the checkout desk.

• Greet Student B and ask if you can help him/her.
• Ask him/her what is wrong with the jacket.
• Ask when he/she bought the jacket.
• Ask if he/she has his/her receipt.
• Offer to exchange the jacket for a new one.
• Agree and give him/her a refund.

Student B

You are a customer in a clothes shop and you want to make a complaint. Talk to Student B, the shop assistant.

• Say yes and explain that you want to return a leather jacket.
• Explain that the zip doesn't work and that you think it's faulty.
• Say that you bought it last week.
• Say yes and give Student A your receipt.
• Say no thank you and explain that you want a refund.

VOCABULARY AND GRAMMAR

1 Complete the mini-dialogues with the correct words. The first letters are given.

Conversation 1

Lydia: Dad, the tablets you bought at the **c**hemist's aren't working. I still feel ill.

Dad: Hmm. Then I'll have to take you to the ¹**h**_____ **c**_____ tomorrow.

Conversation 2

Kim: I saw this advert for an interesting flat. It was in the window of the ²**n**_____ this afternoon when I went to buy my bus ticket and some chocolate.

Mike: I think it's safer to go to an ³**e**_____ **a**_____ when looking for somewhere to live.

Conversation 3

Phil: Do you think this jacket ⁴**s**_____ me? Do I look good in it?

Ron: I think the style is nice but not the size. It's too big. It doesn't ⁵**f**_____ you.

/5

2 Choose the correct words.

All online *payments* /*payers* must give their credit card information.

1 Donatella's sister is a *trade* / *trader* at the local market. She sells cheap perfumes.

2 I don't like being *in debt* / *debtor*, so I'll pay you back tomorrow.

3 Tim is a really high *earnings* / *earner*, so he can afford to buy expensive things.

4 Bjorn runs a factory, but I don't know what his company *produces* / *productions*.

5 I'm thinking of becoming an *investment* / *investor* in a software company. Do you think I will lose my money?

/5

3 Complete the names of the places from the adverts 1–5. The first and last letters are given.

Why not come and buy everything in one big shop? **d**_epartmen_t s_tor_e

1 This week – 20% off all pens and pencils. **s**_____**s**

2 Try delicious locally grown organic pears. **g**_____**s**

3 We offer free eye tests. **o**_____**s**

4 The best sausages in town! **b**_____**s**

5 Today only – 10% off all cakes. **b**_____**s**

/5

4 Complete the sentences and questions with the correct passive form of the verbs in brackets.

Kyle *wasn't chosen* (not/choose) for the football team.

1 The app _____ (design) by a teenager.

2 _____ (you/give) a present?

3 I'm sorry, but the house _____ (sell) last week.

4 _____ (the parcel/deliver) this morning?

5 The students _____ (not/tell) about the new teacher yet.

/5

5 Find and correct the mistakes.

There are too much things on the menu. I can't decide what to order.   *many*

1 There is very few milk left. Can you drink black coffee?   _____

2 How many snow is there in the mountains at the moment?   _____

3 Very little people can afford to buy a private island.   _____

4 Only few very good friends were invited to her party.   _____

5 A lots of the students are sick this week.   _____

/5

6 Complete each pair of sentences with the same answer A–C.

Can we __ window shopping this week?
We need to __ to the shop to buy some bread.
(A) go   B get   C be

1 Mum, I want to go to the toy __ to buy a new game.
Do they sell tennis rackets in the sports __ near you?
A shop   B sale   C agent

2 Unfortunately, I haven't got ___ time for my hobbies.
You've put too __ sugar in this coffee. It's really sweet.
A any   B few   C much

3 Two new cinemas __ built in this town last year.
When __ flat screen TVs invented?
A was   B were   C are

4 You look __ in that hat. Like a movie star!
It's a(n) __ sunny day. Let's go swimming in the sea.
A good   B gorgeous   C original

5 You're lucky, madam. These are the __ pair we have in the shop.
These jeans are such good quality that they should __ for ages.
A final   B end   C last

/5

Total   /30

7 Complete the second sentence so that it has a similar meaning to the first. Use between two and five words, including the word in capitals.

I have got almost no money left. **VERY**

I *have very little* money left.

1 Did we sell the last cashmere jumper to Mr Smith? **WAS**

Do you know if the last _____ Mr Smith?

2 Today, all of the things on this shelf are half-price. **IS**

Today, _____ half-price.

3 I can't find my glasses anywhere. **LOOKED**

I have _____ and still can't find them.

4 There is no cola in the fridge. **NOT**

There _____ in the fridge.

5 The bad news is that almost nobody attended the sales. **FEW**

The bad news is that _____ attended the sales.

/5

8 Complete the text with the correct form of the words from the box. There are two extra words.

any   create   custom   logo
organise   produce   sell   ~~shop~~

Who would buy that?

The online *shopping* website that we know today as eBay was ¹_____ in 1995. Its first name was AuctionWeb, and it started life as a small part of the personal website of the company's inventor, French-American Pierre Omidyar.

The first item for sale on the site was a broken laser pointer. When Pierre found a ²_____ who was happy to pay $14 for this, he asked him why he wanted it. The answer was simple – the man collected laser pointers. Because of this experience, Pierre believed that he could sell ³_____ through his new online shop – and it didn't matter whether the item was working or broken.

Pierre's idea became a huge success and the company grew quickly after he invited other people to sell their items on his website. In 1997, Pierre changed the name to eBay and, one year after this, only three years after the company had started, Pierre was a billionaire.

Today eBay is worth about $10 billion, operates in 30 countries and has between 20–25 million ⁴_____ who advertise their things for sale. And now, you can buy anything from broken laser pointers to the latest ⁵_____ of technology and high street fashions.

/5

9 Choose the correct answers A–C to replace the underlined part of the sentence.

I'm really hungry because I haven't eaten all day.
  A I've had anything to eat
  B I've had something to eat
  Ⓒ I've had nothing to eat

1 Sorry, but I've already sold my watch.
  A my watch has already been sold
  B my watch isn't for sale
  C I'm not selling my watch

2 Is this shirt available in black?
  A Do you make this shirt
  B Do you produce this shirt
  C Do you have this shirt

3 There's a long line of people waiting to buy tickets.
  A checkout   B queue   C rise

4 You look very elegant today. Where are you going?
  A smart   B fashionable   C scruffy

5 Why isn't there anybody working at this checkout desk?
  A is there somebody
  B is there nobody
  C isn't there nobody

/5

10 Complete the text with one word in each gap.

How to shop and save

Most people love spending money *on* clothes. But shopping can be expensive. So here are some tips to help you save money when you go looking to fill up your wardrobe.

Firstly, always remember that there are a ¹_____ of High Street stores that sell clothes that everyone can afford. Plus, they often ²_____ sales at the beginning of each new season. This is because when shops have new and more fashionable clothes coming in, they need to sell older items quickly. So, if you want to ³_____ up a bargain, this can be the best time.

Charity shops and other second-hand shops also offer a variety of cheap clothes. Although they don't usually have items ⁴_____ special offer, it's not difficult to find something at a good price. There's an added advantage too – when you buy second-hand clothes, there's a bigger chance you will find something that looks original compared to clothes from the High Street.

One more way to save money is to buy good quality clothes. Even some expensive designer clothes are not actually very well made. Make sure you buy something that will last. Then, even if it wasn't so cheap to buy, you'll see that the product was ⁵_____ it in the long-term.

/5

Total   /20

8 Well-being

VOCABULARY

8.1 Body parts • symptoms • health • phrasal verbs

SHOW WHAT YOU KNOW

1 Label the body parts. The first letters are given.

f̲orehead

1 e_____
2 f_____
3 n_____
4 s_____
5 c_____
6 h_____
7 k_____
8 b_____
9 l_____
10 f_____

2 Complete the sentences with the correct body parts.

When humans sneeze, air passes out of the _nose_ at over 160 kilometres per hour.

1 In many European countries, male friends kiss female friends – but not on the _____ !

2 Yesterday my granddad bit into a really hard nut and broke his left front _____ .

3 Some geckos, a type of lizard, lick their own eyes clean with their _____ .

4 Camels have beautiful long _____ to protect their eyes from sand.

5 Do you know why we have _____ ? They keep rain and sweat away from our eyes.

6 The bowhead whale has the largest _____ of all animals. It could easily swallow four horses!

WORD STORE 8A | Symptoms

3 Complete the dialogues with the missing words. The first and last letters are given.

Ann: I've got a terrible **h**eadach**e**.
Missy: I'm not surprised. The music on your headphones is too loud.

1 Meg: Are you OK? You nearly fell over.
Ola: Actually, I'm feeling a little **d**_____**y**. I need to sit down.

2 Alan: Dad, I've got a **s**_____**e** now.
Dad: Really? What did you eat?

3 Ed: Feel my head. Have I got a **t**_____**e**?
Stan: You don't feel hot to me but I can get a thermometer if you like.

4 Katy: Where's the bathroom? I feel **s**_____**k**.
Rich: Oh no. Did you eat that three-day old slice of pizza?

5 Dan: I don't think I can do the presentation this afternoon. I've got a bad **c**_____**h**.
Jon: Here, try some of this medicine. It might help.

6 Dr: When did you begin to feel **i**_____**l**?
Pat: Yesterday. After I got home from the skiing trip.

4 Complete the health advice with the words from the box. There are two extra words.

> b̶a̶c̶k̶ chest head leg nose
> shoulder throat thumb

Dr Simple's tips
for curing almost everything

TIP 1: Yoga can really help if your _back_ hurts. Sit correctly on your chair and sleep on a hard floor.

TIP 2: If you've got a runny _____ you should buy a big box of tissues.

TIP 3: Drink lots of water to help with a sore _____ . And only sing when you're in the shower.

TIP 4: You've got a pain in the _____ ? Then maybe you need to see a love doctor!

TIP 5: Sending too many text messages probably created the problem, so try telephoning your friends if your _____ hurts.

TIP 6: A pain in the _____ can be the result of moving your arms too much. My advice – don't move your arms. And if that doesn't help, see tip no. 1!

5 Choose the correct verbs.

Tip-Top Health Q & A

Have you got a health concern? Here are some common questions and their answers.

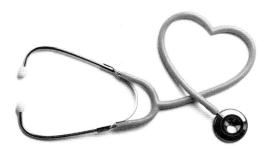

Q: I want to go on a diet. What do I need to know?

A: Right, so you've ¹*made / done* the big decision to ²*keep / lose* weight? Great! Firstly, add some exercise to your daily routine. Join a gym. The high-tech machines will help you to ³*check / keep* your heart rate while you exercise to make sure you don't exercise too hard. Secondly, you need to learn how to ⁴*make / do* the right food choices. There are plenty of diets online if you can't see a dietician.

Q: I think I ⁵*am / have* allergic to something I'm eating. What should I do?

A: Lots of people have allergies. One sign is ⁶*coming / being* out in spots. To identify the problem start by ⁷*keeping / losing* track of what you eat. A food diary will help. Once you know what the problem is, you should visit a doctor.

Q: ⁸*Am / Have* I asthmatic?

A: Only your doctor can tell you if you have asthma. Sometimes, however, breathing problems are the result of stress. Try to ⁹*reduce / lose* the anxiety in your life and ¹⁰*check / make* your pulse regularly. A fast heart rate might show that stress is the problem, not asthma!

Q: I've ¹¹*reduced / lost* my appetite. What's wrong with me?

A: Try to ¹²*reduce / lose* the amount of stress you have. Some people eat more when they are stressed, but others stop eating. Have you ¹³*come / make* out in a rash? A rash can be a sign of stress and anxiety. Also, try to ¹⁴*keep / be* fit. Exercise is a great way to get rid of stress and create a healthy appetite!

6 Complete the sentences with the correct prepositions.

You need to work <u>out</u> regularly if you want to look like Arnold Schwarzenegger.

1 I can't fit into my suit because I'm too fat. I'm going to cut _____ chocolate and sweets.

2 Sandra has decided to take _____ tennis to try and get fit. She's never played before!

3 Joshua returned to work after only three days off work. He always gets _____ the flu quickly.

4 A woman passed _____ on the bus this morning. Luckily, there was a doctor there to help her.

5 I didn't know you suffered _____ a nut allergy. I won't bake this cake again.

6 The exams next week are really stressing Adam _____ . He should learn how to meditate to stay calm.

> **REMEMBER THIS**
>
> The doctor gave me a **prescription** for my headaches.
>
> Here's the **receipt** for your new jacket, madam.
>
> What's the **recipe** for your wonderful pancakes?

> **SHOW WHAT YOU'VE LEARNT**

7 Choose the correct answers A–C.

1 I've got a really bad __ in my shoulder.
   A hurt   B sore   C pain

2 It's important to check your heart __ when you exercise.
   A rate   B pulse   C weight

3 Brad has got a cold. He's got a runny __ .
   A throat   B head   C nose

4 My dad has decided to work __, so he's joined a gym.
   A on   B out   C up

5 The thought of going to the dentist always stresses me __ .
   A out   B with   C over

8 Find and correct the mistakes.

Research says that one in twelve people got asthmatic. <u>are</u>

1 Courtney is allergic from milk, so just give her some water to drink. _____

2 I've a really bad headache. Where's the aspirin? _____

3 How long have you suffered with migraines, Tamara? _____

4 Oh no! I've come up in a rash all over my chest. _____

5 My leg pains. I shouldn't go jogging tomorrow. _____

/10

GRAMMAR

8.2 Past Perfect

SHOW WHAT YOU KNOW

1 Complete the sentences with the Past Simple form of the verbs in brackets.

1 When Nasrine ª*began* (begin) to feel ill, she
   ᵇ_____ (call) for the doctor.
2 When the doctor ª_____ (enter) the room, the nurses ᵇ_____ (not/stop) talking.
3 The pain in his leg ª_____ (get) worse when he ᵇ_____ (stand up).
4 Liz ª_____ (not/feel) well when the plane ᵇ_____ (start) to experience turbulence.
5 When the footballer ª_____ (pass out), the medical team ᵇ_____ (run) onto the pitch.

2 ★ Complete the story with the Past Perfect form of the verbs in brackets.

Maggie lay in bed, but couldn't fall asleep. She thought about everything that *had happened* (happen) that day. She couldn't stop thinking about the car accident that she
¹_____ (be) involved in. Luckily, nobody was seriously hurt and she was certain that she ²_____ (not/do) anything wrong. She ³_____ (drive) the usual route home and, like always, she
⁴_____ (pay) close attention to the road. And then there was the young boy right in front of the car. He was now in hospital with a broken leg. ⁵_____ (she/look) away for a second? No. She was sure. So why couldn't she sleep?

3 ★ ★ Which action happened first in the sentences? Write 1 or 2 after each part of the sentence.

When I arrived [1]ª, the dentist washed her hands [2]ᵇ.
1 When I arrived [ ]ª, the dentist had washed her hands [ ]ᵇ.
2 My legs hurt [ ]ª because I ran too far. [ ]ᵇ.
3 When my legs began to hurt [ ]ª, I stopped running [ ]ᵇ.
4 The trainer had already left the gym [ ]ª when I arrived [ ]ᵇ.
5 The trainer left the gym [ ]ª because I was rude to him [ ]ᵇ.
6 After the referee showed him the red card [ ]ª, the player left the pitch [ ]ᵇ.
7 By the time the referee gave him the red card [ ]ª, the player had already apologised [ ]ᵇ.

4 ★ ★ Choose the correct verb form in each sentence.

1 David found it hard to concentrate because he *didn't meditate* / *hadn't meditated* before.
2 When I got home after jogging, I realised I *had lost* / *lost* my door key.
3 The woman *hadn't eaten* / *didn't eat* vegan food before, so she was pleasantly surprised by how tasty it was.
4 Theo had already begun to feel stressed by the time he *had arrived* / *arrived* at the school.
5 Before Ross *had joined* / *joined* the gym, he had spoken to one of the trainers.
6 Eleanor recognised the yoga instructor. Where *did she see* / *had she seen* her before?
7 When we got to the village, we discovered that the owners of the spa hotel *sold* / *had sold* it. Now it was a large burger bar.
8 After the two women finished the marathon, they *went* / *had gone* for a pizza.

5 ★ ★ ★ Complete the story with the Past Simple or the Past Perfect forms of the verbs in brackets.

Liam sat on the bed in his room and thought about his life. He *had been* (be) a professional athlete for nearly three years. He was only half way through the six-year contract he ¹_____ (sign) with a big sports company which supported him financially. The problem, as usual, was that he ²_____ (feel) sad and lonely. He spent nearly all of his free time in a hotel room with nobody to talk to. He really ³_____ (miss) spending time with his parents and his brother. What's more, before he became a professional runner, he ⁴_____ (have) plenty of friends. Now, he ⁵_____ (realise) that most of them ⁶_____ (get) married and had a family. Of course, none of his old friends were as 'successful' or famous as he was. But he still ⁷_____ (not/be) happy. Why ⁸_____ (he/become) an athlete in the first place? Because he thought being rich and famous was more important than anything else.

SHOW WHAT YOU'VE LEARNT

6 Complete the sentences with the Past Simple or the Past Perfect forms of the verbs in brackets.

1 I ª*was* (be) half way to the gym when I ᵇ_____ (realise) I ᶜ_____ (leave) my trainers at home.
2 ª_____ (Katie/finish) her fitness programme the last time you ᵇ_____ (call) her?
3 Julie ª_____ (not/live) in the countryside for very long when she ᵇ_____ (notice) how much healthier she felt.
4 By the time I ª_____ (get) to the chemist's, my headache ᵇ_____ (go).
5 The doctor ª_____ (not/recognise) the patient because he ᵇ_____ (lose) lots of weight.
6 My neck ª_____ (hurt) because I ᵇ_____ (fall) asleep at my desk.

/6

GRAMMAR: Train and Try Again page 151

LISTENING LANGUAGE PRACTICE

8.3

Collocations • expressing purpose
• places to do sport

1 **Read the interview between a radio presenter and a teenager. In gaps 1–9, choose the correct answers A–C.**

Extract from Students' Book recording 🔊 **3.33**

P: Good morning from Central Park in New York City. I can't ¹___ I'm in the middle of one of the busiest cities in the world, and yet I can't ²___ any ^A^traffic *noise / sound*. ^B^Pollution *levels / scales* are low and the ^C^air *standard / quality* is good. I can ³___ why New Yorkers say that Central Park is their backyard or garden and their escape from ^D^city *activity / life*.
⁴___ around, I'd say it's also their gym – it's where people come to walk, run, cycle, work out, train, climb and ⁵___ football. Central Park is huge! There are over 93 kilometres of pathways, 26 ^E^playing *pitches / fields* and 21 playgrounds for children, and when you ⁶___ a rest, there are 9,000 benches to sit on. There's a zoo, a theatre, a ^F^skating *track / rink*, a reservoir, places to sail and swim, and plenty of places to eat – I could live here! […]
I'm going to talk to a group of young people sitting on the grass over there. Hi! […] Do you ⁷___ if I ask you a few questions? […] I'm recording a podcast about parks. You look very relaxed. Do you ⁸___ to Central Park a lot?

T: Yeah, we hang ⁹___ here all the time in summer. This is Sheep's Meadow – it's a really good place for sitting on a blanket, reading a book, people-watching.

1	A believe	B think	C know
2	A listen	B hear	C observe
3	A understand	B know	C learn
4	A Seeing	B Watching	C Looking
5	A kick	B do	C play
6	A need	B have	C take
7	A like	B mind	C want
8	A come	B visit	C go
9	A up	B in	C out

2 **Read the text again. Choose the correct words A–F to make collocations. Use a dictionary if necessary.**

3 **Complete the sentences with the collocations from Exercise 2 in the correct form.**

My school has an excellent *playing field* to have football matches on.
1 Ambrose loves _____ because he enjoys going shopping and visiting museums and theatres.
2 The _____ in Kraków in Poland is one of the worst in the world. It's really bad if you have asthma.
3 The _____ in cities are much higher than in the countryside because of traffic and factories.
4 There's a great _____ near Tony's house. They have regular discos on ice!
5 I live on a busy street and the _____ from cars and lorries is very loud.

> **REMEMBER THIS**
>
> A skating rink is a good place **for hanging** out / **to hang** out with friends.
>
> Sheep's Meadow is a good place **for sitting** / **to sit** on a blanket.

4 **Read REMEMBER THIS. Complete the sentences with the correct forms of the verbs from the box. There are two extra verbs.**

> borrow   drink   go   listen
> meet   swim   visit   ~~watch~~

The Opollo Cinema is a great place to *watch* films.
1 The lake near my grandma's cottage is a nice place for _____ in the summer.
2 The Tropical Café is a cool place to _____ friends for a chat.
3 The beach is the best place to _____ sunbathing.
4 Club Rocker is the worst place for _____ to live music.
5 My local library is a good place for _____ books and DVDs.

WORD STORE 8D | Places to do sport

5 **Find and correct the mistakes. Two sentences are correct.**

There's an outdoor ice ~~pool~~ in the city centre but it only opens in December. *rink*
1 Do you know how big a regular basketball pitch is?
_____
2 Oh no! I think I left my bag on the tennis court. We need to go back. _____
3 Many people say that the Nürnburgring in Germany is the scariest motor racing ring in the world.
_____
4 There's a full-size boxing rink at my gym but I've never seen anybody fighting there. _____
5 Sean only uses an indoor swimming track because he doesn't like cold water. _____
6 They're building a hockey court near my house. We should learn to play. _____
7 Ross fell over on the handball court today and hurt his leg. _____

1 **Read the text quickly and decide why it was written.**

1 To explain how to do more recycling in cities
2 To present a particular environmental project
3 To give advice on how to save energy at home

Greener and cleaner cities

1 _____
Today, there are around 7.4 billion people living on the planet. The Earth's population, however, is growing at 1.1% each year, which means that by the year 2030 there will be about 8.4 billion people. What's more, most people choose to live in cities because it is easier to find work. Busier and larger cities, however, use a lot of natural resources such as gas and electricity. It also means more vehicles* on the roads and greater use of public transport by people who commute to work.

One key question, then, is this: what can we do to protect the environment and deal with the larger number of people living on the planet?

2 _____
One idea might be the construction of lighthouse* cities. At present, Stockholm, Barcelona and Cologne are part of an experimental project to create cleaner, more energy efficient* cities for people to live in. If the results of these experiments prove successful, the ideas and technology will be transferred to other cities to help the creation of a better, more environmentally friendly Europe.

3 _____
One of the major technological inventions these cities are using is connected to recycling. But not the recycling of plastic, glass and paper which we all know. The lighthouse cities want to recycle heat.

Experts have realised that the great amount of hot air created by computer data centres, stadiums and supermarkets is wasted. But in Stockholm this 'waste heat' is already used to create hot water which is then pumped around the city into private houses and housing estates. This recycling of energy is saving both money and the resources which generate* heat in the first place.

4 _____
When it comes to fighting pollution, lighthouse cities aim to encourage the use of car-sharing to help reduce the number of vehicles on the roads. In Cologne, there are plans to build special car parks for electric cars which local people can 'book' and then share with other passengers on their journeys. When the cars are parked, they transfer energy to each other so that each vehicle is ready for a journey and that energy is used efficiently.

5 _____
Another aim of the lighthouse city project is to make people understand how to save on natural resources. Residents in all cities will be able to use apps to monitor how much energy they are using and when is the best time to clean the house, for example, or do the washing. There may even be prizes for the 'greenest' residents. The idea here is that if people can save money and save the environment at the same time, they will probably act more responsibly.

That's why the lighthouse cities like Stockholm, Cologne and Barcelona, like the lighthouses of the past, are 'showing the way' to a safer future.

GLOSSARY

vehicle (n) – a machine with an engine such as a car, bus, or truckd
lighthouse (n) – a tower with a powerful flashing light that guides ships away from danger

efficient (adj) – if someone or something is efficient, they work well without wasting time, money, or energy
generate (v) – to produce or cause something

2 Read the text again and answer the questions.

1 How many more people than today will live on the Earth by the year 2030?

_____

_____

2 Why is living outside big cities not a very attractive option for many people?

_____

_____

3 On what condition will the new, innovative idea be used in cities across Europe?

_____

_____

4 What do they do in Stockholm to get hot water?

_____

_____

5 In what two ways do lighthouse cities plan to reduce pollution?

_____

_____

6 Why will people feel motivated to behave in a more responsible way?

_____

_____

3 Read the text again. Match headings A–G with paragraphs 1–5. There are two extra headings.

A Cleaner commuting
B Learning to care
C Reusing more than rubbish
D The city of dreams
E More people, more problems
F Gadgets that make life easier
G Modern solutions to city living

4 Find and complete words in the collocations from the text. The first letters are given.

p_opulation_ growth

1 n_____ resources
2 p_____ transport
3 to c_____ to work
4 to p_____ successful
5 t_____ inventions

5 Use the collocations from Exercise 4 in the correct forms to complete the sentences.

I think _population growth_ is a major problem. How can we grow food for so many people?

1 If this experiment _____ , we can help millions of people have healthier lives.
2 I wonder what amazing _____ we will see in the next 50 years.
3 James hates using _____ because he says the buses and trams are too unreliable.
4 Edith likes living in the city centre because she doesn't have to _____ .
5 We need to use renewable energy like solar and wind power because _____ will not last forever.

6 Look at the vocabulary in lesson 8.4 in the Students' Book. Choose the correct words.

The **MegaSuck** vacuum [1]_storm / mask / cleaner_ doesn't just work on your carpet! The powerful **MegaSuck** mechanism also clears the air in your home from vehicle exhaust [2]_fumes / particles / smoke_, dangerous factory [3]_smoke / particles / pollution_, unhealthy smog [4]_particles / storms / fumes_ and other forms of air [5]_particles / pollution / purifiers_. It can also protect you from dust [6]_fumes / smoke / storms_. Clean your house and help with environmental [7]_pollution / storms / protection_. You'll never need to wear a face [8]_mask / protection / cleaner_ in your home again!

Only $250. Order today!!

WORD STORE 8E | Word families

7 Complete the sentences with the correct form of the words in capitals.

The _pollution_ in this city is almost as high as in Beijing! **POLLUTE**

1 I am happy to hear any _____ criticism you may have on the new project. **CONSTRUCT**
2 James has a bottle with a special filter which _____ tap water – it's cheaper and better for the planet. **PURE**
3 There are many _____ ideas which we can use to improve the environment. **CREATE**
4 When a huge ship sank, nearly 200,000 tonnes of oil _____ the nearby ocean waters. **POLLUTION**
5 Tristan has bought an air _____ for his bedroom. Now he sleeps like a baby. **PURE**
6 Environmental _____ is the responsibility of every person on Earth. **PROTECT**
7 You have been very _____ during this difficult time in my life. **SUPPORT**
8 The _____ of World Wide Fund for Nature (WWF) in 1961 meant that the negative influence of people on nature was already visible in the 1960s. **CREATE**

SHOW WHAT YOU KNOW

1 Complete the sentences with the correct form of the verbs in brackets.

Lewis _thinks_ (think) jogging is the best exercise.

1 The volleyball coach _____ (speak) to the players yesterday.

2 The journalists _____ (interview) the team's manager at the moment.

3 Ian _____ (carry) a heavy sports bag when he left the house.

4 I'm looking forward to watching the match. I _____ (never/be) inside a stadium before.

5 The sports shop _____ (already/sell) all their tennis balls by the time I got there.

2 ★ Complete the sentences with _said_ or _told_.

The Prime Minister _said_ that he wanted to improve diets in schools.

1 The doctor _____ the patient that he was perfectly healthy.

2 The team coach _____ we probably wouldn't win the match.

3 The yoga teacher _____ me to touch my toes.

3 ★ Choose the correct forms.

1 'I don't usually eat meat.'
The woman said she _doesn't_ / _didn't_ eat meat.

2 'Ella isn't answering her phone!'
Fay said Ella _wasn't_ / _isn't_ answering her phone.

3 'The referees are late.'
The manager said the referees _were_ / _are_ late.

4 'The kids are playing by the pool.'
Jill said that the kids _are_ / _were_ playing by the pool.

5 'I can almost see the pollution.'
The man said he _can_ / _could_ almost see the pollution.

6 'The nurses aren't doing enough.'
Mrs Jackson said the nurses _weren't_ / _aren't_ doing enough.

4 ★ ★ Complete the sentences with the correct forms of the words in brackets. Use Reported Speech.

1 B: 'I cycled six miles.' / S: 'I rode my bike further.'
Beth said she ª_had cycled_ (cycle) six miles.
Seth told Beth he ᵇ_____ (ride) further.

2 D: 'I haven't eaten meat for a year.' / A: 'I love meat.'
Dan told Ann he ª_____ (not/eat) meat for a year.
Ann said she ᵇ_____ (love) meat.

3 B: 'You've lost a lot of weight.' / J: 'I was on a strict diet.'
Bill told Jill she ª_____ (lose) a lot of weight.
Jill said that she ᵇ_____ (be) on a strict diet.

5 ★ ★ ★ Read the news report and complete the Direct Speech sentences. Include personal pronouns where necessary.

'In the case of the mystery virus at St Mark's Hospital, medical expert Dr Singh said _he was not very worried_ about the problem. He said ¹_he had seen a virus like this_ and that ²_he had confidence in his team_ to find a cure soon. He then told the media that ³_he wasn't giving any further comments._ A number of patients at the hospital said that ⁴_they had felt very sick_ and that ⁵_some of them had suffered terrible headaches._ They also told journalists that ⁶_they hadn't lost hope._ More news to follow.'

'I _'m_ not very worried.'

1 'I _____ like this.'

2 'I _____ team.'

3 'I _____ any further comments.'

4 'We _____ very sick.'

5 'Some _____ terrible headaches.'

6 'We _____ hope.'

SHOW WHAT YOU'VE LEARNT

6 Rewrite the following sentences in Direct Speech as Reported Speech. Change the personal pronouns if necessary.

'I've seen the man', said Edna in court.
Edna told the judge _she had seen_ the man.

1 'Vandals are destroying my school's handball court!', said Carly to the police officer.
Carly told the police officer that vandals _____ handball court.

2 'I didn't take the air purifier', said the nurse.
The nurse said she _____ air purifier.

3 'I don't want to go to the volleyball match', said Mike.
Mike told me _____ to go to the volleyball match.

4 'There has been an accident in your gym', said the women to the fitness trainers.
The women told the fitness trainers there _____ gym.

5 'My father was a professional tennis player', Phillip said to Ella.
Phillip told Ella that _____ a professional tennis player.

6 'We are feeling a little dizzy', said the girls.
The girls said _____ a little dizzy.

/6

GRAMMAR: Train and Try Again page 151

1 ★ **Put the words in the correct order to make sentences. Sometimes there is more than one answer.**

It / Brad / was / passed / hot / out / so / that / .
It was so hot that Brad passed out.

1 Malcom / his / fatty foods / out / cutting / of / is / diet / .
_____

2 Jamie / out / three / a / week / times / works / .
_____

3 Why / take / don't / up / you / a / sport / ?
_____

4 How / have / suffered / long / from / you / asthma / ?
_____

5 I / over / this / to / cold / can't / get / seem / .
_____

2 ★ ★ **Choose the correct answers A–C.**

1 **Davina:** Why are you so stressed?
  Joseph: Because I've ___ my school work.
  A fallen behind with **B** handed in
  C coped with

2 **Lisa:** I've got a problem, Hugo.
  Hugo: Well, you know you can always ___.
  A cut me out **B** talk things over with me
  C deal with me

3 **Ruby:** I've had enough! I can't do this exercise.
  Warren: Don't ___ ! Practice makes perfect.
  A give up **B** turn up
  C cut it out

4 **Ronald:** You're not very good at skating, are you?
  Harriet: Why do you have to ___ all the time? I'm trying!
  A call me down **B** let me down
  C put me down

5 **Lizzy:** I don't ___ my dance instructor very well.
  Angela: Why not? Is she too strict?
  A get on with **B** get in with
  C get with my

6 **Amelia:** Can you ___ my sports bag for a second?
  Nasar: Sure. No problem.
  A look up **B** look for
  C look after

3 ★ ★ ★ **Find and correct the mistakes. Two sentences are correct.**

Can I sign up with your yoga classes, please? *sign up for*

1 I'm staying home tonight to catch up my phrasal verbs. _____

2 Jenny found out the virus about on the Internet. _____

3 Marcus hangs out with Suzie a lot, doesn't he? _____

4 We're going to play volleyball. Do you want to join in? _____

5 You're having a hard time right now but you'll get it through. _____

4 ★ ★ ★ **Complete each pair of sentences with the same answer A–C.**

1 Has the vet turned ___ yet? Poor Mousey is looking pretty ill.
  Who first came ___ with the idea of a vacuum cleaner?
  A over **B** up **C** through

2 Come along to my fitness class. I'm sure you'll fit ___ nicely.
  The woman at the chemist's said I needed to hand ___ a prescription to buy those tablets.
  A up **B** in **C** over

3 Mike's really sad about Molly, but I told him to get on ___ his life.
  How do you cope ___ stress at work, Robert?
  A to **B** with **C** by

4 I closed the window to keep that cat ___ . Did you open it for him?
  This homework assignment is really stressing me ___ .
  A out **B** over **C** up

5 I feel fantastic! There's nothing better than a work ___ in the morning.
  Please keep the children ___ of this room. I've got a terrible headache.
  A up **B** over **C** out

6 Jim's really unhappy because Tina broke ___ with him this morning.
  How do you put ___ with Doctor Savage? He's so unfriendly.
  A on **B** through **C** up

7 Can you go ___ these team instructions again with me? I don't understand them.
  I'm still weak because I haven't got ___ the flu yet.
  A through **B** with **C** over

5 ★ ★ ★ **Complete the sentences with verbs in the correct forms.**

Tori is *looking* after her little sister at the moment because she's feeling ill.

1 Thomas is actually very good at skating. I've no idea why he _____ himself down so often and says he's bad at it.

2 Marta isn't playing today because she's still _____ over the cold she had at the weekend.

3 What did you do yesterday? I _____ out with Jerry and Brendan in the shopping centre all afternoon.

4 Kara and I _____ up for a karate class this morning. It starts on Monday and we're both very excited about it.

5 Mo has _____ up skiing and has just spent all of her money on skis and skiing clothes.

6 I've just _____ out about this sport called zorbing. You get inside a large plastic ball and roll downhill – it sounds great!

WRITING

A reader's comment – linkers

1 Complete the phrases with the words from the box. There are two extra words.

> agree   also   fact   hand   On
> Personally   ~~reason~~   What   why

1 For this _reason_, I …   `C`
2 _____ , I believe that …
3 That's _____ …
4 I _____ agree that …
5 _____ is more, I think that …
6 In _____ , …
7 _____ the other hand, I …

2 Mark the sentences in Exercise 1 as G for giving an opinion, A for adding further points, O for giving an opposite opinion or C for concluding.

3 Put the sentences in a logical order.

Topic 1

   I believe that taking drugs to do better at sports should be illegal.   `1`
A However, I believe that some athletes need drugs for medical reasons.
B I also agree that sports stars who cheat should be banned.
C Therefore, I don't think that use of all drugs should be forbidden in sport.

Topic 2

A In fact, I think PE should be compulsory in schools until the age of 18.
B Personally, I believe that all school children should be more active.
C On the other hand, I think students should be able to choose which sports to do.

4 Replace the underlined phrases in the reader's comment with phrases from Exercise 1. Sometimes more than one answer is possible.

aboutyourschool.edu

——— Add your comments here ———

I enjoyed your article about the benefits of taking part in team sports.

_2_ I think young people nowadays do too little exercise. ¹__ I also think that teenagers can learn a lot of useful skills when they are training for particular sports. ²__ Moreover, I think that young people need to develop a good attitude to team work as this will be valuable later in life.

³__ However, I agree that being too competitive can have negative effects on children. ⁴__ Therefore, I think schools should pay attention to helping young people understand this.

5 Match beginnings 1–6 with endings a–e. There is one extra sentence beginning.

   A calculator would make   `f`
1 Our mum makes us
2 Stewart's jokes always make me
3 The dentist makes me
4 My father often makes me
5 Morning exercise can make you
6 This fitness app has made my

a laugh because they are so silly.
b nervous because I hate pain.
c do our homework before we can watch TV.
d feel healthy the whole day.
e life much better.
f things a lot easier.

6 Complete the sentences with the correct forms of *make* and the words in brackets. Put *make* in the correct place in the sentence.

   If I marry you, will you _make me cut my hair_ (me / cut / my hair)?

1 When we were younger, our parents _____ _____ (us / clean / our room).
2 Sad films _____ _____ (always / Sue / cry). Isn't she silly?
3 Adam's morning meditation _____ _____ (him / feel / relaxed) the whole day.
4 The nurse at the hospital _____ _____ (me / turn off / my smartphone), so I couldn't call you.
5 Doing exams _____ _____ (has never / James / anxious). He's always enjoyed doing them.
6 Next week Dad _____ _____ (will / us / go) fishing with him again. Boring!

7 Read the task below. Then read the email response to the online article and put the verbs in brackets in the correct form. Add any extra words you need.

> You have just read an online article on educating students in schools about the environment. The article says that schools should:
>
> - Teach students more about what pollutes the air.
> - Help students understand more about the dangers of pollution – both now and in the future.
> - Educate students about how to protect the environment.

> Write a reader's comment. Include and develop these points:
>
> - Give your opinion about the article.
> - Say what you agree with and why.
> - Say what you disagree with and why.
> - Give your conclusion.

Sulu93: Thank you ᴬ*for / to / with* the article. It has ¹_____ (make / me / think) about just how ᴮ*far / few / little* my school has ²_____ (do / help) students learn about the causes of air ꟲ*pollution / particles / fumes* and what ³_____ (need / be / do) to protect the environment.

For example, there ᴰ*is a lot of / are lots of / is many* smog and factory ᴱ*smoke / fumes / storms* in the city ꟳ*where / which / who* I live, so the air quality is very poor. But lots of older students ⁴_____ (continue / drive) to school. There are cycle paths and a bus service, so why ⁵_____ (they / choose / travel) by car?

I agree that schools ⁶_____ (need / be) responsible ꟳ*for / to / with* educating students. However, this also ⁷_____ (has / be) the government's responsibility. I think local pollution levels ᴴ*would be / will be / are* much lower if state advertising informed the public more of how important this issue is.

8 Read the email again and choose the correct words A–H.

9 You have just read the article below on a news website. Write a reader's comment. Include and develop these points:

- Give your opinion about the article.
- Say what you agree with and why.
- Say what you disagree with and why.
- Give your conclusion.

NEWSFOCUS.com

Daily Discussion

Accident at school – Who is responsible?

Yesterday, a judge ordered a school to pay £2,000 to the parents of a teenage girl who broke her arm during a school basketball match. The judge said that the school had to ensure the safety of its students and therefore had failed in its duty. But were the school and its staff really responsible?

Personally, I believe that schools need to take care of their students during school hours. However, it is impossible to prevent accidents during a competitive sporting event. When a teacher runs such a class, they are only responsible for making sure there is fair play. In fact, without the element of risk there would be little interest in such activities.

I think the judge was wrong to make the school responsible for this accident.

Join the Daily Discussion and tell us what you think in our Reader's Comments section below.

SHOW THAT YOU'VE CHECKED

Finished? Always check your writing.
Can you tick ✓ everything on this list?

In my reader's comment:

• I have given my opinion about the article.	☐
• I have said what I agree with and why.	☐
• I have said what I disagree with and why.	☐
• I have used phrases such as *However, ...* or *On the other hand, ...* to give opposite opinions.	☐
• I have used phrases such as *Therefore ...* or *That's why ...* to give a conclusion	☐
• I have not used emoticons ☺ or abbreviations (*info / CU / gr8*).	☐
• I have checked my spelling and punctuation.	☐
• My text is neat and clear.	☐

8.8 SPEAKING

A doctor's appointment

1 Translate the phrases into your own language.

SPEAKING BANK

Diagnosis

When did the pain start? _____

I'm going to examine you / take your temperature. _____
_____

I'm going to do a blood test. _____

Breathe in and out. _____
_____
_____

Open wide. _____

Lie down, please. _____

If I press here, does it hurt? _____
_____

I think you've got indigestion / the flu / an infection / a virus. _____
_____

You're probably allergic to ... _____
_____
_____

Treatment

You should eat more slowly / go on a diet. _____
_____

You need to drink more water. _____
_____

I'm going to give you a prescription. _____

I'm going to make an appointment for you (to see the specialist). _____
_____

Take one tablet after each meal. _____
_____

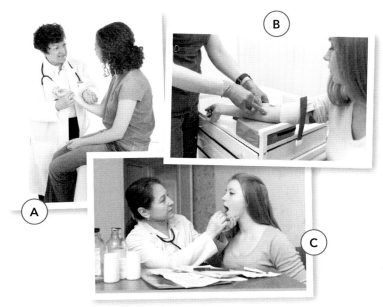

2 Complete the dialogue between Victoria and her doctor with the words from the box. There are two extra words.

cough   flu   ill   prescription   runny   sick
symptoms   temperature   throat   ~~well~~   wide

D: Hello Victoria. What's the problem?

V: Hi, Doctor Jones. I'm not feeling very _well_. I've got a sore ¹_____ and a really bad dry ²_____ .

D: Oh dear. That doesn't sound nice. And do you have any other ³_____ ?

V: Well, I've got a little bit of a ⁴_____ nose too. But it's not too bad.

D: Right, OK. Can you sit here, please? And open ⁵_____ for me. Say 'aaaaaah'. Thank you. And now let me take your ⁶_____ .

V: What is it, doctor?

D: Thankfully, it's nothing too serious. I think you've got the ⁷_____ .

V: Hmm. So what should I do now?

D: I'm going to give you a ⁸_____ for some medicine. Take it to the chemist's, then go home to bed. You need to rest for a few days then you should be fine. One more thing, as soon as you're feeling better, I suggest you buy some trousers that cover your ankles and wear a hat and a scarf. It is winter, you know!

V: Erm, OK. Thank you, doctor. Goodbye.

3 Complete the missing words in the dialogue between Laura and her doctor. The first and last letters are given.

L: Hi, Doctor Adams. How are you?

D: I'm well, thanks. But how can I help you? What's the p_roble_m?

L: I've got a pain in my ¹c_____t. At first I thought it was just ²i_____n because I ate too fast, but it won't go away. And I also feel very weak.

D: Oh dear. When did the pain start?

L: A few days ago.

D: Hmm, OK. Please ³l_____e down here. And now I want you to ⁴b_____e in and out. Nice and deep. Thank you. You can sit up now.

L: And?

D: I think you've got an ⁵i_____n but I'm going to do a ⁶b_____d test to be sure. Please roll up the sleeve on your jumper. This shouldn't hurt too much.

L: Ouch!

D: There you go. That wasn't too painful, was it? The results will be ready tomorrow and I'm going to make an ⁷a_____t for you to see a ⁸s_____t.

L: Oh, no. Is it serious? I'm probably just ⁹a_____c to something, right? Maybe nuts or gluten or something?

D: Well, there's certainly no need to worry just yet. Come back tomorrow and we'll see what we can do.

4 Read the dialogues in Exercises 2 and 3 again and decide which photo A–C shows Victoria and which Laura. There is one extra picture.

1 In pairs, ask and answer the questions.

PART 1

Talk about shopping.
1 Do you ever buy things in vintage shops? Why?/Why not?
2 Do you like picking up a bargain in the sales? Why?/Why not?
3 How do you decide what clothes suit you?
4 Can you describe a situation when you bought a faulty product and needed to make a complaint? What happened?
5 Do you think it's important to wear clothes from special brands? Why?/Why not?

PART 2

Talk about health.
1 What things could you cut out from your diet to make yourself healthier?
2 What do you do when you have a temperature?
3 What sport can you take up to improve your health?
4 How can pollution influence our health?
5 Do you think that social media is bad for your health? Why?/Why not?

2 Some people are visiting the doctor today. They have a lot of different symptoms.

Talk together about the different advice the doctor might give these people.

Talk about health and going to the doctor.
• What do you do when you feel ill?
• How often do you go to the doctor's?
• Do you suffer from any allergies?

• Which do you think is worse: a headache, a stomachache or a sore throat? Why?
• What things can people do to stop themselves from becoming ill?

3 Discuss this question together. 'Exercise is more important than diet if you want to stay healthy.' What do you think?

For exercise:
Exercise … • helps you to lose weight by burning calories. • is good for your heart and lungs. • stops you from getting serious diseases. • makes you feel happy and energetic.

For a healthy diet:
Eating a healthy diet … • keeps your body healthy, e.g. olive oil helps your heart. • improves your skin. • helps your brain to stay healthy. • helps your stomach to work well.

VOCABULARY AND GRAMMAR

1 Choose the odd one out.

runny nose / sore throat / headache / ~~pain in the shoulder~~

1 face mask / factory smoke / air pollution / smog particles
2 create / construct / support / purifier
3 cough / chest / back / leg
4 path / court / pitch / ring
5 feel / hurt / ache / pain

/5

2 Complete the sentences with the correct words from the box. There are two extra words.

> back   dizzy   fumes   head
> rash   ring   ~~sick~~   vacuum

I feel _sick_. I hate being on boats or ships.

1 Sophie felt a little _____ because she stood up too fast.
2 The school has bought a boxing _____ . What do you think about that?
3 Richard thinks his _____ hurts because of the heavy bag he carries to school every day.
4 The exhaust _____ in the city centre make it difficult to breathe.
5 This new _____ cleaner also washes your carpet! That's what the advert says.

/5

3 Complete the missing words in the sentences. The first and last letters are given.

If you want to lose **w**_eigh_**t**, you need to stop eating so much chocolate.

1 Sergio came off the rugby **p**_____**h** covered in thick wet mud.
2 This dust **s**_____**m** is making it difficult to see anything.
3 If you want to reduce **a**_____**y**, you need to learn how to relax.
4 I'd like to be healthier, so I'm going to make better life **c**_____**s** – starting with what I eat!
5 Running around the park once a day is a great way to keep **f**_____**t**.

/5

4 Complete the sentence with the Past Simple or Past Perfect forms of the verbs in brackets.

Connor _had forgotten_ (forgot) to wash his hands before he sat down for dinner.

1 Andrea _____ (be) stressed because she hadn't revised for the test.
2 When Neil arrived at the gym, everyone _____ (already/begin) the fitness class.
3 By the time Jill _____ (get) home, she had started to feel unwell.
4 Linda felt much better after she _____ (speak) to her best friend about the problem.
5 I had just left Jeanette's house when I _____ (realise) I didn't have my sports bag.

/5

5 Complete the second sentence so it has a similar meaning to the first. Use Reported Speech.

Ross said: 'I am the best footballer in the school.'
Ross told me _he was_ the best footballer in the school.

1 Abi said: 'I'm joining a yoga class.'
Abi told us _____ a yoga class.
2 Nick said: 'I didn't swim in the swimming pool.'
Nick said _____ in the swimming pool.
3 Catherine said: 'I've never broken a bone in my body.'
Catherine told them _____ a bone in her body.
4 Amy said: 'I didn't come out in spots until an hour after eating.'
Amy said _____ an hour after eating.
5 Mia said: 'The air pollution in this town is really bad.'
Mia told me _____ really bad.

/5

6 Complete each pair of sentences with the same answer A–C.

We are going to __ the new James Bond film tonight.
I don't need a __ because I've got the time on my phone.

A see   B clock   (C) watch

1 Jenny told __ she was going to go on a diet.
Hey! Those skates belong to __ . You can't just use my things.

A me   B I   C that

2 The teacher said the student was __ well and sent him home.
I didn't recognise the trainer because I had __ seen him before.

A definitely   B not   C never

3 Two cyclists __ they had used drugs to improve their performance.
Grandma __ she took vitamin tablets each day to keep her healthy.

A spoke   B told   C said

4 The boxer __ never lost a professional fight before last night.
The racing driver said he __ driven faster than ever yesterday.

A has   B had   C have

5 The basketball __ in our school are fantastic!
There are some tennis __ next to my house.

A balls   B courts   C tracks

/5

Total   /30

7 Choose the correct answers A–C.

Is there an all-year ____ in your city?
A ice track
B skating track
C ice rink *(circled)*

1 Ed explained that he ____ to school to sit the exam.
A has a temperature and can't come
B has had a temperature and couldn't come
C had a temperature and couldn't come

2 Adriana ____ a stomachache earlier that day, so she was feeling very weak and miserable in the evening.
A has had
B has
C had had

3 That evening Patrick told me that ____ .
A he was bad at making decisions
B he has made a bad decision
C he was making a bad decision

4 Grandma told me she ____ an air purifier for her garage.
A was bought
B was buying
C had bought

5 The nurse ____ my pulse, but the doctor wanted to do it again.
A had checked
B was checking
C has checked

/5

8 Complete the second sentence so that it has a similar meaning to the first. Use between two and five words, including the word in capitals.

I ate ice cream too quickly and got a headache.
EATEN
I got a headache after *I had eaten ice cream* too quickly.

1 It's a good idea to monitor how many calories you eat. **KEEP**
It's a good idea to _____ how many calories you eat.

2 'You have to take the tablets twice a day', the doctor told me. **SAID**
The doctor _____ the tablets twice a day.

3 Rachel was late for the bus, so she missed her fitness class. **BECAUSE**
Rachel missed her fitness class _____ for the bus.

4 Norah told me she had broken her leg on the basketball court. **MY**
'I _____ on the basketball court', said Norah.

5 Allan drank all of the cola in the bottle, then began to feel sick. **DRUNK**
Allan began to feel sick after _____ all of the cola in the bottle.

/5

9 Choose the correct answers A–C.

My day at the races

Last week, I was at the motor racing _A_ watching my friend Jack race his new car. During the race, however, I began to feel quite **¹__** . It started with a cough and a headache but by the time I got home I had got a **²__** throat too.

I **³__** never had such symptoms before that day, so I was a little confused and worried. When I went to the doctor, he told me that I probably had an allergy to something but he didn't know what. I told him I had been to see the race and he asked me about the place where the motor racing was.

I told him that there was a new **⁴__** there that hadn't been fully built yet. I think they were making the stadium bigger so more people could watch the races. 'Ah', he said, 'that's the problem.' New building work often leads to the **⁵__** of lots of dust and dirt in the air, he explained. I probably had an allergy to that, he said. Now I try to avoid places where they are doing building works.

	A	B	C
	track *(circled)*	court	ring
1	hurt	ill	pain
2	sore	hurting	painful
3	have	had	did
4	construct	construction	constructive
5	creating	creative	creation

/5

10 Choose the correct answer A–C to replace the underlined part of the sentence.

The woman in the theatre <u>passed out</u> during the final scene.
A became unconscious *(circled)*   B decided to leave
C began to complain

1 Ian has just <u>taken up badminton</u>.
A started playing badminton for the first time.
B stopped playing badminton forever.
C won a game of badminton.

2 Most people are <u>cutting out</u> smoking now that they know the health risks.
A stopping   B reducing
C checking

3 Can you give me some <u>constructive</u> advice on how to improve my fitness?
A negative   B critical
C useful

4 Thomas says he <u>always loses his appetite</u> when he's depressed.
A goes on a diet   B doesn't like to eat
C is never very hungry

5 My girlfriend left me! How will I ever <u>get over it</u>?
A suffer from it   B recover from it
C stress out about it

/5

Total   /20

VOCABULARY BANK

Translate the phrases into your own language.

People

Age

adult
average age
birth certificate

elderly
grow up
old age

Personality

active
adaptable
adventurous
ambition
ambitious
be passionate about sth

be popular with

be positive
be serious about

be successful

be the centre of attention

brave
caring
charm (n)
charm (v)
charming
cheerful
clever
communicative
competition
competitive
confident
creative
dependent
determination
polite
popular
protective
quiet
reliable
reliance on

rely on
responsible
rude
selfish
sensible
sensitive
serious
shy
silly

sociable
stupid
successful
supportive
sure of yourself

talkative
team-player
unadventurous

unfit
unpopular
unwise
visual thinker

wise

Feelings and emotions

anger
ashamed
bad mood
bad-tempered
be afraid of
be crazy/mad about
be into/keen on
be obsessed with

be relieved
bored
can't wait
confused
confusing
delighted
disappointed with

disgusted
disgusting
embarrassed
encouraging
excited about
exhausting
feel at home
feel homesick
frightened
frozen
get nervous
grateful
hate
look forward to

make fun of
moved
nightmare
prefer
shocked
surprised
useless at
worry about

Appearance

get a tattoo
look bored
look cheerful
look fashionable

look good
look gorgeous

look original
look scruffy
look smart
look tired
suit

Clothes and accessories

casual clothes
comfortable
designer clothes

fit
friendship bracelet

hoodie
jacket
leather
purse
put on
second-hand clothes

silver cross
skinny jeans
sweatpants
tie
uniform
winter coat

Shoes

ballet flats
boots
flip-flops
high heels
knee-high
sandals
slippers
trainers
wellington boots

Personal values

be in favour of
be involved in
care about
support (v)
protect

Home

Types of houses and location

block of flats _____

bridge _____

bungalow _____

cottage _____

detached house _____

_____

houseboat _____

in a village _____

in the city centre _____

in the countryside _____

in the suburbs _____

natural light _____

near the sea _____

on a housing estate _____

_____

on the edge of the city _____

_____

pavement _____

semi-detached house _____

_____

studio apartment _____

terraced house _____

treehouse _____

Building materials

brick _____

concrete _____

glass _____

metal _____

stone _____

wood _____

Rooms, furniture and equipment

basement _____

beanbag _____

bedside table _____

blinds _____

bookcase _____

carpet _____

ceiling _____

chest of drawers _____

_____

cooker _____

couch _____

cupboard _____

cushion _____

desk _____

electricity _____

fridge/refrigerator _____

front door _____

interior wall _____

kitchen sink _____

ladder _____

lamp _____

sheet _____

shelf/shelves _____

stairs _____

upstairs _____

vacuum cleaner _____

wardrobe _____

wooden floor _____

Description

comfortable _____

cosy _____

luxury _____

modern _____

on the first floor _____

_____

on the ground floor _____

on the second floor _____

_____

on the third floor _____

_____

on the top floor _____

_____

open-plan _____

peaceful _____

spacious _____

traditional _____

uncluttered _____

wide _____

Moving house

house-warming party _____

_____

move (house) _____

neighbour _____

neighbourhood _____

Housework

do the cooking _____

do the gardening _____

_____

do the housework _____

_____

do the ironing _____

do the washing _____

do the washing-up _____

_____

make a mess _____

make dinner _____

make your bed _____

School

Subjects

academic subject _____

architecture _____

Music _____

PE/Physical Education _____

Science _____

Educational system

A levels _____

_____

apply for (a place) _____

_____

be/become a professor of _____

_____

compulsory _____

curriculum _____

do a degree _____

_____

elementary/primary school _____

_____

entrance exam _____

get/have a degree _____

_____

get into university/a place at university

_____

_____

graduate from _____

_____

nursery _____

secondary school _____

single-sex school _____

_____

Places at school

canteen _____

library _____

playground _____

school gate _____

School life

after-school activity _____

_____

attend school _____

be a fast learner _____

be an expert on _____

break up _____

catch up on _____

classmate _____

college graduate _____

_____

concentrate on _____

connect with _____

demanding _____

depend on _____

_____

do a course _____

do/take an exam _____

_____

do your homework _____

_____

VOCABULARY BANK

Translate the phrases into your own language.

drop a subject

fail an exam

fall behind

fancy-dress party

field trip

finish school
fit in
focus on
gap year

get a lot out of something

get good grades

get into trouble

get over a difficulty with the support of

get through
go to school
grade/mark
hand in homework

interactive experiment

keep up with
learn by heart/memorise

learn from one's mistakes

learning disorders

leave school

line up
listen to
look up
make mistakes
mark homework

mentor
miss/skip lessons

misunderstand
mixed-ability class

move up
pass an exam
revise for an exam

revision
role model
schedule
school uniform
schoolwork

set homework

sign up
socialise with

stand up
start school
struggle with
swipe card
take a break
take a subject
take it easy

talk something over

term
timetable
tuition fee

Work

Jobs

accountant
airline pilot
analyse data
analyse evidence

archaeologist
astronaut
astronomer
babysitter
be in (IT)
beautician
biologist
bus driver
businessperson

camp supervisor

carer
carpenter
chemist
collect data
collect specimens

computer science
computer scientist

conservation
conservationist

cook (n)
designer
develop a theory
do an experiment

driving instructor

editor
electrician

engineer
entrepreneur
estate agent
fashion magazine

fire-fighter
food industry
geologist
interpreter
invent
journalist
lifeguard
linguist
linguistics
marine biologist

marine biology
mathematician
mechanic
military leader

model
musician
nurse
office assistant

photographer
physicist
psychologist
psychology
publish a research paper

publish evidence

receptionist
sales representative

scientist
secretary
shop assistant

skiing instructor

social worker

software developer

specialist
take measurements

take notes
taxi driver
work in (IT)

Looking for a job

application form
apply for a job
at any time
at present

at the moment ___
attach ___
available ___
be capable of doing something ___

be confident that ___

get a job ___
have experience of ___

in connection with ___
interview ___
job advert ___
look for a job ___
obtain ___
opportunity ___
possess skills ___

succeed in ___
suitable candidate ___

with reference to ___

work experience ___

Working conditions and employment

association ___
away from home ___
be badly-paid ___
be employed ___
be responsible for/be in charge of ___

be self-employed ___

be unemployed ___
be well paid ___
benefit ___
challenging ___

conference call ___

daily ___
decent job ___
decision maker ___
do/work long hours ___

do/work night shifts ___

do/work overtime ___

do training ___
earn ___
earner ___
earnings ___
employ (v) ___
employee ___
employer ___

flexible hours ___

full-time job ___
get/have a day off ___

get fired/the sack ___

get five weeks' paid holiday ___

give up ___
have a job ___
have five weeks' paid holiday ___

inside ___
make a living ___

male-dominated job ___

manual job ___
office ___
part-time job ___
position ___
promotion ___
put up with ___
repetitive ___
resign from a job ___

retire ___
rewarding ___
run a business/a company ___

salary ___
staff ___
stressful ___
suitable ___
take somebody on ___

take time off ___
tiring ___
waste of time ___
work from home ___
work indoors ___
work on ___
work outdoors ___

work outside ___

Family and social life

Family and friends

fiancé(e) ___
generation ___
stepfather ___
wedding ___

Relationships

adapt to ___
admire ___
get married ___

get on with ___
impress ___
inspire ___
inspired by ___
make a good impression ___

have something in common ___

Everyday life

do sport ___
follow somebody on Twitter ___

get up ___
have a shave ___
play the violin/guitar ___

take the underground ___

wake up ___

Free time

chill out ___
come round ___
do bungee jumping ___

follow your own interests ___

entertainment ___
go shopping ___
go out ___
go window shopping ___

have a good time ___
have a party ___
jigsaw puzzle ___
make a noise ___
stay up ___
take something up ___

tend to ___

Food

Food and drinks

a selection of ___
chutney ___

cola ___
drinking water ___
herbal ___
local speciality ___

mineral water ___

Eating out

meal ___
service ___
waterfront restaurant ___

VOCABULARY BANK

Translate the phrases into your own language.

Shopping and services

Types of shops

baker's _____
bookstore _____
butcher's _____
charity shop _____
chemist's _____
clothes shop _____
computer shop _____
department store _____
DIY store _____
florist's _____
greengrocer's _____
High Street store _____
_____
jeweller's _____
newsagent's _____
optician's _____
pet shop _____
shoe shop _____
sports shop _____
stationer's _____
store _____
street market _____
supermarket _____
toy shop _____
vintage shop _____
_____

Services

bank _____
estate agent's _____
_____
hairdresser's _____
post office _____

Buying and selling

availability _____
available _____
barcode _____
be worth it _____
can't afford _____
_____
changing room _____
checkout desk _____
consumer _____
cost a fortune _____
customer _____
delivery _____
do the shopping _____
free _____
have a sale _____
on (special) offer _____
_____
out of stock _____
payer _____
payment _____

pick up a bargain _____
_____
provide _____
quality _____
queue _____
reduced _____
sell _____
sell out _____
sell-by date _____
seller _____
ship (v) _____
shop online _____
_____
size _____
subscription _____
try on _____
value _____
wait in line _____

Advertising

advertising _____
attract _____
competitive _____
give out _____

Complaints

apologise for _____
broken _____
complain _____
complaint _____
damaged _____
exchange something for something
_____
faulty _____
get a refund _____
keep the receipt _____
make a complaint _____
_____
receive _____
return _____
ripped _____
some parts are missing _____
_____
swap _____

Money

be in debt _____
billionaire _____
cash _____
debtor _____
invest in _____
investment _____
spend money on _____

Travelling and tourism

Sightseeing, trips and excursions

(it's) a must _____
_____
accommodation _____
ancient _____
arch _____
arrive _____
attraction _____
be famous for _____
breathtaking view _____
_____
busy _____
castle _____
crowded _____
direct sunlight _____
_____
don't mind _____
enormous _____
fascinating _____
go backpacking _____
_____
historic monument _____
_____
historic site _____
_____
host _____
impressive _____
keep sb out _____
let sb in _____
look forward to _____
_____
lovely _____
narrow _____
nightlife _____
passenger _____
reach the South Pole _____
_____
recommend _____
return to _____
rough _____
ruins _____
sailing _____
show somebody around _____
_____
slum _____
souvenir _____
stay in _____
tourist destination _____
_____
tourist highlight _____
_____
tower _____
travel agent _____
turquoise ocean _____

Forms of transport

aisle
GPS
on foot
take the underground

traffic jam

Culture

Art

at a museum
art gallery
brush
classic oil painting

creation
exhibition
household name

join a band

landscape
modern abstract painting

paint
painter
photo/photograph
photographer
photography
portrait
sculptor
sculpture
street art

Film, theatre, books

A-list actors

act
acting
animation
audience
autobiography
binge watcher

biography
blockbuster
bookworm
box office
chapter
character
classic novel
clip
come out
comedy
comic book
computer-generated images

costume

crime novel
documentary
drama series
ending
escapism
fairy tale
fantasy
genre
historical fiction

horror
horror fiction
in the background
in the foreground

incidentally
loss
movie
musical
paste on buildings/walls

perform
period drama
play
plot
poem
producer
put on (a play)
relate to
romantic comedy
scene
science fiction
script
setting
short story
soundtrack
special effects
stage
take on (a role)
thriller
trailer
travel show
TV drama/series
X-rated

Media

chat show
cooking programme

crime drama
episode
game show
light entertainment

news bulletin
on-demand TV

reality TV
sitcom
soap (opera)
talent show

telly
weather forecast

Music

the charts
gig
live
music award
record
rock
vocal range

Description

best-selling

complex
disappointing
engaging
entertaining
excellent
factual
gripping
imaginative
inspiring
moving
ordinary

Sport

Sports

climbing
cycling
cricket
hockey
horse riding
netball
rugby

Doing sport

bad at
badminton court

basketball court

bench
boxing ring
break a record
cheer
compete against
cross the finishing line

do sport
enjoy
football pitch

handball pitch

hockey pitch

VOCABULARY BANK

Translate the phrases into your own language.

ice rink _____
keep fit _____
kit _____
marathon _____
motor racing track _____

pathway _____
pitch _____
rugby pitch _____
running track _____
skateboard _____
skating rink _____

swimming pool _____
tennis court _____
unicyclist _____
volleyball court _____

work out _____

Health

Illnesses, symptoms and treatment

addictive _____
ambulance _____
be allergic to _____
be asthmatic _____
blood test _____
breathe in _____
breathe out _____
burn yourself _____
cardiologist _____
check your pulse/heart rate _____

come out in a rash/spots _____

condition _____
cough _____
cut something out _____
disease _____
do harm _____
drop _____
equipment _____
examine _____
feel dizzy _____
feel ill _____
feel sick _____
first aid _____
flu _____
get ill _____
go on a diet _____
headache _____
healthy _____
(make) healthy choices _____

(make) healthy decisions _____

heart attack _____

hospital _____
hurt _____
indigestion _____
keep track of _____
lie down _____
look after _____
lose one's appetite _____

lose weight _____
make an appointment _____

my back hurts _____
my head hurts _____
my thumb hurts _____
pain in the chest _____

pain in the leg _____
pain in the shoulder _____

pass out/faint _____
physiotherapist _____

prescription _____
recover from/get over an illness _____

reduce anxiety _____
reduce stress _____
runny nose _____
sore throat _____
stomachache _____
suffer from _____
take somebody's temperature _____

Science and technology

Electronic devices and IT technology

broadband _____
crash _____
desktop computer _____

digital _____
download music _____
e-book _____
e-ink _____
e-reader _____
electronic _____
go dead _____
keyboard _____
laptop _____
laser printer _____
mobile (phone) _____
mouse _____
password _____
screen _____
search engine _____

smartphone _____
tablet _____
text message _____
text somebody _____

update your profile _____

username _____
virus _____
visit a website _____

web browser _____

Scientific discoveries

analysis _____
ancestor _____
archaeology _____
astronomy _____
black hole _____
chemistry _____
collect evidence _____
come up with _____

discover _____
discovery _____
do research _____
environment _____
evolution _____
exploration _____
explore _____
figure out _____
find a solution _____
geology _____
gravity _____
imagination _____
imagine _____
mathematics _____
observation _____
observe _____
physics _____
planet _____
researcher _____
science _____
scientist _____
solution _____
solve _____
space _____
technology _____

The natural world

Landscape

cave _____
coast _____
crater _____
dense rainforest _____
desert _____

dry _____
hill _____
hot springs _____
humid _____
island _____
lush _____
mountain _____
river _____
rock _____
soil _____
vegetation _____
volcanic _____
volcano _____

Animals and plants

camel _____
plant _____
shell _____

The weather

average temperature _____
_____
below zero _____
boiling _____
chilly _____
cold _____
degrees centigrade _____
_____
fall _____
freezing _____
hot _____
minus 25 degrees _____
plus 25 degrees _____
rise _____
scorching _____
warm _____

Environmental protection

(air) pollution _____
air purifier _____
at risk _____
blow out _____
construct _____
construction _____
constructive _____
dust storm _____
environmental protection _____
_____
exhaust fumes _____
face mask _____
factory smoke _____
global warming _____
permanent _____
pollute _____
protect the environment _____
_____
pure _____
purification _____
purify _____

recorded _____
_____
run a research station _____
_____
save _____
smog particle _____
waste _____

State and society

Social groups and issues

abandon _____
background _____
capital (city) _____
charity _____
citizen _____
civil rights _____
community _____
developing country _____
_____
donation _____
foreign country _____
immigrant _____
increase _____
manifesto _____
member _____
nationwide _____
nomadic tribe _____
old people's home _____
_____
peace _____
population _____
relevant _____
royal family _____
soup kitchen for homeless people _____
_____
voluntary work _____
volunteer _____

The problems of the modern world

bully _____
homeless _____
identity _____
poor _____
prison _____
tell lies _____
thirsty _____
unemployment _____

VOCABULARY BANK

Culture of English-Speaking Countries

Adele (Adele Laurie Blue Atkins) a contemporary British pop singer

Aguilera, Christina an American pop singer and songwriter

Amazon an American dot-com established in Seattle in 1994 focusing on e-commerce; It owns the biggest on-line shop in the world.

American civil rights movement a social movement popular in the USA in the 50's and 60's of the 20th century; It aimed at abolishing racial segregation in the US using peaceful methods.

Bath a town in England famous for its numerous monuments, which include the Roman Baths

Batman a fictional superhero appearing in a series of comic books and many film adaptations

the BBC (The British Broadcasting Corporation) the main British public radio and television broadcaster

Bezos, Jeff the founder, Chief Executive Officer and president of Amazon.com

Bond, James a fictional agent working for the British Secret Service who appears in many novels by Ian Fleming as well as a series of films starring various actors, most recently Daniel Craig

Branson, Richard a British businessman and founder of Virgin Group

the Brit School (The BRIT School for Performing Arts and Technology) a British secondary school which provides education and training for young people interested in a career in the arts, entertainment and communications industries

Cambridge University the second oldest university in Great Britain, the first being Oxford University

Camden Market a famous market located in one of London's districts

Captain America a fictional character who appeared in numerous comic books published by Marvel Comics and many film adaptations

Carey, Mariah an American singer, composer, songwriter who is well-known for her extraordinary voice of a five-octave range

Central Park a park in New York City located in the centre of Manhattan

Coober Peddy a town in South Australia which is often called the 'opal capital of the world'; it is because of the mines where the most precious and expensive opals are found

Cyrus, Miley an American actress, singer and songwriter

Darwin, Charles a British naturalist, biologist and geologist; he is well-known for his book *The Origin of Species* and the scientific theory of evolution by natural selection

DiCaprio, Leonardo an American actor; he won an Oscar in 2016

Edinburgh the capital of Scotland

Edinburgh Castle a castle in Edinburgh; it is one of the oldest fortresses in Great Britain

the FA Cup (The Football Association Challenge Cup) a football competition which takes place in England every year; it is the oldest national football competition in the world

Glastonbury Festival one of the biggest festivals of performing arts and music in the world; it is organised near the village of Pilton in Somerset, England

Grandin, Temple an American psychologist and professor of animal science at Colorado State University; she is one of the first autistic people who has a successful professional career and is able to share insights from her autistic experience; she is known as a speaker on animal welfare and autism

Harry Potter a series of very popular fantasy novels about the adventures of a young wizard, Harry Potter, written by J. K. Rowling

Hidden Figures an American film from 2016 directed by Theodore Melfi

Hubble, Edwin an American astronomer

Hulk a fictional superhero and Bruce Banner's alter ego, who appears in numerous comic books published by Marvel Comics and many film adaptations

Humans a science fiction TV series produced in the USA and the UK

Iron Man a fictional superhero and Tony Stark's alter ego, who appears in numerous comic books published by Marvel Comics and many film adaptations

Jackson, Michael an American musician, dancer, composer, singer, songwriter and entertainer who is often called the 'King of Pop'

Jessie J a contemporary British pop singer

Johnson, Katherine an African-American mathematician, also known as 'human computer'; Her work contributed greatly to the development of NASA's Space Shuttle Programme.

Knightley, Keira a British actress who was nominated for an Oscar for her role in the film *Pride and Prejudice*

Lake District Cumbria a region in the county of Cumbria in England; The Lake District National Park is located in its central part.

Lake Windermere a lake in the Lake District National Park

Leibovitz, Annie an American portrait photographer who has received many prestigious photography awards

Lewis, Leona a British singer, songwriter and composer who was the winner of the third series of *The X Factor*

the London Dungeon an interactive museum in London where infamous historical events from the British history are recreated with the help of actors and special effects

the London Eye an observation wheel located by the River Thames from which it is possible to see the panoramic view of London; It was opened in 1999.

Madame Tussauds a museum of wax figures in London

Manhattan the smallest and the most populated district of New York City located on the island of Manhattan; the name of a county in the state of New York

Massachusetts Institute of Technology (MIT) a private polytechnic university founded in the USA in 1861; It is located in Cambridge, Massachusetts.

Muamba, Fabrice a retired English football player who moved to England at the age of 11 from the Democratic Republic of the Congo

The Musketeers a British TV series – an adaptation of the novel *The Three Musketeers* by Alexander Dumas

NASA   National Aeronautics and Space Administration) an agency of the US Federal Government, which is responsible for the space exploration programme

National Museum of Scotland   a museum located in Edinburgh; It houses the collections of Scottish antiquities, culture and history as well as science and technology, natural history and world cultures.

National Portrait Gallery   an art museum in London

Newton, Isaac   an English physicist, mathematician, astronomer, philosopher, historian and theologian

Obama, Barack   an American politician; he was the 44th president of the USA (2009-2017)

Obama, Michelle   First Lady of the USA (2009-2017); She is a lawyer and married to Barack Obama, ex-president of the USA.

Oliphant, Sarah   a backdrop painter who creates scenic backdrops for top photographers, film producers and fashion designers

the Oscars   the Academy Awards which are given by the Academy for Motion Picture Arts and Sciences every year to recognise achievements in the film industry

the Oscars ceremony   an event organised by the Academy for Motion Picture Arts and Sciences every year; During the ceremony, Oscars are given to the winners in 24 film categories.

Oxford Street   the main shopping street in London

Phelps, Michael   an American swimmer, 23 times Olympic champion, 26 times world champion

Pirates of the Caribbean   a series of American adventure films

Queen Elizabeth II   the head of the British Royal Family, who has been the Queen of the United Kingdom since 1953

the Roman Baths   a site located in Bath; it includes buildings which were used for public bathing in the Roman times

Rowling, J.K.   a British writer and author of the *Harry Potter* series of novels

the Royal Family   Queen Elizabeth II and members of her close family

Sally Lunn bun   a type of sweet cake; it is the specialty of the town of Bath

Science Museum   a museum in London

Scotland   a country located to the north of England; It is part of the United Kingdom of Great Britain and Northern Ireland.

Scottish   coming from Scotland

Segregation   legally approved racial separation of people into 'colored' and 'white' in the USA until the middle 60's

Shakespeare, William   an English playwright, poet and actor; he wrote plays, such as *Hamlet, Macbeth, Romeo and Juliet* and *A Midsummer Night's Dream*

Shakespeare's Globe   a theatre in London; It is a contemporary reconstruction of the Globe Theatre from Queen Elizabeth I and Shakespeare's time.

Somerset   a county in South West England

Sparrow, Jack   the main character of a series of adventure films, *Pirates of the Caribbean*, who is played by Johnny Depp

Spiderman   a fictional superhero and Peter Parker's alter ego, who appears in comic books published by Marvel Comics and in many film adaptations

Star Wars   a famous series of science fiction films

Superman   a fictional superhero and Clark Kent's alter ego, who appears in comic books and film adaptations

Tate Modern   a British national gallery of international contemporary art in London

Thriller   Michael Jackson's 6th solo album, which is the bestselling album in history

Turing, Alan   a British mathematician, cryptoanalyst; he is considered to be the father of theorethical computer science and artificial intelligence

Twitter   a social networking site

the UK   the United Kingdom of Great Britain and Northern Ireland

War Horse   a war film directed by Steven Spielberg which was produced in the USA and the UK

Watson, Emma   a British actress and model who first appeared in the *Harry Potter* film series

Welsh   coming from Wales

Wonder Woman   an American action film inspired by a series of comic books about a female superhero

The X Factor   a reality TV programme whose aim is to find singing talents

The X-Files   a very popular American TV series including elements of horror, thriller, drama, mystery and supernatural

The X-Men   a group of fictional superheroes who appear in comic books published by Marvel Comics and in film adaptations by Marvel Studios

PEOPLE

1 Complete the descriptions with words from the box.

> adventurous ambitious brave caring
> cheerful communicative confident creative
> ~~energetic~~ generous hard-working imaginative
> impatient independent irresponsible lazy
> lonely outgoing protective quiet reliable
> rude selfish sensitive

Aries: You are full of energy. _energetic_
But you never feel like working.
¹ _____

Taurus: You will leave a young child alone near
a swimming pool. ² _____
But when the child falls into the water, you will
rescue him. ³ _____

Gemini: You are always smiling and happy.
⁴ _____
You don't need help or advice from other
people. ⁵ _____

Cancer: You easily get upset and embarrassed when
people criticise you. ⁶ _____
But you often make people angry by saying
something impolite. ⁷ _____

Leo: You always want to try new and exciting
things. ⁸ _____
It is very difficult for you to wait for things.
⁹ _____

Virgo: You take hot soup to your grandmother when
it's cold. ¹⁰ _____
You never stop believing in your own abilities.
¹¹ _____

Libra: You are always ready to find an original
solution to a problem. ¹² _____
You don't say much. ¹³ _____

Scorpio: You don't take a break until the job is finished.
¹⁴ _____
You find it easy to talk and explain things to
people. ¹⁵ _____

Sagittarius: You always buy great birthday presents.
¹⁶ _____
You like meeting new people and talking to
them. ¹⁷ _____

Capricorn: You want to be successful, rich and powerful.
¹⁸ _____
People can trust you. ¹⁹ _____

Aquarius: You think about yourself but not about how
other people feel. ²⁰ _____
You have no friends. ²¹ _____

Pisces: You can make a wonderful meal out of the last
three things in the fridge. ²² _____
You like to take care of other people.
²³ _____

HOME

1 Match the types of houses with their definitions.

studio apartment ☐h
1 cottage ☐
2 detached house ☐
3 bungalow ☐
4 houseboat ☐
5 semi-detached house ☐
6 terraced house ☐
7 a block of flats ☐

a a house in a line of houses joined together
b a house with only one floor
c a large building with many levels, in which there are
many separate flats/apartments
d a small house in the country
e a house which is not joined to another house
f a house joined to another house on one side
g a house on water
h a small flat with one main room

2 Choose the correct answer.

The place in the house which is below the ground
floor is called a
A shed. (B) basement. C toilet.

1 The piece of furniture you sit on is a
A cooker. B beanbag. C wardrobe.

2 To reach high places, you climb a
A desk. B bookcase. C ladder.

3 A couch is a kind of
A furniture. B material. C wall.

4 You use a vacuum cleaner to clean
A the dishes. B the carpet. C the windows.

5 To keep food cool you put it in the
A library. B couch. C fridge.

6 A wardrobe is a large
A storage area. B lamp. C armchair.

7 To make your couch more comfortable and
decorative, you use
A sheets. B cushions. C posters.

8 To be able to read in the evening, you turn on
A a cupboard. B a ladder. C a lamp.

9 You enter the building through the
A interior wall. B front door. C fridge.

10 The soft cover on your floor is called a
A floorboard. B blind. C carpet.

11 You wash the dishes in the kitchen
A sink. B cupboard. C washing machine.

12 The ceiling is the part of a room
A under your feet. B above your head.
C where you hang pictures.

13 Before you go to bed, it needs a clean
A ceiling. B sheet. C floor.

14 A piece of furniture with open shelves is called a
A cooker. B cupboard. C bookcase.

SCHOOL

1 Match the words to make expressions. You can use some of them more than once.

attend — *i*

1 take — — | a homework
2 fail — — | b good grades
3 drop — | c a subject
4 graduate — | d from university
5 get — — | e lessons
6 learn — — | f a break
7 skip — — | g an exam
8 pass — — | h a degree
9 do — — — | i by heart
| j school

2 Tick (✓) the true and cross (x) the false sentences. Correct the false sentences.

A gap year is a break between primary school and secondary school. [x]

A gap year is a break between secondary school and college or university.

1 A timetable is a list of the times when classes in school happen. ☐

_____

2 Learning by heart means memorising. ☐

_____

3 An entrance exam is an exam you have to take at the end of your education. ☐

_____

4 A tuition fee is the money you pay for college or private school. ☐

_____

5 A swipe card is a special plastic card that you use to get into a building or open a door. ☐

_____

6 A field trip is a trip to a field. ☐

_____

3 Complete the sentences with the words from the box. There are two extra words.

> classmate   degree   canteen   knowledge
> term   nursery   ~~Science~~   single-sex

What did you do in your *Science* class today?

1 _____ schools are only for girls or only for boys.

2 We have lunch at the _____ .

3 A _____ is one of the periods of time the school year is divided into.

4 A _____ is a place where parents leave their small children when they go to work.

5 When you pass an exam at the end of university, you get a
_____ .

WORK

1 Complete the names of jobs with the missing letters.

'Some people think it's an unimportant job, but in my case it's just the opposite – it seems I'm responsible for everything – phone calls, emails, my boss's coffee and even Christmas presents for his wife ...' **s** *e c r e t a r y*

1 I've always been good at numbers, but it is not what people think: it's not that you only have to count in this job. Calculators and computers count, but we use intelligence to make good business decisions.'
a _ _ _ _ _ _ _ _

2 'I make people happy in my job. My clients are usually women. I make their skin look younger and healthier. I also paint their nails and put their make-up on before a special occasion like a wedding or New Year's Eve party.' **b** _ _ _ _ _ _ _ _

3 'I need to make a good first impression, because I'm the first person the customers see when they enter the hotel. I greet the customers, answer phone calls and emails, do the paperwork and accept the payments.' **r** _ _ _ _ _ _ _ _ _ _

4 'People call me or visit my office when they want to buy, sell or rent a flat, a house or a piece of land. I help them find the best offer and negotiate the price. I don't have many clients in a month, but when I sell or buy a house for someone, I earn a lot.'
e _ _ _ _ _   **a** _ _ _ _

5 'My job is very stressful. I often go to conferences and have to speak in front of a lot of people. I change a person's words from one language into another when they speak. I never do it in writing because I think that's boring.'
i _ _ _ _ _ _ _ _ _ _

6 'I can work for a newspaper, a magazine, television or radio. I like my job because every day is different. I usually go to places where something interesting is happening and then write a news report. This means I have to travel a lot to collect information and then I work from home when I write.' **j** _ _ _ _ _ _ _ _

7 'Summer is a busy time for me. I work ten hours a day, seven days a week when it's warm and sunny. I spend the whole day at the beach and can sunbathe, which is great! But I can't fall asleep because I'm responsible for the lives of all the people swimming and playing in the water.' **l** _ _ _ _ _ _ _ _

2 Match the verbs and noun phrases from the box to make collocations. You can use some of them more than once.

> ~~badly-paid~~   a day off   a job   fired   from home
> in debt   a living   long hours   night shifts   overtime
> outside   self-employed   training   unemployed

1 be   *badly-paid* _____
2 do   _____
3 earn   _____
4 get   _____
5 make   _____
6 work   _____

FAMILY AND SOCIAL LIFE

1 Complete the letter with the correct words.

> Dear Amanda,
>
> I've got a problem and I don't know what to do.
> I can't adapt _to_ my new town. Everybody here
> ¹_____ time ²_____ somebody on Twitter,
> but I'm not inspired by social media. I don't get
> ³_____ with anyone! I've tried talking to a few
> boys, but we have nothing ⁴_____ common.
> They listen ⁵_____ hip hop all the time and
> ⁶_____ bungee jumping. They don't ⁷_____
> a good time doing jigsaw puzzles like me. What
> can I do? Please, help!
>
> Patrick

2 Choose the correct answer.

When you admire someone, it means that you
(A) like them because they have done something good.
B dislike them because they have done something bad.
C don't respect them.

1 When you text somebody, it means that you
A read what someone has written.
B send them a letter.
C send them a short message on your mobile.

2 When you stay up, it means that you
A wake up and leave the bed.
B don't go to bed.
C sleep upstairs.

3 When you come round, it means that you
A talk to people.
B visit people in their homes.
C move in a circle.

4 When you refuse to do something, it means that you
A say you won't do something for somebody.
B say you can do something for somebody.
C say you will do something for somebody.

3 Match the words to make expressions. You can use some of them more than once.

	get	[f]	a	time
1	come	☐	b	a party
2	have	☐☐	c	round
3	make	☐	d	a good time
4	spend	☐	e	a good impression
5	inspired	☐	f	by

FOOD

1 Complete the sentences with the correct words and phrases from the box.

> drinking water   herbal   local speciality
> meal   ~~mineral water~~

Don't drink cola – _mineral water_ is much healthier.
1 Fish and chips is a very popular type of _____ in the UK.
2 Paella is a _____ in Spain.
3 In the jungle, it's important to carry some _____ with you. Water from the muddy streams can be unsafe.
4 My family enjoys drinking _____ tea instead of black tea.

SHOPPING AND SERVICES

1 Complete the text with the correct words.

Yesterday, my mum gave me a shopping list and sent me to the nearest department _store_. She asked me to buy some birthday presents for my twin brothers and some food for the birthday party. I didn't want to go because I always buy things that aren't ¹_____ it and spend too much ²_____ unnecessary things. I prefer sitting at home at my computer and shopping ³_____ . When I was passing a clothes shop, I saw a beautiful dress ⁴_____ special offer, so I decided to try it ⁵_____ . Unfortunately, it didn't ⁶_____ me and the dress in my size was ⁷_____ of stock. On my way to the toy shop, I also had to pass a jeweller's. I saw a silver bracelet there which attracted my ⁸_____ . The price was reduced – I had never picked ⁹_____ such a bargain! I didn't have my ¹⁰_____ card with me, so I paid in ¹¹_____ with my mum's money. When I got out of the shop I realised it was almost closing time. I quickly bought some food from the shopping list and two toy cars for the boys. When my mum saw what I had bought, she was angry – the toys were broken and the food was past its sell-by ¹²_____ . I couldn't return the food or exchange the toys ¹³_____ something else because I hadn't kept the ¹⁴_____ . I had to apologise ¹⁵_____ the shopping mistake again and again!

2 Choose the correct answer.

When you complain,
A you are happy about something.
(B) you are unhappy about something.

1 When you get a refund,
A the shop gives you the money back.
B the shop offers you something at a reduced price.

2 When parts of something are missing,
A there are too many of them.
B there aren't enough of them.

3 When a price is competitive,
A it's higher than other prices.
B it's lower than other prices.

VOCABULARY BANK

TRAVELLING AND TOURISM

1 Choose the correct answer.

A place for someone to stay or live is called
A a host.   **B** a historic site.
C accommodation.

1 The part of a town next to the sea or river is called a
A chapel.   **B** waterfront.   **C** bridge.

2 A building with strong walls built in the past by a king is called a
A temple.   **B** castle.   **C** monument.

3 A road that is not very pleasant to use is
A rough.   **B** slum.   **C** enormous.

4 A place where you borrow books is called a
A theme park.   **B** post office.   **C** library.

5 A place where you go on holiday is called a
A harbour.   **B** tourist destination.
C tourist attraction.

6 A little gift that you buy during a holiday is called a
A must.   **B** memory.   **C** souvenir.

7 A very tall building that stands alone is called a
A stilt.   **B** tower.   **C** historic site.

2 Match the words to make expressions and then complete the sentences.

tourist   g   **a** view
1 traffic   **b** sunlight
2 turquoise   **c** ocean
3 breathtaking   **d** jam
4 historic   **e** monument
5 direct   **f** agent
6 travel   **g** highlight

A well-known *tourist highlight* in Scotland is Loch Ness.

1 The journey took us so long because of a huge _____ .

2 I will never forget the view of the greenish-blue _____ from my hotel window.

3 In the future, I'd like to see a _____ of the Namib Desert in southern Africa.

4 Palace of Versailles near Paris is a well-known _____ .

5 Tessa's hotel room was bright in the daytime although there was no _____ .

6 My _____ takes care of booking the flights.

3 Choose the odd one out.

carriage / ferry / aisle / car
1 backpacking / sailing / sightseeing / wedding
2 camera / view / nightlife / sight
3 tent / sailing / caravan / campsite
4 ruins / passenger / castle / museum
5 host / harbour / waterfront / bridge
6 aquarium / canal / ferry / attraction

CULTURE

1 Put the words in the box into the four categories. You can use some of them more than once.

acting   animation   biography   chapter
chat show   clip   comic book   documentary
editor   episode   exhibition   gig   movie
musical   news bulletin   novel   painter
play (noun)   poem   producer   reality show
script   sculptor   short-story   sitcom
soap opera   soundtrack   special effects
street art   symphony   talent show   the charts
vocal range   weather forecast

1 Things you can read: *short story,* _____
_____
_____
_____

2 Things you can watch/see: _____
_____
_____
_____

3 Things you can listen to: _____
_____
_____
_____

4 People: _____
_____
_____
_____

2 Complete the names of the film types.

a film about elves and dragons:
a **f***antasy* film
1 a series in which a detective solves a crime:
a **c**_____ drama
2 a film in which people live on Mars:
a **s**_____-**f**_____ film
3 a film in which there is a lot of singing and dancing:
a **m**_____
4 a film about funny people and humorous situations:
a **c**_____
5 a film about facts:
a **d**_____

3 Choose the correct adjective from the box to describe a book. There are three extra adjectives.

best-selling   complex   disappointing
engaging   entertaining   excellent   factual
imaginative   inspiring   moving

It's based on what really happened.   *factual*
1 It is bought by a lot of people.   _____
2 It is difficult to understand because it has a lot of details.   _____
3 It makes you feel strong emotions.   _____
4 It's full of new and interesting ideas.   _____
5 It's amusing and interesting.   _____
6 It's not as good as you expected.   _____

129

SPORT AND HEALTH

1 Match the words to make expressions and complete the sentences. There are three extra expressions.

skating	h	a track
1 keep	☐	b fit
2 running	☐	c aid
3 first	☐	d court
4 tennis	☐	e dizzy
5 hockey	☐	f pitch
6 feel	☐	h rink

1 When an accident happens, everyone should be able to give _____ .
2 There are two tennis players on the _____ .
3 You need to exercise regularly to _____ .
4 If you want to be a professional sportsperson, you need to practise running on a _____ .

2 Choose the correct answer.

Who doesn't work with the sick?
(A) spectator **B** nurse **C** surgeon

1 Which is not a person?
A referee **B** triathlete **C** bench

2 Which is a symptom?
A runny nose **B** ring **C** deaf

3 What do we need to buy some types of medicine?
A blood **B** aid **C** a prescription

4 Which doesn't mean the same as 'ill'?
A healthy **B** unhealthy **C** sick

SCIENCE AND TECHNOLOGY, THE NATURAL WORLD

1 Choose the correct form.

Archaeology /(Archaeologists) have just discovered some human bones in the ruins of the city.
1 *Biologist / Biology* is the study of life on earth.
2 Darwin collected evidence for *evolution / exploration*.
3 Authors use their *imagine / imagination* when they write.
4 The ship sank and the sea got *purified / polluted*.
5 Scientists *discover / discovery* new stars every day.
6 *Physics / Physicist* was my least favourite subject at school.
7 Before the scientists could decide how to cure the disease, they had to do a genetic *analyse / analysis* of the virus.

2 Complete the puzzle. What's the hidden word?

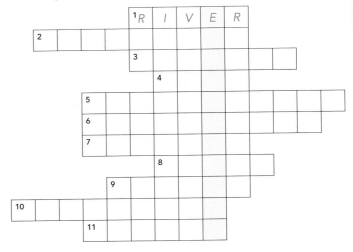

1 The Thames or the Nile
2 Very hot
3 The force that makes things fall to the ground
4 What plants grow in
5 A device that makes the air cleaner
6 A forest in a tropical area where it rains a lot
7 A mountain with a hole at the top, through which hot gases and lava are thrown out from time to time
8 Hot and wet (for example about air and weather)
9 The hole at the top of a volcano
10 Dangerous chemicals in the air or water
11 An area where there is almost no greenery and where temperatures are very high

3 Complete the sentences with the correct words.

A h<u>ill</u> is a small mountain.
1 A c_____ is a deep hole in a big piece of rock or a mountain.
2 A d_____ is some land with almost no plants and animals, where it rarely rains.
3 A r_____ is a large piece of stone.
4 An i_____ is a small piece of land in the sea.
5 A m_____ is some land that is much higher than the usual level of land.

4 Choose the correct answer.

A system of sending information online at a very high speed is called
(A) broadband. **B** a blog. **C** a desktop.
1 If your computer suddenly stops working, it has
A splashed down. **B** crashed. **C** tweeted.
2 If a camera records information in the form of numbers, it means it's
A technological. **B** electronic. **C** digital.
3 If a battery stops working and has no power, it's
A dead. **B** switched off. **C** scrolled down.
4 A secret group of letters or numbers is called (a)
A document. **B** e-ink. **C** password.
5 A special word that shows who you are and allows you to enter a computer system is called a/an
A search engine. **B** username. **C** icon.
6 When you add new information to your profile, you
A update it. **B** follow it. **C** download it.

5 Match the verbs with the nouns to make expressions.

make	f	a a research station
1 protect	☐	b research
2 run	☐	c evidence
3 find	☐	d the environment
4 do	☐	e a solution
5 collect	☐	f a discovery

6 Put the words from the box into the six categories. There are two words in each category.

> black hole   broadband   ~~camel~~   cave
> donkey   engineer   field   geologist
> keyboard   planet   screen   website

1 Animal: _camel_ _____
2 Computer equipment: _____ _____
3 Internet: _____ _____
4 Jobs: _____ _____
5 Landscape: _____ _____
6 Space: _____ _____

STATE AND SOCIETY

1 A politician is giving a speech. Complete the letters to make the missing words.

'Dear _c i t i z e n s_!

I'm making this speech because I feel that we need to change a lot for this ¹**c_ _ m _ _ _ _ y**. We should fight for the ²**c _ _ _ rights** of all our citizens if we have a chance to do so. Because everybody deserves to be fed, live in peace and have a job. There are a lot of people who are ³**a _ _ _ d _ _ _ d** and poor – they have nobody to help them. They need our ⁴**d _ _ _ t _ _ _ s** and care. Because if we have money and ⁵**v _ _ _ _ _ ee _** to do the work, we'll be able to build ⁶**s _ u _ kitchens** for ⁷**h _ _ _ _ _ s _ people** and help ⁸**i _ m _ _ _ a _ _ _** to become a part of our community. And we should do this!

2 Answer the questions.

What do you call someone who:
has no place to live in? _homeless_
1 works for free to help others? A _____
2 has left their country to live in another one? An _____
3 has no money? _____
4 belongs to a group? A _____

3 Match the words to make expressions.

nomadic	e	a country
1 developing	☐	b work
2 royal	☐	c rights
3 civil	☐	d family
4 voluntary	☐	e tribe

4 Match the words to make expressions.

foreign	f	a race
1 human	☐	b city
2 political	☐	c kitchen
3 old people's	☐	d home
4 soup	☐	e system
5 capital	☐	f country

5 Match the nouns from the box with the definitions. There is one extra word.

> background   bully   capital   charity
> community   donation   identity   lies
> manifesto   ~~market~~   peace   population
> prison   segregation   tribe   volunteer

An area where a country or company sells its products _market_
1 Things you say that are not true _____
2 The most important city in a country, where the country's government is _____
3 A large group of families with the same language, beliefs and customs _____
4 The number of people living in a country _____
5 An organisation which helps people in need _____
6 A formal statement of a political party _____
7 Someone's history – their family, education, work, etc. _____
8 The place where criminals are kept as a form of punishment _____
9 Someone who hurts people weaker than him/her _____
10 A time without wars _____
11 Who you are _____
12 Someone who does some work for free, to help others _____
13 A situation in which people have to live, work, study, etc. separately because of their race, sex or religion _____
14 The money you give to a person or organisation to help them _____

CULTURE OF ENGLISH-SPEAKING COUNTRIES

1 **Match the words to make the names of tourist attractions in the UK and then match them with their descriptions.**

Roman ⟨e⟩   a Castle
1 Madame ◯   b Dungeon
2 London ◯   c Street
3 Edinburgh ◯   d Tussauds
4 Oxford ◯   e Baths

  This is a public place for bathing located in one of the UK's cities and built by the ancient Romans. _Roman Baths_
1 This is a wax museum in London showing historical figures, film and sports stars and other celebrities. _____
2 This is an interactive museum of London's macabre history, with actors playing some of London's bad guys such as Jack the Ripper. _____
3 This is the busiest shopping street in Europe. _____
4 This is the most frequently visited paid tourist attraction in Scotland which is located on a volcanic hill. _____

2 **Complete the crossword. Then arrange the letters in the grey boxes to make the name of a city in the UK.**

1▶ B R O A D C A S T I N G

Across

1 The BBC is short for the British _Broadcasting_ Corporation.
2 Another name for the Academy Award.
3 The surname of the 44th President of the USA
4 The Queen and her relatives are the _____ Family.
5 The capital city of Scotland.
6 Connected with Scotland and people who live there.
7 The act and practice in the USA in the sixties of separating people into racial groups.
8 The well-known British author of _Romeo and Juliet_.

The city is __ __ __ __ __ __ .

Down

9 The well-known British band from Liverpool, that started their career in the sixties.
10 A wheel which is the most popular tourist attraction in the United Kingdom is called the London _____ .
11 The author of the _Harry Potter_ series.
12 One of the best-known markets in London is called the _____ Market.
13 The secret agent, code name 007.
14 Where you can see wax figures – Madame _____ .
15 The original language spoken in Wales.
16 English naturalist and biologist, known for his studies of evolution.

Present Simple and Present Continuous

We use the **Present Simple** to talk about:
- regular activities:
  *I often **go** to the gym.*
- states and permanent situations:
  *My uncle **lives** in Toronto.*
- preferences, with verbs like *love, hate, like, prefer, etc.*:
  *I **love** Chinese food.*

Affirmative			Negative	
I/You/We/They	run.		I/You/We/They	don't (do not) run.
He/She/It	runs.		He/she/It	doesn't (does not) run.

Yes/No questions			Short answers
Do	I/you/we/they	run?	Yes, I/you/we/they do. No, I/you/we/they don't.
Does	he/she/it	run?	Yes, he/she/it does. No, he/she/it doesn't.

Common time phrases in the Present Simple: *always, every day/week/year, never, often, on Sundays, sometimes, usually.*

We use *always, usually, often, sometimes* and *never*:
- after the verb *be*:
  *Tom is **usually** late to school.*
- before the main verb:
  *My dad **usually** reads at home.*

We usually use *every day, **every Sunday**, every weekend* at the end of the sentence:
My dad washes his car every Sunday.

We use the **Present Continuous** to talk about:
- activities taking place at the moment of speaking:
  *My grandfather **is sleeping**.*
- temporary situations:
  *I'm **saving** for a new game.*

NOTE: With some verbs (e.g. *like, hate, know, love, need, prefer, understand, want*) we don't use the Present Continuous:
*I really **don't understand** you.*

Affirmative			Negative		
I	'm (am)		I	'm not (am not)	
You/We/They	're (are)	running.	You/We/They	aren't (are not)	running.
He/She/It	's (is)		He/She/It	isn't (is not)	

Yes/No questions			Short answers
Am	I		Yes, I am. / No, I'm not.
Are	you/we/they	running?	Yes, you/we/they are. No, you/we/they aren't.
Is	he/she/it		Yes, he/she/it is. No, he/she/it isn't.

Common time phrases in the Present Continuous: *at present, at the moment, (right) now, these days, this morning/month/year/summer, today.*

1 Make positive sentences (+), negative sentences (–) and questions (?) in the Present Simple.

Monkeys / like / bananas (+)   *Monkeys like bananas.*

1 he / watch TV / in the evenings (+)
_____

2 my mother / drink / coffee (–)
_____

3 Donald / spend / Christmas / at home / every year (+)
_____

4 you / often / go / shopping (?)
_____

5 my aunt / work / at school (–)
_____

6 he / speak French (?)
_____

2 Complete the sentences with the Present Continuous forms of the verbs in brackets.

Andy *is looking* (look) at the watch now.

1 My mum _____ (have) lunch in the kitchen.

2 The cat _____ (run) round the garden.

3 He _____ (not/work) now, he _____ (swim) in the pool.

4 _____ you _____ (read) at the moment?

5 This summer my sister _____ (work) in a restaurant.

6 _____ your best friend _____ (laugh) now?

3 Complete the dialogue with the correct Present Simple or Present Continuous forms of the verbs in brackets.

A: Hi Louisa, what *are you doing* (you/do)?
   ¹_____ you _____ (watch) TV?

B: No, I'm not. You can turn it off.

A: Why ²_____ you _____ (pack) your bag?

B: I need to go. My friend ³_____ (wait) for me. Today we ⁴_____ (study) for the big test.

A: Oh, I see. Yes, you often ⁵_____ (have) tests at the beginning of the week.

B: Yeah. Before I go, I ⁶_____ (want) to talk to Jane. Where is she?

A: She ⁷_____ (play) in the garden.

B: Right. She always ⁸_____ (play) basketball after dinner. Anyway, I ⁹_____ (need) to go now. Please tell Mum that I ¹⁰_____ (study) with Steve.

A: You often ¹¹_____ (study) with Steve!

B: Erm, I have to go. Bye!

4 Put the words in the correct order to make questions in the Present Simple or Present Continuous. Make any changes if necessary.
Then ask and answer the questions in pairs.

Andy / watch / what / now
What is Andy watching now?

1 you / what / today / wear / ?

_____

2 live / your / near / school / ? / you

_____

3 what / like / ? / most / console games / you

_____

4 usually / what / you / for breakfast / ? / have

_____

5 book / you / ? / read / what / now

_____

6 to school / ? / wear / what / you / usually

_____

7 right now / ? / work / anywhere / you

_____

8 play / ? / the guitar / any of your friends

_____

5 Make sentences in the Present Simple or Present Continuous that are true for you, your family or friends. Use the words and phrases from the two boxes. Then make questions to compare your answers in pairs.

> always   at the moment   every day   never
> often   on Sundays   sometimes   this morning
> this summer   today   usually

> be late for school   get up early   go to the gym
> have a shower   help my parents at home
> play chess   post on Facebook   study a lot
> visit friends   watch TV   wear jeans
> work in a restaurant

I go to the gym every day.
Do you often go to the gym?

6 Complete the sentences with the words from the box. Then discuss the sentences in pairs.

> at   days   every   every day
> never   on   ~~usually~~

My sister *usually* helps our mum.

1 We often clean the bathroom _____ Saturdays.

2 My parents don't like rock music. They _____ go to concerts with me.

3 _____ the moment we are learning English.

4 My friend goes to school by bus _____ .

5 My mum is working a lot these _____ .

6 I watch my favourite TV show _____ Sunday.

Past Simple

We use the **Past Simple** to talk about finished actions in the past. We often say when they happened:
*My friend **went** to London last summer.*

Regular verbs

Most often: + *-ed*:
finish – finished

Ending in *-e*: + *-d*:
like – liked

Consonant +*-y*: *-ied*:
cry – cried

One vowel + one consonant:
double the consonant + *-ed*:
stop – stopped

Irregular verbs

e.g.
*become – became,
break – broke, buy – bought,
do – did, find – found,
go – went, have – had,
put – put, meet – met,
run – ran, say – said,
see – saw*

Affirmative

I/You/He/She/It/We/They	worked.

Negative

I/You/He/She/It/We/They	didn't (did not) work.

Yes/No questions

Did	I/you/he/she/it/we/they	work?

Short answers

Yes, I/you/he/she/it/we/they **did**.

No, I/you/he/she/it/we/they **didn't**.

Wh- questions

When **did** I/you/he/she/it/we/they **work**?

The Past Simple form of *be* is *was/were* and we do not use *did* in questions and negative sentences:

Were you at school yesterday?

The Past Simple form of *can* is *could* and we do not use *did* in questions and negative sentences:

Could you ride a bike when you were five?

Common time phrases in the Past Simple: *yesterday (morning/evening), in 2015, days/years ago, last night/week.*

1 Complete the sentences with the Past Simple forms of the regular verbs in brackets.

His father *worked* (work) yesterday.

1 His grandfather _____ (live) in Germany many years ago, but he _____ (not/work) there.

2 _____ you _____ (stay) long at the party on Saturday?

3 Caroline _____ (not/study) hard for the exam last week and she _____ (fail).

4 Jane's boyfriend _____ (stop) playing the piano when he _____ (start) high school.

5 I _____ (follow) his fanpage during his trip to Asia.

6 _____ he _____ (play) basketball yesterday?

2 Complete the sentences with the Past Simple forms of the irregular verbs in brackets and short answers.

I _sent_ (send) him a letter a week ago.

1 A: _____ you _____ any souvenirs when you _____ in England? (buy, be)
   B: No, I _____ . I _____ time. (not/have)

2 A: _____ you at the concert with Ben? (be)
   B: No, I _____ with Alan and Sue. (go)

3 A: Tina _____ her leg when she _____ in the Alps. (break, be)
   B: _____ she _____ to hospital? (go)
   A: Luckily, yes, she _____ .

4 A: _____ you _____ your keys yesterday? (find)
   B: Yes, I _____ . I _____ them in my bag. (find)

5 A: _____ Mr Kay _____ marathons when he _____ younger? (run, be)
   B: Yes, he _____ . He also _____ a lot. (swim)

6 A: _____ your brothers _____ when they _____ children? (fight, be)
   B: Yes, they _____ . My younger brother always _____ . (win)

7 A: _____ your primary school teachers nice to you? (be)
   B: Yes, they _____ . I _____ them a lot. (like)

8 A: _____ you _____ a nice present for your birthday? (get)
   B: No, I _____ a new dress but I _____ some books. (want, get)

3 Complete the story with the Past Simple forms of the verbs in brackets.

Alan's weekend

Last weekend, I _visited_ (visit) my grandparents. I ¹_____ (take) a train after school. It ²_____ (snow) a lot, so we ³_____ (want) to go skiing on Saturday. When I ⁴_____ (arrive), we all went to bed early. Unfortunately, I ⁵_____ (forget) to set the alarm clock and we didn't wake up on time. It ⁶_____ (be) already 10 a.m! We ⁷_____ (not/have) breakfast. We ⁸_____ (be) in a hurry because the weather ⁹_____ (be) fantastic and we ¹⁰_____ (want) to spend a lot of time outside. We ¹¹_____ (run) to the car and ¹²_____ (drive) to the slope. When we ¹³_____ (get) out of the car, my grandfather ¹⁴_____ (look) at the beautiful mountain and ¹⁵_____ (say): 'I love skiing. Let's start!' Then he ¹⁶_____ (turn) back. I ¹⁷_____ (can) see his face. It ¹⁸_____ (be) red. He ¹⁹_____ (start) to shout: 'Skis! Where are the skiis?' There ²⁰_____ (be) no skis. We ²¹_____ (not/pack) our skis. When we ²²_____ (come) home, we ²³_____ (have) warm tea and ²⁴_____ (laugh) a lot. The weekend was very funny!

4 Write questions in the Past Simple about the underlined parts of the answers.

They were at home at 5.
Where were they at 5?

1 Sophie went to a great party yesterday.
_____

2 He watched a comedy last night.
_____

3 My favourite subject at school was Science.
_____

4 Alice read more than fifty books last year.
_____

5 Sue's parents bought a big house in 2015.
_____

6 I didn't go shopping because I felt sick.
_____

7 Yesterday I sent more than fifty emails.
_____

8 My sister could swim when she was six.
_____

5 Make questions about the text in Exercise 3 in the Past Simple. Then ask and answer the questions about your weekend in pairs.

snow a lot / at the weekend / ?
Did it snow a lot at the weekend?

1 set / the alarm clock / on Friday / ?
_____

2 have / breakfast / on Saturday / ?
_____

3 be / the weather / nice / ?
_____

4 go / to the mountains / ?
_____

5 laugh / a lot / ?
_____

6 Put the prompts in the correct order to make questions in the Past Simple. Then ask and answer the questions in pairs.

last / good / a / night / watch / movie
Did you watch a good movie last night?

1 yesterday / what / school / to / wear / ?
_____

2 go / where / last / on / holiday / year / ?
_____

3 who / weekend / meet / at / the / ?
_____

4 what / yesterday / time / get / up / ?
_____

5 busy / be / Saturday / at / 6 p.m. / on / ?
_____

6 child / what / time / doing / in / be / your / like / free / when / you / a / ?
_____

7 night / what / last / do / ?
_____

8 like / school / primary / your / ?
_____

Present Perfect

We use the **Present Perfect** to talk about actions which finished in the past, but we don't know or it is not important exactly when they happened:

*Kate **has visited** Edinburgh.*

have/has + past participle of the main verb

Regular verbs	Irregular verbs
The same as the Past Simple forms + -ed	e.g. break – broken, buy – bought, do – done, find – found, have – had, put – put, meet – met, say – said

Affirmative		Negative	
I/You/We/They	've (have) worked.	I/You/We/They	haven't (have not) worked.
He/She/It	's (has) worked.	He/She/It	hasn't (has not) worked.

Yes/No questions			Short answers
Have	I/you/we/they	worked?	Yes, I/you/we/they have. No, I/you/we/they haven't.
Has	he/she/it	worked?	Yes, he/she/it has. No, he/she/it hasn't.

Wh- questions

Why have I/you/we/they worked?

Common time phrases in the Present Perfect:
ever (in questions), *never* (in negative sentences; remember not to use *never* and *not* together), *just* (in affirmative sentences), *yet* (in questions and negative sentences), *already* (in affirmative sentences).

*Have you **ever** been to Italy?*
*He has **never** tried onion soup.*
*We have **just** arrived.*
*Have you finished your dinner **yet**?*
*I have **already** seen this film twice.*

been to	gone to
We are no longer in the place: **Have** you **been** to Italy? Yes, I**'ve been** there twice.	We are still in the place: *Is Tom in? No, he isn't. He **has gone** to the library.*

1 Complete the sentences with the Present Perfect forms of the verbs in brackets.

I *have* already *finished* (finish) my homework.
1 I _____ (not/do) my homework yet.
2 What _____ you _____ (change) in your room?
3 We _____ already _____ (read) this article.
4 They _____ (be) to America twice.
5 _____ you _____ (water) the flowers?
6 _____ her sister _____ (cut) her hair very short?

2 Make questions in the Present Perfect. Then complete the short answers.

your dog / be / for a walk
Has your dog been for a walk? Yes, it has.
1 your parents / book / a trip to Asia
_____ Yes, _____
2 you / see / Mary
_____ Yes, _____
3 Mark / buy / a new bike
_____ No, _____
4 your best friend / try / kitesurfing
_____ Yes, _____
5 Fiona / go shopping
_____ Yes, _____

3 Write true affirmative or negative sentences about your partner. Use the Present Perfect and the phrases below.

see a movie more than three times
My partner has never seen a movie more than three times.
1 be camping
_____
2 write a poem
_____
3 sing in a karaoke bar
_____
4 ride a camel
_____
5 win a medal
_____
6 go bungee jumping
_____

4 Ask and answer the questions in Exercise 3.
A: Have you ever been camping?
B: Yes, I have.
A: Oh, I was wrong.

5 Use the words to make true sentences about someone you know. Use the Present Perfect, *never*, *yet* and *already*. Make changes if necessary.

book / a ticket online
My mum has never booked a ticket online.
1 take / the dog / for a walk
_____
2 eat / in / a Chinese restaurant
_____
3 bag / leave / at the airport
_____
4 go / to / a pyjama party
_____
5 fail / an exam
_____
6 talk / to / a famous actor
_____

be going to

We use **be going to** + infinitive to talk about intentions and plans which may change:

*My sister **is going to study** law.*

Affirmative				Negative			
I	am			I	'm not (am not)		
You/ We/ They	are	going to	run.	You/ We/ They	aren't (are not)	going to	run.
He/ She/ It	is			He/ She/ It	isn't (is not)		

Yes/No questions				Short answers
Am	I			Yes, I am. No, I'm not.
Are	you/ we/ they	going to	run?	Yes, you/we/they are. No, you/we/they aren't.
Is	he/ she/it			Yes, he/she/it is. No, he/she/it isn't.

Wh- questions

Why	am	I	going to	run?
	are	you/we/they		
	is	he/she/it		

1 Complete the sentences with *be going to* and the correct forms of the verbs in brackets.

She *is going to go* (go) to a concert on Saturday.

1 We _____ (visit) a lot of museums this summer.
2 _____ your brother _____ (watch) a football match tonight?
3 _____ we _____ (have) a break soon?
4 Sheila _____ (not/cook) dinner.
5 Donald _____ (spend) his holidays at home.
6 What _____ (you/do) after class?
7 I _____ (not/wait) for you any longer.

2 Complete the telephone conversation with the words and phrases from the box. There are two extra words.

> am   are (x2)   aren't   be   do   going
> I   is   isn't   not   to   you   we

M: Hi, Susan! It's Mary. How are you?
S: Hi, love! I'm good! I'm getting ready to go out for the concert. What <u>are</u> you going to do tonight?
M: I'm going ¹_____ go shopping with my sister.
S: Oh, great! Are you ²_____ to buy the new dress we talked about last week?
M: No, I'm ³_____ . My sister Sue ⁴_____ going to visit our aunt in Spain, and she needs some clothes.
S: Are ⁵_____ going to help her?

A: Yes, I ⁶_____ . ⁷_____ 'm also going to look for a pair of new shoes for her. What time are you going to ⁸_____ back from the concert?
M: ⁹_____ 're going to be back before 8 p.m.
S: ¹⁰_____ you going to take a taxi home?
M: No, we ¹¹_____ .
S: OK, have fun, Mary, and call me when you are back!
M: Sure! Bye!
S: Bye!

3 Complete the dialogues with *be going to* and the correct forms of the verbs in brackets.

A: Brian is poor at Maths. <u>Are you going to help</u> (you/help) him?
B: Of course <u>I am</u>!

1 **A:** _____ Neil _____ (be) at your wedding?
  B: No, _____ .
2 **A:** What _____ (he/do) with his old car?
  B: He _____ (not/sell) it. He _____ (keep) it in his garage.
3 **A:** _____ (they/stay) with us for dinner?
  B: No, _____ . They _____ (leave) early.

4 Make true sentences. Use *I'm going to* or *I'm not going to*.

I'm not going to stay for dinner.

1 _____ sleep after school.
2 _____ visit my dentist this month.
3 _____ have guests at the weekend.
4 _____ buy a new smartphone this year.
5 _____ do the shopping on Friday.
6 _____ be rich one day!

5 Ask and answer questions about the sentences in Exercise 4 in pairs.

A: Are you going to sleep after school?
B: Yes, I am.

6 Make questions with *be going to* and the words. Then ask and answer the questions in pairs.

what / study / ?
What are you going to study?

1 what / do / tomorrow / ?
_____
2 what / eat / tonight / ?
_____
3 where / travel / next summer / ?
_____
4 what / buy / at the weekend / ?
_____
5 visit a doctor / this month / ?
_____
6 start / a summer job / in July / ?
_____

137

FOCUS 1 GRAMMAR REVIEW

will for predictions

We use **will/won't** to make predictions based on our opinions, feelings or experiences:

*I think he **will finish** the test on time.*

Affirmative			Negative			
I/You/ He/She/ It/We/ They	'll (will)	change.	I/You/He/ She/ It/We/ They	won't (will not)		change.

Yes/No questions			Short answers	
Will	I/you/ he/she/ it/we/ they	change?	Yes, I/you/he/she/it/we/they will. No, I/you/he/she/it/we/they won't.	

Wh- questions

When will I/you/he/she/it/we/they change?

The future form of *can/can't* is *will/won't be able to*:
People will be able to travel fast.

We use **will** + *get/become* + comparative adjective to say that a situation is going to change:

*Food **will become** more expensive.*

1 Complete the sentences with *will* and the correct forms of the verbs in brackets.

There *will be* (be) taxis to the moon.

1 I hope tigers _____ (not/die) out.
2 _____ the icebergs _____ (melt)?
3 People _____ (not/use) mobile phones.
4 A lot of things _____ (not/change).
5 _____ oceans and lakes _____ (disappear)?
6 What _____ the cheapest means of transport _____ (be)?

2 Make predictions about fifty years from now. Use the future form of *can/can't* and the words below.

Robots can't think.

In fifty years, *robots will be able to think.*

1 We can't travel in time.
In fifty years, _____
2 People can't breathe under water.
In fifty years, _____
3 Scientists can't find a cure for cancer.
In fifty years, _____
4 We can't stop a hurricane.
In fifty years, _____
5 We can't see through walls.
In fifty years, _____
6 Cars can't fly.
In fifty years, _____

3 Make predictions about the year 2100 with *will + get/ become* + comparative adjective. Then discuss the predictions in pairs.

food / cheaper *Food will become cheaper.*

1 pollution / bad _____
2 petrol / expensive _____
3 schools / good _____
4 temperatures / high _____
5 intelligent technologies / popular _____
6 electric cars / available _____

4 Make predictions about your partner. Use *I think you will / I don't think you will.*

go to the USA *I think you will go to the USA one day.*

1 learn to speak Chinese

_____

2 be a famous actor

_____

3 write a book

_____

4 study with me at the same university

_____

5 live and work in a foreign country

_____

6 become the president

_____

7 live with your parents

_____

5 Make predictions about people's lives in 200 years. Write at least one sentence for each category. Then discuss the predictions in pairs.

Travel: *In 200 years, planes will not have pilots.*

1 Shopping

_____

2 Nature

_____

3 Free time

_____

4 Education

_____

5 Work

_____

6 Transport

_____

7 Food

_____

8 Family

_____

9 Health

_____

must, have to and should

We use **must** to express obligation and necessity; the speaker feels it is necessary or important:
*We **must** hurry.*

We use **mustn't** to express prohibition:
*We **mustn't** smoke here.*

We use **should/shouldn't** to give advice:
*You **should** drink it.*

Must, mustn't, should and *shouldn't* are modal verbs and have the same form for every person.

Affirmative			Negative		
I/You/He/She/It/We/They	must / should	go.	I/You/He/She/It/We/They	mustn't / shouldn't	go.

We use **have to** to talk about rules, regulations and orders from other people; it is necessary because of a rule or law or because somebody else says so:
*We **have to** wear uniforms.*

We use **don't have to** to say that something is not necessary (not *mustn't*):
*We **don't have to** get up early tomorrow.*

Affirmative			Negative		
I/You/We/They	have to	go.	I/You/We/They	don't have to	go.
He/She/It	has to	go.	He/She/It	doesn't have to	go.

Yes/No questions			Short answers
Do	I/you/we/they	have to go?	Yes, I/you/we/they do. No, I/you/we/they don't.
Does	he/she/it		Yes, he/she/it does. No, he/she/it doesn't.

Wh- questions

Why **do** you **have to** go? Why **does** she **have to** go?

1 Make questions with *have to* and the phrases below. Then ask and answer the questions in pairs.

parents / visit school regularly
Do parents have to visit your school regularly?
Yes, they do.

1 policemen / wear uniforms
_____

2 a secretary / be good at swimming
_____

3 a teacher / prepare for lessons
_____

4 students / pay for sandwiches in your school
_____

5 you / do your homework every day
_____

2 Your friend has some problems. Give him/her advice. Make sentences with *should/shouldn't* and the phrases in brackets.

'I have a problem with my computer.' (buy)
You should buy a new one.

1 'It's 8 o'clock. I will be late for school!' (hurry)
_____

2 'I have a terrible toothache.' (go to a dentist)
_____

3 'My school grades are poor.' (worry about your grades)
_____

4 'I don't have enough money to go on holiday.' (spend)
_____

5 'I am tired because I go to bed late every night' (go to bed early)
_____

3 Make sentences you would say to your little brother/sister. Use *must, mustn't* and the phrases below.

argue with Mum
You mustn't argue with Mum.

1 open the door to strangers
_____

2 go to bed before 9 p.m.
_____

3 go to school
_____

4 take my phone
_____

5 eat too much chocolate
_____

6 brush your teeth every day
_____

7 be nice to your friends
_____

4 Rewrite the sentences about rules in a library. Use *should, shouldn't, mustn't* and *have to*.

It is necessary to give books back on time.
You have to give books back on time.

1 It is necessary to be quiet.
You _____

2 If you are younger than eight, don't go there alone.
You _____

3 It's a good idea to listen to your friends' advice.
You _____

4 When you are at the library, don't speak.
You _____

5 It isn't a good idea to take more than two books at a time.
You _____

5 Make true sentences with *must*, *should* or *have to* in the correct form and the phrases below.

help my sister with her homework

I must help my sister with her homework.

1 do the washing up / every day

_____

2 go to bed / early

_____

3 my parents / go to work / every day

_____

4 go to school / on Saturday

_____

5 my best friend / be home before 10 p.m.

_____

6 cook / for my family

_____

7 go / to school / on foot

_____

6 Your friend wants to study at a very good university. Give him/her advice. Make sentences with *must*, *mustn't, have to, don't have to, should* and *shouldn't* and the phrases below.

You must study Maths. You don't have to be good at swimming.

1 study Maths/Biology/History/Geography/… a lot

_____

2 study at weekends/at nights

_____

3 be good at Biology/swimming/computers/Maths/ History/…

_____

4 be creative/well-organised/…

_____

5 do extra homework in …

_____

6 practise your English/German/… a lot

_____

7 be late for school

_____

8 be active during lessons

_____

9 party all night long

_____

10 read articles on foreign websites

_____

11 be interested in current affairs

_____

12 go to art galleries and museums

_____

Countable and uncountable nouns, articles

Countable nouns can be counted and have plural forms, e.g.: *banana, egg, bottle, girl.*

Uncountable nouns cannot be counted and do not have plural forms, e.g.: *milk, meat, cheese.*

With countable nouns we can use:

With uncountable nouns we can use:

Singular
- a / an
- the

Plural
- some / any
- how many, a lot of

- the
- some / any
- how much, a lot of

We use **some** with positive sentences and **any** with negative sentences and questions.

*There are **some** bananas on the table. Are there **any** eggs?*

***How many** bananas are there?*

*There are **a lot of** bananas left.*

*We don't have **any** milk but we have **some** cheese.*

***How much** milk is left?*

*There is **a lot of** meat on the plate.*

We use **a/an** with singular countable nouns when:
- we talk about a thing or a person for the first time: *There is **a banana** in the fridge.*
- when the thing or the person is one of many: *He is **a nice man.***

We use **the** with singular and plural countable nouns and with uncountable nouns when:
- we mention a thing or a person again: ***The banana** is fresh.*
- when something is specific and unique: *This pizza is the best in **the world.***

We do not use an article when:
- We talk about things in general: ***Bananas** are healthy.*
- We talk about days, months, cities and most countries, e.g. *August, Monday.*

1 Write C (countable) or U (uncountable) next to the words below.

girl   Ⓒ

1 banana   ☐

2 meat   ☐

3 water   ☐

4 tomato   ☐

5 egg   ☐

6 rice   ☐

7 bread   ☐

8 time   ☐

9 cherry   ☐

10 money   ☐

11 jam   ☐

12 butter   ☐

13 black pepper   ☐

2 Complete the questions with *how many* and *how much*.

How much milk do you drink a week?

1 _____ apples do you eat a week?
2 _____ juice is there in your fridge?
3 _____ tea do you usually drink a day?
4 _____ potatoes do you need for dinner?
5 _____ bread have you bought this month?
6 _____ bottles of ketchup do we need for the hotdogs?
7 _____ sugar do we have in the cupboard?
8 _____ hamburgers does he eat a month?

3 Complete the sentences with *a, an, some* and *any*.

There is *a* nice book on the shelf.

1 She always has _____ egg and _____ coffee for breakfast.
2 Adam wanted to make _____ cake, but there isn't _____ milk.
3 Look! There is _____ bottle of water on the floor.
4 There are _____ books on his desk.
5 Hi, Mum. Could you make _____ sandwich for me, please?
6 There isn't _____ cheese on the pizza.
7 There aren't _____ reporters in front of the house.
8 Is there _____ jacket in the wardrobe?

4 Complete the sentences with *a, an, the* and Ø (no article).

Ø London is beautiful.

1 It was _____ good day. We went shopping to _____ Leeds and bought _____ nice sofa.
2 There is _____ famous restaurant in my area. _____ restaurant serves tasty _____ Indian food.
3 Thanks, Mum. _____ sandwiches were delicious.
4 There is _____ very good school of English in _____ city centre.
5 He is _____ vegetarian and he doesn't eat _____ meat.
6 It is usually very hot in _____ Italy in _____ June.
7 She bought _____ packet of excellent _____ tea in _____ supermarket yesterday.
8 On _____ Monday, I am going to visit my _____ uncle who lives in _____ countryside and has a lot of _____ horses.

5 Complete the sentences with the words from the box.

> a   an   any   many   much   some   the

The baby wants *some* milk.

1 I don't want _____ soup. I don't like it.
2 How _____ carrots are there in the bag?
3 Brian's mum is _____ famous doctor.
4 How _____ chocolate do you want on your ice-cream?
5 Thank you! _____ meal was great!
6 There is _____ egg in the bowl.

6 Make questions with *how much* and *how many* and the phrases below. Then ask and answer the questions in pairs. In your answers, use *a, an, some, any, a lot of, the* and Ø (no article).

time / to get dressed / ?

How much time do you need to get dressed?

I need a lot of time to get dressed.

1 books / on your shelf / ?
_____

2 snow / outside / ?
_____

3 balloons / for your birthday party / ?
_____

4 shoes / in your wardrobe / ?
_____

5 homework / for tomorrow / ?
_____

6 films / a year / ?
_____

7 money / for the holidays / ?
_____

8 music / listen / ?
_____

7 Complete the sentences with *a, an, the* and Ø (no article). Then discuss the statements in pairs.

I love reading Ø books.

1 There are a lot of good shops on _____ main street in our _____ town.
2 Sopot Festival attracts a lot of famous _____ musicians. I want to go to _____ festival next year.
3 _____ dogs are great pets.
4 _____ chocolate is bad for you.
5 _____ women drive better than _____ men.
6 Yesterday was _____ great day.
7 I love watching _____ films. _____ film I watched last weekend was great.
8 I would love to visit _____ London in _____ summer.
9 _____ fast food is good for active people.
10 _____ one and only play I saw last year was interesting.
11 Mexican cuisine is _____ best in _____ world.
12 It's easier to concentrate at _____ night than in _____ morning.

Revision of tenses

We use the **Present Simple** to talk about: regular activities, states, permanent situations and preferences (with verbs like *love, hate, like, prefer*, etc.).

We use the **Present Continuous** to talk about: activities taking place at the moment of speaking and temporary situations. With some verbs (e.g. *like, hate, prefer, understand*) we don't use the Present Continuous.

1 **Make questions about the underlined parts of the sentences.**

She is waiting <u>for her boyfriend</u>.
Who is she waiting for?

1 Maria often goes <u>to the cinema</u>.
_____

2 We are drinking <u>coffee</u>.
_____

3 He trains every day <u>because he wants to become a professional footballer</u>.
_____

4 Her aunt visits her <u>twice a month</u>.
_____

5 I am reading <u>a great thriller</u> now.
_____

6 We live <u>in Italy</u>.
_____

7 Tom usually wears <u>black jeans</u> to school.
_____

8 He goes to the gym <u>on Mondays</u>.

9 Tim and Sue are revising for an exam <u>because they want to get good marks</u>.
_____

10 Sarah likes <u>vegetarian food</u>.
_____

2 **Complete the sentences with the verbs from the box in the correct form of the Present Simple or Present Continuous.**

be (x2)   eat   not be   not watch   play
revise   sleep   talk (x2)   watch   work

1 Sally *is* a doctor. She _____ in a hospital.
2 Her baby _____ in the bedroom right now.
3 At the moment, they _____ about the last exercise.
4 They often _____ comedies together.
5 The children _____ in the house. They _____ football outside.
6 Alex _____ the match now because he _____ for the test.
7 We _____ vegetarians. We never _____ meat.
8 I always _____ to my mum when I have a problem.

We use **be going to** and **will/won't to talk** about the future.

We use **be going to** + infinitive to talk about intentions and plans which may change.

We use **will/won't** to make predictions based on our opinions, feelings or experiences.

3 **Complete the sentences with the correct forms of the verbs in brackets. Use *will* or *be going to*.**

1 A: Why is Mum going out?
   B: She _____ (go) to the jeweller's. Perhaps she _____ (find) a nice watch there.

2 A: Jessica _____ (be) a model and she goes to the gym every day to keep fit. I think she _____ (be/good) at modelling. What do you think?
   B: Yes, I am sure, she _____ (be). _____ (you/be) a model too?

3 I don't like Mathematics. I _____ (not/study) it. What _____ (you/study)?

We use the **Past Simple** to talk about finished actions in the past. We often say when they happened. To make questions in the **Past Simple**, we **usually** use *did*.

However, the Past Simple form of *be* is *was/were* and then, we do not use *did* in questions and negative sentences.

4 **Make *yes/no* questions with the words from the box and the phrases below. Then, ask and answer the questions in pairs.**

a month ago   at the weekend   last week   last year
two days ago   yesterday   yesterday morning

go / you the library / ?
Did you go to the library yesterday?
Yes, I did.

1 watch / a good film / ?
_____

2 cook / your mum / ?
_____

3 go / to the party / ?
_____

4 learn / for the test / ?
_____

5 be / grandfather / on holiday / ?
_____

6 get / a present / for your birthday / ?
_____

7 get up / early / ?
_____

8 go / for a walk / ?
_____

9 meet / friends / ?
_____

10 buy / a great book / ?
_____

5 Write *wh-* questions for the sentences in Exercise 4. Use the words in brackets.

Did you go to the library yesterday? Yes, I did.
How many (borrow)
How many books did you borrow?
I borrowed five books.

1 What (watch)
_____

2 What (cook)
_____

3 How many people (be)
_____

4 How long (learn)
_____

5 Where (go)
_____

6 What present (get)
_____

7 What time (get up)
_____

We use the **Present Perfect** to talk about actions which finished in the past, but we don't know or it is not important exactly when they happened.

6 Complete the sentences with the words from the box.

been (x2)   ever   gone   has
have   just   never   yet

Has Megan *ever* been abroad?

1 My boyfriend has _____ taken me to the theatre.
2 We haven't finished this project _____ .
3 I have _____ made a huge mistake.
4 Your trousers are all dirty. Where have you _____ ?
5 They have never _____ to Rome.
6 _____ you tried skiing?
7 His parents have _____ to the UK. They are in London now.

7 Make short answers to the questions.

Do you like horror films?
Yes, I do.

1 Will people use pens in the future?
No, _____ .
2 Have you read his latest book?
No, _____ .
3 Does she often log in to this computer?
No, _____ .
4 Is he listening to the radio now?
Yes, _____ .
5 Has she opened the letter yet?
Yes, _____ .
6 Did you play the guitar when you were a child?
Yes, _____ .
7 Will there be books at schools in 2100?
No, _____ .

8 Make true sentences in the Present Perfect with the phrases below. Then compare the sentences in pairs.

the most expensive car / drive
The most expensive car I have ever driven is a Ferrari.

1 the best teacher / know
_____

2 the cheapest restaurant / eat
_____

3 the best song / listen to
_____

4 the most beautiful city / be
_____

5 the most expensive ticket / buy
_____

6 the best mobile app / use
_____

7 the best friend / have
_____

8 the most interesting book / read
_____

9 Complete the sentences with the correct forms of the verbs in brackets. Then change the underlined words and phrases to make true sentences about you, your family and friends.

They *drink* (drink) a lot of coffee every day.
My mum drinks a lot of coffee every day. I don't drink a lot of coffee every day.

1 I _____ (already/pass) the driving test.
_____

2 When I _____ (be) five, I _____ (read) a lot of books.
_____

3 My sisters often _____ (go) shopping for clothes.
_____

4 Susan _____ (spend) last weekend in the mountains.
_____

5 My father _____ (can/speak) two foreign languages when he finishes his language course next year.
_____

6 I _____ (use) a great app to learn English now.
_____

7 At the moment, I _____ (not/work) anywhere.
_____

8 John _____ (not/have) lunch yet.

1.2 Present tenses – question forms

1 Ask *yes/no* questions for the answers below.

1 _____ ?
   No, she doesn't enjoy cooking.

2 _____ ?
   Yes, he's studying for his exams.

3 _____ ?
   No, I have never met him.

4 _____ ?
   No, I don't like shopping.

5 _____ ?
   Yes, David has visited Paris and London.

6 _____ ?
   Yes, we go to the gym at the weekend.

7 _____ ?
   No, they aren't having dinner.

8 _____ ?
   Yes, they do aerobics twice a week.

2 Ask *wh-* questions for the answers below.

1 _____ ?
   Tom helps old people in the local area.

2 _____ ?
   Tom helps <u>old people in the local area</u>.

3 _____ ?
   I enjoy <u>music</u>.

4 _____ ?
   <u>Sue</u> is keen on music.

5 _____ ?
   I'm reading <u>a book by Stephen King</u> at the moment.

6 _____ ?
   <u>Sue</u> is reading a book by Stephen King at the moment.

7 _____ ?
   <u>Stephen King</u> wrote the book.

8 _____ ?
   I'm from <u>London</u>.

9 _____ ?
   I'm phoning <u>Sue</u>.

10 _____ ?
   The charity helping mothers with children is in <u>Africa</u>.

11 _____ ?
   <u>Frank</u> has borrowed this game from Lilian.

12 _____ ?
   Frank has borrowed this game <u>to play it with Alex</u>.

1.5 Verb + *-ing* form or *to* infinitive

3 Choose the correct forms.

1 Karen really enjoys *reading / to read* poetry.
2 Would you like *going / to go* to the cinema?
3 Pete can't stand *wearing / to wear* formal clothes.
4 We can't avoid *telling / to tell* him the truth.
5 I've decided *going / to go* abroad.
6 They can't afford *buying / to buy* this house.
7 I'd love *working / to work* in a clothes shop.
8 Do you ever miss *to go / going* surfing in summer?
9 Tim always manages *arriving / to arrive* at the office on time.
10 Have you ever considered *leaving / to leave* your country to live abroad?

Summative Practice Unit 1

4 Complete the sentences with one word in each gap.

1 _____ he work here?
2 What _____ she like doing at weekends?
3 _____ you ever seen that film?
4 _____ game is she playing?
5 I can't afford _____ buy a bike this year.
6 Who _____ reading a book by Dan Brown now?
7 What do you _____ during the weekend?
8 I hope _____ find a part-time job soon.
9 What _____ you doing at the moment?
10 _____ is sitting in that armchair? Your grandma?
11 We _____ not planning to visit Madrid this year.
12 What time _____ you get up on Sundays?

5 Find the mistakes and correct the sentences.

1 From where is Karen?
   _____

2 She'd like wearing a uniform.
   _____

3 Who like you?
   _____

4 How much time do he spend doing sports?
   _____

5 What you do after dinner?
   _____

6 They have ever given money to charity?
   _____

6 Complete the interview with David and Janet with the correct form of the verbs in brackets. Use the Present Simple, the Present Continuous, *-ing* form or *to* infinitive.

I: Hi, David, what do you like [1]_____ (do) in your free time?

D: I love [2]_____ (do) sports.

I: What sports [3]_____ (you/do)?

D: I really enjoy [4]_____ (play) basketball and volleyball.

I: How about you, Janet? [5]_____ (you/have) any hobbies?

J: Of course I do. I [6]_____ (play) the guitar. And I really like [7]_____ (listen) to music.

I: What about reading?

J: Well, yes, I don't mind [8]_____ (read), but I only [9]_____ (read) novels. I refuse [10]_____ (read) poetry.

I: Why is that?

J: Well, because you need [11]_____ (concentrate). And I want [12]_____ (relax) in my free time!

I: What [13]_____ (you/read) now?

J: I [14]_____ (read) a novel by Patricia Highsmith.

I: What about you, David?

D: Reading? I don't mind [15]_____ (read) novels, but I [16]_____ (not/read) much, I admit. I prefer social networking or [17]_____ (go) out with friends.

2.2 Past Continuous and Past Simple

1 Find the mistakes and correct the sentences.

1 When the fire-fighters were arriving, she was listening to music.

_____

2 I was having a shower when the phone was ringing.

_____

3 Susan was lying on the beach when she was hearing someone calling for help.

_____

4 What you were doing when the police arrived?

_____

5 I didn't work when you called me.

_____

2 Complete the dialogue with the Past Simple or the Past Continuous forms of the verbs in brackets.

A: Hello Sue. I ¹_____ (phone) you yesterday, but nobody answered. What ²_____ (you/do)? Were you at home?

B: What time ³_____ (you/phone)?

A: At four, I think.

B: Oh! I ⁴_____ (watch) a soap opera at that time. That's why I ⁵_____ (not/hear) the phone.

A: I ⁶_____ (call) you because I'm going to the mountains for the weekend. Would you like to come?

B: I'd love to, but I gave up skiing two years ago. I ⁷_____ (ski) a lot before the accident.

A: An accident? Oh dear! I ⁸_____ (not/know) about an accident! What happened?

B: I ⁹_____ (ski) down a slope when I ¹⁰_____ (collide) with another skier and I ¹¹_____ (break) my leg. Before the accident I ¹²_____ (be) very good at skiing!

2.5 Used to

3 Choose the correct forms. In two sentences, both forms are correct.

1 The children *didn't use to get up / weren't getting up* early.

2 I *used to work / worked* in a travel agency, but two weeks ago I managed to get a job in the media.

3 Last week I *bought / used to buy* a new tablet.

4 In those times, I *was going to / used to go* to Barcelona every summer.

5 I *used to go / went climbing* alone, but now I always climb with somebody else.

6 In 2015, George *went / used to go* to Africa for the first time.

Summative Practice   Units 1–2

4 Write *wh-* questions for the answers below using the question words in brackets.

1 We were watching a film when David arrived. (What)

_____

2 My cousins speak English. (Who)

_____

3 I speak French, German and English. (How many)

_____

4 Laura likes reading detective stories. (Who)

_____

5 Barbara enjoys swimming. (What)

_____

6 I've been to London and Paris. (Where)

_____

5 Complete the sentences with *used to* (where possible), the Present Simple, the Present Continuous, the Past Simple or the Past Continuous forms of the verbs in brackets.

1 Don't wait for Paul. He never _____ (come) home before 6 p.m.

2 He _____ (wait) for us when we _____ (arrive) last night.

3 I _____ (visit) my school website three days ago.

4 'What _____ (Paul/do) at the moment?' 'He _____ (work).'

5 '_____ (you/work) at the supermarket all day?' 'No, it's a part-time job.'

6 I _____ (work) in a supermarket, but now I work in a bank.

6 Complete the story with *used to*, the Present Simple, the Present Continuous, the Past Simple or the Past Continuous forms of the verbs in brackets.

It was a very stormy night near the end of November. Sherlock Holmes and I ¹_____ (read) by the fire. It was late, and most people ²_____ (be) in bed. Holmes put down his book, and said: 'I'm glad that we aren't going out tonight, Watson'. Just then we ³_____ (hear) a carriage stop outside the house. Someone ⁴_____ (get) out. I went to the window and ⁵_____ (look) out into the darkness. 'Someone ⁶_____ (come) here,' I said. Very soon we ⁷_____ (know) who our visitor was. It was Stanley Hopkins, a young detective from Scotland Yard. Holmes and I ⁸_____ (help) him in the past. 'Have you seen the newspapers this evening, Mr Holmes?', he asked. 'No,' said Holmes.

Hopkins said, 'The case is very new and the police at Yoxley ⁹_____ (investigate)'.

'Where is Yoxley?' I asked.

'It's in Kent,' he replied. 'It's a very small place. It looks like a difficult case. A man is dead, and I really ¹⁰_____ (not/know) why anyone wanted to kill him.'

From Sir Arthur Conan Doyle, The Return of Sherlock Holmes, simplified by Alan Pugh

3.2   Comparative and superlative adjectives

1 Complete the second sentence so that it means the same as the first.

1 Air travel is faster than any kind of transport.
Air travel is the _____ kind of transport.

2 This restaurant has better food than any other restaurant in the area.
This restaurant has the _____ food in the area.

3 Going to a concert is more exciting than going to the cinema.
Going to the cinema isn't _____ going to a concert.

4 I am better at Maths than any other subject.
Maths is my _____ subject.

5 James isn't as tall as Ben.
James is _____ Ben.

6 Mobile phones are much cheaper now than a few years ago.
Mobile phones used to be far _____ a few years ago.

2 Find the mistakes and correct the sentences.

1 *Star Wars* is further more exciting than *Game of Thrones*.
_____

2 My little sister is funnyer than my older brother.
_____

3 He's one of the more interesting characters I've ever seen on screen.
_____

4 *The Hobbit* is one of the worse books we read last year.
_____

5 This is the nicest book I ever read.
_____

6 Mont Blanc isn't high as Mount Everest.
_____

7 Colin Firth is more tall than Tom Cruise.
_____

3.5   Present Perfect with *just, already, (not) yet* and Past Simple

3 Complete the sentences. Use the Present Perfect or the Past Simple and the words in brackets.

1 I _____ (already/buy) tickets for the U2 concert. How about you?

2 A: ᵃ_____ (you/see) Margaret yet?
B: I ᵇ_____ (just/say) goodbye to her. She ᶜ_____ (be) in the hall downstairs.

3 A: Guess what!
B: I know, you ᵃ_____ (just/win) a million dollars.
A: Sounds good! Actually, I ᵇ_____ (buy) a lottery ticket last weekend but I ᶜ_____ (not/hear) about my win yet. Anyway, I ᵈ_____ (talk) to Jim the other day and ᵉ_____ (invite) him to the party. He ᶠ_____ (be) surprised but more than happy.

Summative Practice   Units 1–3

4 Choose the correct forms.

1 What *do / does* he want to be?
2 Who are you working *at / with*?
3 Kate doesn't mind *to get up / getting up* early.
4 When we got up, the sun *shone / was shining*.
5 She used to *working / work* for the BBC.
6 He hasn't finished his homework *already / yet*.
7 John *has joined / joined* the football club two weeks ago.
8 He's *the youngest / younger* in his class.

5 Complete the dialogue. Use the correct tenses of the verbs and the correct comparative or superlative forms of the adjectives.

A: I ¹_____ (just/be) to the movies.
B: Really? What ²_____ (you/see)?
A: I ³_____ (see) Steven Spielberg's last film. ⁴_____ (you/see) it?
B: No, I ⁵_____ . What is it like?
A: I think it's his ⁶_____ (good) film. Have you been to the movies recently?
B: No, I haven't. But I ⁷_____ (watch) *The King's Speech* on TV last night. It's one of the ⁸_____ (interesting) films I ⁹_____ (ever/see).
A: Oh, I prefer films with lots of action. I think historical dramas are boring. They are certainly ¹⁰_____ (boring) than adventure stories.

6 Complete the text with *used to* (where possible), the Present Simple, the Present Perfect, the Past Simple or the Past Continuous of the verbs in brackets.

I ¹_____ (always/enjoy) going to the mountains. When I was a child, I ²_____ (go) to the mountains with my dad. Now I ³_____ (go) to the mountains with my son. We usually ⁴_____ (go) for long summer walks. Last year we ⁵_____ (go) to the French Alps. One day, we ⁶_____ (walk) along the path that led to our mountain chalet when it ⁷_____ (begin) to rain. It was a real mountain storm, with thunder and lightning. My son ⁸_____ (be) really frightened. When we ⁹_____ (get) to the chalet, we were completely wet. But it ¹⁰_____ (be) nice and warm inside, and we ¹¹_____ (have) a wonderful dinner with soup and cheese. Then we ¹²_____ (go) to bed. The next day we ¹³_____ (walk) back to the village when my son ¹⁴_____ (ask) me about our next trip. We ¹⁵_____ (just/decide) on our next mountain walk. It's Ben Nevis next time.

4.2 Present Perfect with *for* and *since*

1 Ask questions for the answers below.

1 _____ ?
We have known each other <u>since we were children</u>.

2 _____ ?
Shannon has been in the waiting room <u>for two hours</u>.

3 _____ ?
<u>Michael</u> has had this Jaguar for more than a decade.

4 _____ ?
The Smiths have lived <u>in this building</u> since they came to our town.

5 _____ ?
Adam has had this book <u>since his 10th birthday</u>.

2 Complete the second sentence so that it means the same as the first. Use the words in brackets in the correct form and any other words you need.

Today is Monday, 25 June

1 Anne arrived here on Saturday.
Anne _____ (be/here) _____ days.

2 It hasn't stopped raining for two hours.
It _____ (start raining) _____ ago.

3 We bought the new computer for the children yesterday.
The children _____ (have/the new computer) _____ yesterday.

4 I fell in love with this song when I heard it at the party last Friday.
I _____ (love/this song) _____
I heard it at the party last Friday.

5 Our parents have known each other since Christmas Day last year.
Our parents _____ (meet/the first time) _____ ago.

4.5 Present Continuous, *be going to* and *will*

3 Choose the correct forms.

1 We had a discussion and we've decided we *are not going to / will not* attend the meeting.

2 Don't worry. *I'll phone / I'm phoning* to tell you the news.

3 Wait a moment! *I'll help / I'm going to help* you.

4 What *are you doing / are you going to do* after high school?

5 We *leave / are leaving* from the school at nine.

6 What time *will you meet / are you meeting* them tomorrow?

7 *We're meeting / We meet* at four at Ken's today because he needs to go out at seven.

8 I'm bored. I think *I'm going to make / I'll make* a cake.

4 Find the mistakes and correct the sentences.

1 'Who Emma likes?' 'She likes Tim.'
_____

2 'Who does like Emma?' 'Paul likes Emma.'
_____

3 On what singers are you keen?
_____

4 I don't mind to study after dinner.
_____

5 I walked along the mountain path when you were phoning me.
_____

6 The Petersons used to move out of that house only a few months ago.
_____

5 Complete the sentences with *be going to, will*, the Present Continuous or the Present Perfect forms of the verbs in brackets.

1 I promise I _____ (send) you a message when I get there.

2 Mr Jenkins _____ (live) in this house since he was born.

3 _____ (Pat/organise) a party for her birthday next week?

4 How long _____ (you/know) your coach?

5 Pete _____ (know) his best friend since they were in primary school together.

6 OK, I _____ (go) for a short walk with you.

7 Buster, our dog, _____ (be) with us for ten years now.

6 Choose the correct forms.

A: We [1]*are going / will go* camping in the Lake District this weekend. What [2]*are you doing / will you do*?

B: I [3]*'m going to stay / will stay* at home. I have plenty of work to do.

A: [4]*Have you ever been / Did you ever go* there?

B: Yes, I have. I [5]*used to go / was going* there with my dad.

A: When [6]*have you / did you* last go?

B: We last [7]*went / have been* there five years ago.

A: Where [8]*did you use to go / were you going*?

B: We [9]*used to go / have been* to Lake Windermere. But we also [10]*have been / used to go* climbing. Once we [11]*climbed / used to climb* Scafell Pike. Scafell Pike is the Lake District's [12]*higher / highest* mountain. I remember we [13]*were climbing / climbed* when all of a sudden the weather [14]*changed / was changing*. It got really foggy, but eventually Dad [15]*found / has found* the way down. We were lucky.

A: What a pity you [16]*aren't coming / don't come* along with us!

B: Well, I promise I [17]*come / 'll come* with you next time you go. I [18]*haven't been / didn't go* to the Lake District [19]*for / since* that time and I really miss the place.

A: Don't worry, next time we go, we [20]*are letting / 'll let* you know!

5.2 First Conditional

1 Complete the sentences with the correct form of the verbs from the box.

enjoy   go (x4)   like   listen   meet   visit

1 Australia is the country I would like to visit if I _____ abroad.

2 If you _____ thrillers, you _____ the book I gave you.

3 If you _____ to the party, you _____ Lisa, the girl that paints beautiful pictures.

4 If Joe _____ to Stratford-upon-Avon, he _____ Shakespeare's birthplace.

5 If you _____ to the concert, you _____ to the winner of the *X Factor* competition last year.

2 Choose the correct forms.

1 If it *don't / doesn't* rain, we *go / 'll go* to the beach.

2 Jenny and I *won't go / don't go* for a walk in the park if it *snows / will snow* as heavily as now.

3 If Jan *will call / calls*, I *won't / don't* answer.

4 If Tim's brother *won't / doesn't* go to university, he *works / 'll work* in his uncle's office.

5 The workers *will protest / protest* if the negotiations between the management and the employees *will break down / break down*.

5.5 Defining relative clauses

3 Match the items from the box to the definitions. There are three extra items.

chemist   password   sale   sculpture
shelves   sitcom   USB port   wardrobe

1 This is a large piece of furniture where you keep your clothes. _____

2 This is a person who works in a laboratory. _____

3 This is something which helps to keep your data safe. _____

4 This is a TV programme that makes you laugh. _____

5 This is a time when there are reductions in the prices of many items in shops. _____

4 Complete the sentences with the missing relative pronouns. Sometimes there is more than one answer.

1 I will never forget the town _____ we had our motorcycle accident.

2 Did you talk to Marty about the book _____ the teacher asked us to read?

3 A: Do you know the woman _____ is smiling at us? B: Yes, that's my mum.

4 That's the boy _____ found the wallet.

5 The young man _____ lives next door is a police officer.

6 This is the place _____ I first met your father.

Summative Practice   Units 1–5

5 Match phrases 1–7 with a–g to form sentences.

1 If my mum doesn't agree,
2 A flexible school is a school
3 You'll get a much better job
4 India is a part of the world
5 I like talking to people
6 If you don't study hard,
7 This is the book

a who travel a lot.
b which I read last week.
c that I'd like to visit one day.
d I won't be able to go.
e if you go to university.
f where you don't have timetables.
g you won't pass your exam.

6 Complete the sentences with the correct forms of the verbs in brackets. Use present, past, future tenses and *used to* (where possible).

1 Who _____ (he/enjoy) working with?

2 I _____ (walk) to school when suddenly I _____ (see) them. They _____ (hide) around the corner.

3 I _____ (smoke) when I was younger, but the doctor told me to give up.

4 'Pete _____ (just/come back) from Australia.' 'Really? When _____ (he/arrive)?'

5 They _____ (leave) for their weekend trip tomorrow morning.

6 'This box is heavy.' 'Don't worry! I _____ (carry) it for you.'

7 What _____ (you/do) for your birthday?

8 If you _____ (not/go) abroad, you _____ (not/learn) a foreign language.

7 Find the mistakes and correct the sentences.

1 'What you do?' 'I'm an actor.'

_____

2 She would prefer taking a gap year before going to university.

_____

3 They were watching a horror film when the light was going out.

_____

4 He didn't use to liking horror films.

_____

5 Of all the students in the class, Janet is the more responsible.

_____

6 I haven't been to the Science Museum for I was a child.

_____

7 If the bus will be late, we walk to school.

_____

8 She works for a company sells shoes.

_____

GRAMMAR: Train and Try Again

UNIT 6

6.2 Second Conditional

1 Choose the correct forms.

1 If I had a good job, I *will* / *would* be happier.
2 I'd go out for a walk if I *didn't* / *don't* work in an office.
3 If Sarah didn't earn enough money, she *wouldn't* / *won't* travel abroad.
4 My brother *would sleep* / *slept* at night if he had a different job.
5 If our education system *was* / *is* better, we'd choose better politicians.

2 Put the words in the correct order to form sentences.

1 took / If / car / the / would / we / problems / have / parking / we / it
_____

2 advice / I / I / If / ask / would / brother / my / wanted
_____

3 waste / not / it / we / would / food / own / grew / we / If / our
_____

4 in / lower / many / If / there / so / were / not / cities / the / cars / level / would / smog / be
_____

5 from / in / would / plastic / not / people / to / shopping / home / they / buy / ones / remembered / bags / shops / If / take
_____

6.5 Modal verbs for obligation and permission

3 Choose the correct forms.

1 You *can't* / *don't have to* smoke in this area.
2 People working in hospitals *have to* / *can* wear uniforms.
3 You *mustn't* / *don't have to* finish the food if you don't like it.
4 We *must* / *can* finish the work today. The boss won't wait!
5 You *mustn't* / *must* wait here. Please move to the waiting room.
6 You *don't need to* / *mustn't* tell him. He already knows.

4 Find and correct the mistakes.

1 Teachers mustn't wear a suit to work, but they usually choose to wear nice clothes. _____
2 You don't have to talk on your phone and drive at the same time. It's illegal. _____
3 Annie don't must do the English test because she's half Australian. _____
4 Is it true that we not have to go to school until 11 a.m. tomorrow? Cool! _____

Summative Practice

Units 1–6

5 Match phrases 1–10 with a–j to form sentences.

1 What time ☐
2 What would you do ☐
3 Do nurses ☐
4 If we went by coach, ☐
5 If you needed a ticket for the disco, ☐
6 I had to leave early last night ☐
7 Do you have to do military service ☐
8 The world would be a better place ☐
9 You mustn't eat or drink ☐
10 Would you wear a tie ☐

a have to wear uniforms?
b I could get you one.
c it would be cheaper.
d if you lost your passport?
e can you get up at weekends?
f if everybody had a job.
g because I wasn't well.
h in your country?
i if you worked in an office?
j anything at your desk.

6 Complete the dialogue with the words and expressions from the box.

> can't 'd be 'd buy 'd give up
> don't have to 'd look for have to
> have you asked have you worked
> 'll have to since 've worked were

A: What would you do if you won the lottery, Sue?
B: If I won the lottery, I ¹_____ a larger house. What would you do?
A: Oh, if I won the lottery, I ²_____ my job immediately. I hate doing the same things day after day.
B: You ³_____ win the lottery to change your life! If you just changed your job, you ⁴_____ much happier! How long ⁵_____ for that company?
A: I ⁶_____ for them ⁷_____ three years now. ⁸_____ 2015. Every day I ⁹_____ get up at six, be there at eight, work long hours, get back home at eight, eat something and go to sleep … I ¹⁰_____ go on like this!
B: ¹¹_____ for a pay rise?
A: Yes, I have. But when I asked, they answered that money doesn't grow on trees, so I ¹²_____ wait till next year …
B: Well, if I ¹³_____ you, I ¹⁴_____ for another job.

149

7.2 The Passive

1 Turn the sentences into *yes/no* questions.

1 The car is cleaned once a month.

_____

2 Fresh, soft butter is needed to make that chocolate cake.

_____

3 The cakes have been eaten during the party.

_____

4 The most important work has already been done.

_____

5 The lives of hundreds of people were transformed by Fairtrade in Africa in the 1990s.

_____

6 All the shoes in this shop are made of plastic.

_____

7 This painting was sold yesterday.

_____

8 This plum jam was produced in Turkey last September.

_____

2 Use the verbs in brackets in the correct active or passive form.

1 A new shopping centre _____ (open) in our neighbourhood last weekend.

2 _____ (the people/ask) about the tickets yet?

3 The parcels _____ (already/deliver). They're in the hall.

4 The criminal _____ (stop) by police officers at the end of last year.

5 This construction company usually _____ (build) all the offices in the area.

6 _____ (your name/write) with a single or double 's'?

7.5 Quantifiers

3 Find the mistakes and correct the sentences.

1 There isn't many time left.

_____

2 Can I ask you a little questions?

_____

3 Sean gave the cat any milk in the morning.

_____

4 There isn't many food in the fridge.

_____

5 I've got a few change.

_____

6 How much is the trousers?

_____

7 They paid me a little pounds to do the job.

_____

Summative Practice

Units 1–7

4 Choose the correct forms.

1 *How much / How many* books have you got in your library?

2 The orchestra *conducted / was conducted* by Claudio Abbado.

3 Who was the soundtrack composed *by / with*?

4 There were *a few / a little* pairs left in your size, but they *have just been / were just sold* to another customer.

5 This marmalade was *making / was made* by my aunt.

6 I've got *a little / a few* milk but no coffee.

7 *How much / How many* beef have you bought?

8 I didn't get *some / any* cheese.

9 We've got *too few / a few* eggs to make the cake.

10 This shop sells clothes which *have worn / have been worn* by famous people.

11 She wanted *to know / knowing* the answer.

12 'What *did you do / were you doing* when the fire started?' 'I *was buying / bought* some food in the supermarket next to the station.'

13 *Have you ever been / Did you ever go* to Paris?

14 England is *bigger / the biggest* than Wales. It is *bigger / the biggest* country in the UK.

15 'How long *have you had / do you have* this hobby?' 'I've had this hobby *since / for* I retired.

16 'Are you going to / Will you* drive to Scotland?' 'No, *we're going to / we will* travel by train this time.'

17 If I see Tom, *I'll give / I'd give* him your message.

18 If Susan were ill, she *would / will* go to the doctor's.

5 Complete the text with the words from the box.

| are | by | few | little | lot of | lots of |
| some | used to | was | who | | |

Growing up in Africa, I ¹_____ spend a ²_____ time with my aunts in their villages. As a child, I saw country life as an adventure. The village was a place where ³_____ exciting things happened and where I was loved as part of a community. Now I know that my fondness for village life ⁴_____ encouraged by my relationship with ⁵_____ of the women that lived there. Women ⁶_____ were physically strong and positive. Women that never forgot any of our past traditions, and who preserved community values and passed them on to the next generation. These women still exist. They work hard but ⁷_____ of them see the benefits of their work. ⁸_____ has been done to help them. But they have a vision; a vision where poverty and hunger ⁹_____ reduced, where communities are supported ¹⁰_____ investments in education, health, water and food, and finally where more resources are set apart to help women gain equality.

8.2 Past Perfect

1 Complete the sentences with the Past Simple or the Past Perfect forms of the verbs in brackets.

1 When I _____ (finish) washing, I _____ (have) breakfast.
2 He _____ (tell) me this before his brother _____ (go) out.
3 By the age of five, my younger brother _____ (learn) to read and write.
4 After the man _____ (deny) stealing the money, the police officer _____ (show) him a recording from the shop camera. The man _____ (be) silent.
5 By the time Greg _____ (leave) work, he _____ (come) up with a solution to the problem.
6 When I _____ (get) to their house, they _____ (already/have) lunch.

2 Read the sentences. In each sentence decide which activity happened first.

1 Before the dentist came up to me [ ], I had opened my mouth [ ].
2 I felt sick [ ] when I lay down [ ].
3 Joe had come out in a rash [ ] by the time the doctor took him to hospital [ ].
4 The concert began [ ] when we arrived at the concert hall [ ].
5 When Tessa stepped on a stone and fell over [ ], she decided to take better care of her health [ ].
6 When the patient woke up [ ], the nurse had opened the window in the room [ ].

8.5 Reported Speech

3 Choose the correct forms.

1 'I've finished': He said he *had finished / has finished*.
2 'Jack found the book': She said Jack *found / had found* the book.
3 'We locked the door': They *said / told* me they *locked / had locked* the door.
4 'I'm very pleased to meet you': She said she *was / had been* very pleased to meet me.
5 Why *had he said / had he told* you that?
6 He said he *was working / is working*.
7 The man said he *hadn't had / hasn't had* time to put money in the meter.
8 I told them I *enjoy / had enjoyed* their stories.

4 Find the mistakes and correct the sentences.

1 They said me that they had repaired the clock.

_____

2 She said she hasn't done her homework.

_____

3 I said the policeman my address.

_____

4 After we have walked for about two hours, we stopped for a rest.

_____

5 I went to bed after I have locked the door.

_____

Summative Practice Units 1–8

5 Complete the sentences with the correct forms of the verbs in brackets.

1 He _____ (work) here ever since I can remember.
2 He _____ (work) here a couple of years ago.
3 We _____ (not/see) her yet.
4 We _____ (just/see) her.
5 'Something's wrong with the laptop.' 'Yes, I know. I _____ (take) it to the computer shop tomorrow morning.'
6 'Oh, this laptop is always going wrong!' 'All right; I _____ (take) it to the computer shop right away.'
7 If an election is held now, Mr Hilton _____ (be) elected.
8 If an election were held now, Mr Hilton _____ (be) elected.
9 The men who tried to break into the bank _____ (arrest) the next day.
10 When I arrived, she _____ (already/leave).

6 Choose the correct forms.

'The professor ¹*wrote / was writing* a book. He decided that he needed a secretary to help him. A man came, but he wasn't very good. The second man ²*who / which* came was called Smith. But now this young man is dead, and I think someone killed him,' Detective Hopkins ³*said / told*. '⁴*Tell / Say* me everything', said Sherlock Holmes.

'The servant girl ⁵*told / said* me that she ⁶*was working / worked* in one of the bedrooms between eleven and twelve o'clock this morning. The professor was still in bed. Suddenly she ⁷*heard / was hearing* a loud cry. She ⁸*ran / was running* down and found Mr Smith lying on the floor. There was a wound in his neck, and ⁹*a lot of / much* blood on the floor. He was dead. The professor was frightened because he ¹⁰*had heard / heard* the loud cry. He cannot think of ¹¹*any / some* reason why Mr Smith ¹²*was killed / had been killed*. When I arrived, I saw that everyone ¹³*had been / has been* careful not to walk on the garden path. And that no one ¹⁴*had moved / moved* anything either,' Hopkins said.

From Sir Arthur Conan Doyle, The Return of Sherlock Holmes, simplified by Alan Pugh

WRITING BANK

Accepting suggestions

That sounds fantastic!

I'd love to (go).

Well, it's worth a try.

I suppose it'll work.

Agreeing with an opinion

I (completely) agree that/with …

I couldn't agree more that/with …

That's fine with me.

I think so too.

Apologising

Informal phrases

I'm really sorry (that) …

Sorry to bother you.

Sorry I haven't written for so long./Sorry for not writing for so long.

I'm writing to tell you how sorry I am to … (about) … It will never happen again.

Formal phrases

I apologise for …

Please accept my apology for …

Closing formulas: emails and letters

Informal phrases

Best wishes,

Bye for now/See you!

Love,/Take care!/All the best,

Formal phrases

Yours sincerely,

Regards,

Contacting people

Ways to contact people

If you have any information, please contact/call/leave a message for Alison on (0961224466).

If you are interested in …, call (John/Ms White) on (0961224466).

To join us, call …

If you have seen it, please …

Call me on … for more details.

Maintaining contact

Drop me a line sometime.

I hope to hear from you soon.

Give me a call later.

Let me know if you can make it or not.

I was glad to hear about …

Let me know as soon as possible.

Describing lost property

Description

I lost (my bag/passport/coat/dog).

Describing features

It is/was …

Size   huge/tiny/35cm x 25cm

Shape   round/rectangular/square/narrow

Colour   white/red and brown/light/dark green

Material   made of leather/plastic/linen

Age   new/young/old/six years old/modern/ancient It has/had (two handles/a leather strap/a blue cover two pockets/short sleeves/a black tail).

Reasons for search

I keep (all my files there).

It was something I borrowed/got as a birthday present.

It is of great value./It's a really precious thing.

I can't live without it.

It means a lot to me.

Disagreeing with an opinion

I disagree that/with …/ I don't agree that/with …

I am totally against …

I see what you mean but …

I see your point but …

I'm afraid I can't agree with …

I'm not convinced about …

I don't think it's the best solution.

Encouraging participation

Come on, don't be afraid/it's not difficult/it's easy!

Why don't you come and meet some interesting people/ see some great things?

Come and tell us what you think.

Come and have fun!

Don't miss it!

Ending emails and letters

Informal phrases

It was good to hear from you.

Email me soon.

I'd better get going./I must be going now./Got to go now.

Looking forward to your news/to hearing from you again.

Say hello to …

Give my love/my regards to (everyone at home).

Have a nice (trip).

See you (soon/in the summer).

Write soon.

Keep in touch!

Formal phrases

I look forward to hearing from you/your reply.

I hope to hear from you soon.

Expressing opinion

I believe/think/feel (that) …

I really believe (that) …

In my opinion/view, …/To my mind, …

The way I see it, …

It seems/appears to me (that) …

My opinion is that …

As far as I am concerned, …

Expressing preferences

I really enjoy/like/love … because …

I prefer … to …

I'd like to …/I hope to …

I find … boring/dull.

I don't like/I can't stand/I really hate …

It's not really my thing.

Giving advice

You should/ought to …

You'd better …

If I were you, I would …

It might be a good idea (for you) to …

Why don't you …?

Have you thought of/about …?

Inviting

I'd like to invite you to …

I'd like you to come …

Would you come to …? If you want, you can bring a friend.

I'm writing to invite you to (Madrid/my party).

I'm having (a party).

I hope you'll be able to join us/to make it.

You are welcome to …

Join us today!

Come and meet me …

Why don't you come …?

Making requests and enquiries

Informal phrases

Can you …, please?/Could you …?

Do you think you could …?

Let me know if you can (come).

Could you tell me …?

Formal phrases

Would it be possible for you to …?

I'd be grateful if you could …

I wonder if I could ask you to/for …

I'm writing to ask for your help/advice …

I'm writing to enquire about …

WRITING BANK

Making suggestions

I think I/you/we should (go to) …

Perhaps I/you/we could (go to) …

What do you think about (going to) …?

What/How about (going to) …?

How do you feel about …?

Would you like me to …?

Why don't we (go) …?

Let's (go to) …

Shall we (go to) …?

Do you fancy (going to) … ?

Opening formulas: emails and letters

Informal phrases

Dear Margaret,

Hi Anne,

Neutral phrases

Dear Mr and Mrs Edwards,

Dear Ms Brennon,

Refusing suggestions

It doesn't sound very good.

I don't think I fancy it.

I'm sorry, but I can't join you.

I'm not really into …

I've got some doubts about it.

I don't see how it could work.

Actually, I would prefer not to.

Starting emails and letters

Informal phrases

It was good to hear from you.

I hope you're doing well/you're fine/you're OK.

How are things with you?

I'm writing to tell you …

Thanks for your letter.

I wonder if you remember/have heard …

I wanted to/must tell you about …

I just wanted to ask/remind/thank you …

Just a quick email to tell you …

Neutral phrases

I am writing to thank you for …

Telling a story

It all happened some time ago.

It was three years ago.

While I (was playing), …

First,

Then,

Finally,

Suddenly,

Unfortunately,

Fortunately,

It was the best/worst time ever.

We had a great/awful time when we were …

Thanking

Informal phrases

Thank you so much.

It was so/really/very kind of you to …

Neutral phrases

I really appreciate your help.

Thank you for sending it back to me.

I am really grateful for your help.

Thank you for doing me a favour.

It's very kind of you.

Present Simple and Present Continuous

Exercise 1
1 He watches TV in the evenings.
2 My mother doesn't drink coffee.
3 Donald spends Christmas at home every year.
4 Do you often go shopping?
5 My aunt doesn't work at school.
6 Does he speak French?

Exercise 2
1 is having
2 is running
3 is not working, is swimming
4 Are you reading
5 is working
6 Is your best friend laughing

Exercise 3
1 Are you watching   2 are you packing
3 is waiting   4 are studying   5 have
6 want   7 is playing   8 plays   9 need
10 am studying   11 study

Exercise 4
1 What are you wearing today?
2 Do you live near your school?
3 What console games do you like most?
4 What do you usually have for breakfast?
5 What book are you reading now?
6 What do you usually wear to school?
7 Are you working anywhere right now?
8 Do any of your friends play the guitar?

Exercise 5
Students' own answers.

Exercise 6
1 on   2 never   3 At   4 every day
5 days   6 every

Past Simple

Exercise 1
1 lived, didn't work   2 Did you stay
3 didn't study, failed   4 stopped, started
5 followed   6 Did he play

Exercise 2
1 A: Did you buy, were
   B: didn't, didn't have
2 A: Were
   B: went
3 A: broke, was
   B: Did she go
   A: did
4 A: Did you find
   B: did, found
5 A: Did Mr Kay run, was
   B: did, swam
6 A: Did your brothers fight, were
   B: did, won
7 A: Were
   B: were, liked
8 A: Did you get
   B: wanted, got

Exercise 3
1 took   2 snowed   3 wanted
4 arrived   5 forgot   6 was
7 didn't have   8 were   9 was
10 wanted   11 ran   12 drove
13 got   14 looked   15 said
16 turned   17 could   18 was
19 started   20 were   21 didn't pack
22 came   23 had   24 laughed

Exercise 4
1 Where did Sophie go yesterday?
2 What did he watch last night?
3 What was your favourite subject at school?
4 How many books did Alice read last year?
5 When did Sue's parents buy a big house?
6 Why didn't you go shopping?
7 How many emails did you send yesterday?
8 What could your sister do when she was six?

Exercise 5
1 Did Alan set the alarm clock on Friday?
2 Did they have breakfast on Saturday?
3 Was the weather nice?
4 Did they go to the mountains?
5 Did they laugh a lot?
Students' own answers.

Exercise 6
1 What did you wear to school yesterday?
2 Where did you go on holiday last year?
3 Who did you meet at the weekend?
4 What time did you get up yesterday?
5 Were you busy on Saturday at 6 p.m.?
6 What did you like doing in your free time when you were a child?
7 What did you do last night?
8 Did you like your primary school?
Students' own answers.

Present Perfect

Exercise 1
1 haven't done   2 have you changed
3 have already read   4 have been
5 Have you watered   6 Has her sister cut

Exercise 2
1 Have your parents booked a trip to Asia? Yes, they have.
2 Have you seen Mary? Yes, I have.
3 Has Mark bought a new bike?
   No, he hasn't.
4 Has your best friend tried kitesurfing?
   Yes, he /she has.
5 Has Fiona gone/been shopping?
   Yes, she has.

Exercise 3
Example answers:
1 My partner has never been camping.
2 My partner has written a poem.
3 My partner has never sung in a karaoke bar.
4 My partner has never ridden a camel.
5 My partner has won a medal.
6 My partner has gone/been bungee jumping.

Exercise 4
Students' own answers.

Exercise 5
Students' own answers.

be going to

Exercise 1
1 're/are going to visit
2 Is your brother going to watch
3 Are we going to have
4 isn't/is not going to cook
5 is going to spend
6 are you going to do
7 'm/am not going to wait

Exercise 2
1 to   2 going   3 not   4 is
5 you   6 am   7 I   8 be   9 We
10 Are   11 aren't

Exercise 3
1 A: Is Neil going to be at   B: he isn't
2 A: is he going to do   B: is not going to sell, is going to keep
3 A: Are they going to stay   B: they aren't, are going to leave

Exercise 4
Students' own answers.

Exercise 5
Students' own answers.

Exercise 6
1 What are you going to do tomorrow?
2 What are you going to eat tonight?
3 Where are you going to travel (to) next summer?
4 What are you going to buy at the weekend?
5 Are you going to visit a doctor this month?
6 Are you going to start a summer job in July?
Students' own answers.

will for predictions

Exercise 1
1 won't die   2 Will the icebergs melt
3 won't use   4 won't change
5 Will oceans and lakes disappear
6 will the cheapest means of transport be

Exercise 2
Example answers:
1 we will be able / won't be able to travel in time.
2 people will be able / won't be able to breathe under water.
3 scientists will be able / won't be able to find a cure for cancer.
4 we will be able / won't be able to stop a hurricane.
5 we will be able / won't be able to see through walls.
6 cars will be able / won't be able to fly.

Exercise 3
Example answers:
1 Pollution will become worse.
2 Petrol will become less expensive.
3 Schools will become better.
4 Temperatures won't get higher.
5 Intelligent technologies will become more popular.
6 Electric cars will become more available.

Exercise 4
Students' own answers.

Exercise 5
Students' own answers.

must, have to and should

Exercise 1
1 Do policemen have to wear uniforms? Yes, they do.
2 Does a secretary have to be good at swimming? No, he/she doesn't.
3 Does a teacher have to prepare for lessons? Yes, he/she does.
4 Do students have to pay for sandwiches in your school? Students' own answers.
5 Do you have to do your homework every day? Student's own answers.

Exercise 2
Example answers:
1 You should hurry.
2 You should go to a dentist.
3 You shouldn't worry about your grades.
4 You shouldn't spend all your money.
5 You should go to bed early every night.

Exercise 3
1 You mustn't open the door to strangers.
2 You must go to bed before 9 p.m.
3 You must go to school.
4 You mustn't take my phone.
5 You mustn't eat too much chocolate.
6 You must brush your teeth every day.
7 You must be nice to your friends.

Exercise 4
1 You have to be quiet.
2 You mustn't go there alone if you are younger than eight.
3 You should listen to your friends' advice.
4 You mustn't speak at the library.
5 You shouldn't take more than two books at a time.

Exercise 5
Students' own answers.

Exercise 6
Students' own answers. Examples:
1 You must study Maths a lot.
2 You don't have to study at weekends.
3 You must be good at computers.
4 You don't have to be creative.
5 You should do extra homework in Maths.
6 You should practise your English a lot.
7 You mustn't be late for school.
8 You should be active during lessons.
9 You mustn't party all night long.
10 You should read articles on foreign websites.
11 You should be interested in current affairs.
12 You should go to art galleries and museums.

Countable and uncountable nouns, articles

Exercise 1
1 C 2 U 3 U 4 C 5 C 6 U 7 U
8 U 9 C 10 U 11 U 12 U 13 U

Exercise 2
1 How many   2 How much
3 How much   4 How many
5 How much   6 How many
7 How much   8 How many

Exercise 3
1 an, some/a 2 a, any 3 a 4 some
5 a 6 any 7 any 8 a

Exercise 4
1 a, Ø, a 2 a, The, Ø 3 The
4 a, the 5 a, Ø 6 Ø, Ø 7 a, Ø, a/the
8 Ø, Ø, the, Ø

Exercise 5
1 any 2 many 3 a 4 much 5 The 6 an

Exercise 6
Example answers:
1 How many books are there on your shelf?
2 How much snow is there outside?
3 How many balloons do you need for your birthday party?
4 How many shoes are there in your wardrobe?
5 How much homework have you got for tomorrow?
6 How many films do you watch a year?
7 How much money do you need for the holidays?
8 How much music do you listen to?
Students' own answers.

Exercise 7
1 the, Ø 2 Ø, the 3 Ø 4 Ø
5 Ø, Ø 6 a 7 Ø, The 8 Ø, the/Ø
9 Ø 10 The 11 the, the 12 Ø, the
Students' own answers.

Revision of tenses

Exercise 1
1 Where does Maria often go?
2 What are you drinking?
3 Why does he train every day?
4 How often does her aunt visit her?
5 What are you reading now?
6 Where do you live?
7 What does Tom usually wear to school?
8 When does he go to the gym?
9 Why are Tim and Sue revising for an exam?
10 What does Sarah like?

Exercise 2
1 works
2 is sleeping/is playing
3 are talking
4 watch
5 are not, are playing
6 is not watching, he is revising
7 are, eat
8 talk

Exercise 3
1 is going to go, will find
2 is going to be a model, will be good, will be, Are you going to be
3 'm/am not going to study, are you going to study

Exercise 4
Students' own answers.

Exercise 5
1 What did you watch?
2 What did you cook?
3 How many people were there?
4 How long did you learn?
5 Where did you go?
6 What present did you get?
7 What time did you get up?
Students' own answers.

Exercise 6
1 never / just 2 yet 3 never / just
4 been 5 been 6 Have 7 gone

Exercise 7
1 No, they won't.   2 No, I haven't.
3 No, she doesn't.   4 Yes, he is.
5 Yes, she has.   6 Yes, I did.
7 No, there won't.

Exercise 8
1 The best teacher I have ever known is/was …
2 The cheapest restaurant I have ever eaten at is/was …
3 The best song I have ever listened to is/was …
4 The most beautiful city I have ever been to is/was …
5 The most expensive ticket I have ever bought is/was …
6 The best mobile app I have ever used is/was …
7 The best friend I have ever had is/was …
8 The most interesting book I have ever read is/was …
Students' own answers.

Exercise 9
1 have already passed 2 was, read
3 go 4 spent 5 will be able to speak
6 'm/am using 7 'm/am not working
8 hasn't/has not had
Students' own answers

Unit 1

Exercise 1
1 Does she enjoy cooking?
2 Is he studying for his exams?
3 Have you ever met him?
4 Do you like shopping?
5 Has David (ever) visited Paris and London?
6 Do you go to the gym at the weekend?
7 Are they having dinner?
8 Do they do aerobics twice a week?

Exercise 2
1 Who helps old people in the local area?
2 Who does Tom help?
3 What do you enjoy?
4 Who is keen on music?
5 What are you reading at the moment?
6 Who is reading a book by Stephen King at the moment?
7 Who wrote the book?
8 Where are you from?
9 Who are you phoning?
10 Where is the charity helping mothers with children?
11 Who has borrowed this game from Lilian?
12 Why has Frank borrowed this game?

Exercise 3
1 reading 2 to go 3 wearing
4 telling 5 to go 6 to buy 7 to work
8 going 9 to arrive 10 leaving

Exercise 4
1 Does 2 does 3 Have 4 What
5 to 6 is 7 do 8 to 9 are
10 Who 11 are 12 do

Exercise 5
1 Where is Karen from?
2 She'd like to wear a uniform.
3 Who likes you? / Who do you like?
4 How much time does he spend doing sports?
5 What do you do after dinner?
6 Have they ever given money to charity?

Exercise 6
1 doing
2 doing
3 do you do
4 playing
5 Do you have
6 play
7 listening
8 reading
9 read
10 to read
11 to concentrate
12 to relax
13 are you reading
14 'm reading
15 reading
16 don't read
17 going

Unit 2

Exercise 1
1 ~~were arriving~~ arrived 2 ~~was ringing~~ rang 3 ~~was hearing~~ heard
4 ~~you were~~ were you 5 ~~didn't work~~ wasn't working

Exercise 2
1 phoned 2 were you doing 3 did you phone 4 was watching 5 didn't hear
6 called 7 skied 8 didn't know 9 was skiing 10 collided 11 broke 12 was

Exercise 3
1 didn't use to get up 2 both 3 bought
4 used to go 5 both 6 went

Exercise 4
1 What were you watching/doing when David arrived?
2 Who speaks English?
3 How many languages do you speak?
4 Who likes reading detective stories?
5 What does Barbara enjoy (doing)?
6 Where have you been?

Exercise 5
1 comes 2 was waiting, arrived
3 visited 4 is Paul doing, is working
5 Do you work 6 used to work

Exercise 6
1 were reading 2 were 3 heard
4 got 5 looked 6 is coming
7 knew 8 used to help/helped
9 are investigating 10 don't know

Unit 3

Exercise 1
1 fastest 2 best 3 as exciting as
4 best 5 shorter than
6 more expensive

Exercise 2
1 ~~further~~ far 2 ~~funnyer~~ funnier 3 ~~more~~ most 4 ~~worse~~ worst 5 I I've 6 ~~high as~~ as high as 7 ~~more tall~~ taller

Exercise 3
1 have already bought 2a Have you seen
2b 've just said 2c was 3a 've just won
3b bought 3c haven't heard 3d talked
3e invited 3f was

Exercise 4
1 does 2 with 3 getting up
4 was shining 5 work 6 yet
7 joined 8 the youngest

Exercise 5
1 've just been 2 did you see
3 saw 4 Have you seen 5 haven't
6 best 7 watched 8 most interesting
9 have ever seen 10 more boring

Exercise 6
1 have always enjoyed 2 went
3 go 4 go 5 went 6 were walking
7 began 8 was 9 got 10 was
11 had 12 went 13 were walking
14 asked 15 've just decided

Unit 4

Exercise 1
1 How long have you known each other?
2 How long has Shannon been in the waiting room?
3 Who has had this Jaguar for more than a decade?
4 Where have the Smiths lived since they came to our town?
5 How long has Adam had this book?

Exercise 2
1 Anne has been here for two days.
2 It started raining two hours ago.
3 The children have had the new computer since yesterday.
4 I have loved this song since I heard it at the party last Friday.
5 Our parents met for the first time six months ago.

Exercise 3
1 are not going to 2 I'll phone
3 I'll help 4 what are you going to do
5 are leaving 6 are you meeting
7 We're meeting 8 I'll make

Exercise 4
1 Who does Emma like?
2 Who likes Emma?
3 What singers are you keen on?
4 I don't mind studying after dinner.
5 I was walking along the mountain path when you phoned me.
6 The Petersons moved out of that house only a few months ago.

Exercise 5
1 'll send
2 has lived
3 Is Pat organising
4 have you known
5 has known
6 I'll go
7 has been

Exercise 6
1 are going
2 are you doing
3 'm going to stay
4 Have you ever been
5 used to go
6 did you
7 went
8 did you use to go
9 used to go
10 used to go
11 climbed
12 highest
13 were climbing
14 changed
15 found
16 aren't coming
17 I'll come
18 haven't been
19 since
20 'll let

Unit 5

Exercise 1
1 go
2 like, 'll enjoy (any order)
3 go, 'll meet
4 goes, 'll visit
5 go, 'll listen

Exercise 2
1 doesn't, 'll go
2 won't go, snows
3 calls, won't
4 doesn't go, 'll work
5 will protest, break down

Exercise 3
1 wardrobe
2 chemist
3 password
4 sitcom
5 sale

Exercise 4
1 where
2 which/that
3 who/that
4 who/that
5 who/that
6 where

Exercise 5
1 d **2** f **3** e **4** c **5** a **6** g **7** b

Exercise 6
1 does he enjoy
2 was walking, saw, were hiding
3 used to smoke
4 has just come back, did he arrive
5 are leaving
6 'll carry
7 are you doing/are you going to do
8 don't go, won't learn

Exercise 7
1 What do you do?
2 to take
3 went out
4 like
5 the most
6 since
7 is, will walk
8 which/that sells

Unit 6

Exercise 1
1 would **2** didn't **3** wouldn't
4 would sleep **5** was

Exercise 2
1 If we took the car, we would have problems parking it.
2 If I wanted advice, I would ask my brother.
3 If we grew our own food, we would not waste it.
4 If there were not so many cars in cities, the smog level would be lower.
5 If people remembered to take shopping bags from home, they would not buy plastic ones in shops.

Exercise 3
1 can't
2 have to
3 don't have to
4 must
5 mustn't
6 don't need to

Exercise 4
1 ~~mustn't~~ don't have to
2 ~~don't have to~~ mustn't
3 ~~don't must~~ doesn't have to
4 ~~not have to~~ don't have to

Exercise 5
1 e **2** d **3** a **4** c **5** b
6 g **7** h **8** f **9** j **10** i

Exercise 6
1 'd buy
2 'd give up
3 don't have to
4 'd be
5 have you worked
6 've worked
7 for
8 Since
9 have to
10 can't
11 Have you asked
12 'll have to
13 were
14 'd look

Unit 7

Exercise 1
1 Is the car cleaned once a month?
2 Is fresh, soft butter needed to make that chocolate cake?
3 Have the cakes been eaten during the party?
4 Has the most important work been done yet?
5 Were the lives of hundreds of people transformed by Fairtrade in Africa in the 1990s?
6 Are all the shoes in this shop made of plastic?
7 Was this painting sold yesterday?
8 Was this plum jam produced in Turkey last September?

Exercise 2
1 was opened
2 Have the people asked
3 have already been delivered
4 was stopped
5 builds
6 Is your name written

Exercise 3
1 ~~many~~ much
2 ~~little~~ a few
3 ~~any~~ some
4 ~~many~~ much
5 ~~a few~~ a little
6 ~~is~~ are
7 ~~a little~~ a few

Exercise 4
1 How many **2** was conducted
3 by **4** a few, have just been sold
5 was made **6** a little
7 How much **8** any **9** too few
10 have been worn **11** to know
12 were you doing, was buying
13 Have you ever been
14 bigger, the biggest
15 have you had, since
16 Are you going to, we're going to
17 I'll give
18 would

Exercise 5
1 used to **2** lot of **3** lots of
4 was **5** some **6** who **7** few
8 Little **9** are **10** by

Unit 8

Exercise 1
1 (had) finished, had
2 (had) told, went
3 had learnt
4 had denied, showed, was
5 left, had come
6 got, had already had

Exercise 2
1 came up to me, [2] had opened my mouth [1] **2** felt sick [2], lay down [1]
3 had come out in a rash [1], took him to hospital [2] **4** began [2], arrived [1]
5 stepped ... fell over [1], decided [2]
6 woke up [2], had opened [1]

Exercise 3
1 had finished
2 had found
3 told, had locked
4 was
5 had he told you
6 was working
7 hadn't had
8 had enjoyed

Exercise 4
1 ~~said~~ told **2** ~~hasn't~~ hadn't done
3 ~~said~~ told **4** ~~have~~ had walked
5 ~~have~~ had locked

Exercise 5
1 has worked/has been working
2 worked
3 haven't seen
4 have just seen
5 'm going to take/'m taking
6 'll take
7 will be
8 would be
9 were arrested
10 had already left

Exercise 6
1 was writing **2** who **3** said
4 Tell **5** told **6** was working
7 heard **8** ran **9** a lot of
10 hadheard **11** any **12** was killed
13 had been **14** had moved

1.10 Self-check

Vocabulary and Grammar

Exercise 1
1 mean 2 unpopular 3 silly 4 lazy
5 dishonest

Exercise 2
1 deal 2 selfish 3 active
4 independent 5 communicative

Exercise 3
1 nurseries 2 libraries 3 kitchen
4 countries 5 home

Exercise 4
1 C 2 C 3 A 4 B 5 B

Exercise 5
1 to learn 2 playing 3 to carry
4 studying 5 to walk/walking

Exercise 6
1 C 2 B 3 B 4 C 5 A

Use of English

Exercise 7
1 C 2 C 3 B 4 A 5 A

Exercise 8
1 B 2 A 3 A 4 C 5 A

Exercise 9
1 A 2 A 3 C 4 B 5 C

Exercise 10
1 stand 2 with 3 such 4 to 5 in

2.10 Self-check

Vocabulary and Grammar

Exercise 1
1 layers 2 laser printer 3 specimens
4 jigsaw 5 password

Exercise 2
1 Chemistry 2 Mathematics/Maths
3 Computer scientists 4 centigrade
5 below

Exercise 3
1 archaeology 2 psychologist
3 geologists 4 astronomy 5 linguist

Exercise 4
1a was doing 1b called
2a were sleeping 2b rang
3a Did they find 3b closed
4a were dancing 4b stopped
5a Was Shelly waiting 5b crashed

Exercise 5
1 ~~used to go~~   went
2 ~~used~~   use
3 ~~used to invent~~   invented
4 ~~use to be milk~~   milk use to be
5 ~~were~~   used to be

Exercise 6
1 B 2 A 3 A 4 A 5 C

Use of English

Exercise 7
1 B 2 B 3 C 4 A 5 B

Exercise 8
1 planning to publish a research paper
2 didn't use to like
3 as soon as it downloaded
4 used to work
5 were you going

Exercise 9
1 to do 2 remains 3 were sitting
4 collected 5 developed

Exercise 10
1 C 2 B 3 A 4 C 5 B

3.10 Self-check

Vocabulary and Grammar

Exercise 1
1 musicals 2 news bulletins 3 cooking
programme 4 portraits 5 gripping

Exercise 2
1 modern abstract paintings
2 A-list
3 tales
4 plot
5 out

Exercise 3
1 photographer
2 costumes
3 box office
4 comic books
5 documentary

Exercise 4
1 far 2 fitter 3 furthest
4 more 5 the

Exercise 5
1 I've just finished
2 Eileen has already seen
3 Has Rosa looked at a travel guide for
Spain yet?
4 Mum's / has already paid
5 We haven't met any of the other
guests yet.

Exercise 6
1 B 2 C 3 B 4 A 5 C

Use of English

Exercise 7
1 A 2 C 3 A 4 A 5 B

Exercise 8
1 trailer
2 sculptor
3 soundtrack
4 landscapes
5 imaginative

Exercise 9
1 far worse
2 much earlier than
3 just as excited as
4 has just finished
5 a much better actor than

Exercise 10
1 A 2 B 3 B 4 C 5 A

4.10 Self-check

Vocabulary and Grammar

Exercise 1
1 cooker
2 fridge
3 stilts
4 ruins
5 bookcase

Exercise 2
1 scorching temperatures
2 decision
3 must
4 historic sites
5 suburbs

Exercise 3
1 drawers
2 cosy
3 breathtaking
4 ladder
5 ironing

Exercise 4
1 The statue of the King has been in the
square since 1754.
2 The river has not had fish in it for two
years.
3 We have/'ve known about the problem
since this morning.
4 Nina has lived in a flat for ten years.
5 I haven't/have not felt well since last
weekend.

Exercise 5
1 A 2 B 3 C 4 A 5 A

Exercise 6
1 B 2 A 3 A 4 C 5 A

Use of English

Exercise 7
1 B 2 B 3 A 4 C 5 C

Exercise 8
1 is coming for dinner
2 did the shopping really quickly
3 is a traditional building
4 going to make a complaint
5 is making his bed

Exercise 9
1 hasn't visited us since
2 far earlier than
3 cooks extremely well
4 get away from the city
5 is going to buy

Exercise 10
1 housing
2 countryside
3 wooden
4 spacious
5 gardening

5.10 Self-check

Vocabulary and Grammar

Exercise 1
1 grades 2 job 3 nervous
4 bully 5 compulsory

Exercise 2
1 am dreaming of going
2 breaks up on
3 encouraged me to be/become
4 moving up to
5 make fun of

Exercise 3
1 visual thinker 2 timetable
3 curriculum 4 mentor 5 expert

Exercise 4
1 will rent 2 'll/will save 3 get
4 won't / will not pass 5 fails

Exercise 5
1 who   that/which
2 that   where
3 which   that/who
4 where   that/which
5 what   that/who

Exercise 6
1 A 2 B 3 A 4 B 5 C

Use of English

Exercise 7
1 B 2 A 3 A 4 C 5 C

Exercise 8
1 A 2 C 3 B 4 C 5 C

Exercise 9
1 A 2 C 3 B 4 A 5 C

Exercise 10
1 D 2 C 3 B 4 A 5 B

6.10 Self-check

Vocabulary and Grammar

Exercise 1
1 d 2 a 3 b 4 c 5 e

Exercise 2
1 social 2 unemployed 3 the sack
4 puts 5 solver

Exercise 3
1 work   have
2 to   for
3 creating   creative
4 repeating   repetitive
5 rely   reliance

Exercise 4
1 wouldn't feel exhausted all the time if she went
2 I invited you, would you come
3 Laura and Kath worked from home, they would miss
4 wouldn't go out with him again if I were
5 you give me some money if you won

Exercise 5
1 need to 2 can 3 can't
4 must 5 needn't

Exercise 6
1 C 2 B 3 A 4 C 5 B

Use of English

Exercise 7
1 challenging
2 determination
3 reliable
4 demanding
5 competitive

Exercise 8
1 they would come to the festival
2 would need to have
3 doesn't have to bring
4 if you took time off
5 got on well/better with

Exercise 9
1 A 2 B 3 A 4 C 5 C

Exercise 10
1 has (got) perfect eyesight/vision
2 have to do training/must do training
3 would study abroad if he spoke
4 to resign from her
5 such a nature lover

7.10 Self-check

Vocabulary and Grammar

Exercise 1
1 health centre
2 newsagent's
3 estate agent's
4 suits
5 fit

Exercise 2
1 trader
2 in debt
3 earner
4 produces
5 investor

Exercise 3
1 stationer's
2 greengrocer's
3 optician's
4 butcher's
5 baker's

Exercise 4
1 was designed/has been designed
2 Were you given/Have you been given
3 was sold
4 Was the parcel delivered
5 haven't been told

Exercise 5
1 few   little
2 many   much
3 little   few
4 few   a few
5 A lots of   Lots of/A lot of

Exercise 6
1 A 2 C 3 B 4 B 5 C

Use of English

Exercise 7
1 cashmere jumper was sold to
2 everything on this shelf is
3 looked everywhere for my glasses
4 isn't/is not any cola
5 (very) few people

Exercise 8
1 was created 2 customer
3 anything 4 sellers
5 products

Exercise 9
1 A 2 C 3 B 4 A 5 B

Exercise 10
1 lot 2 have 3 pick 4 on 5 worth

8.10 Self-check

Vocabulary and Grammar

Exercise 1
1 face mask
2 purifier
3 cough
4 path
5 pain

Exercise 2
1 dizzy
2 ring
3 back
4 fumes
5 vacuum

Exercise 3
1 pitch 2 storm 3 anxiety
4 choices 5 fit

Exercise 4
1 was
2 had already begun
3 got
4 had spoken
5 realised

Exercise 5
1 she was joining
2 he hadn't/had not swum
3 she'd/had never broken
4 she hadn't/had not come out in spots until
5 the air pollution in that town is/was

Exercise 6
1 A 2 B 3 C 4 B 5 B

Use of English

Exercise 7
1 C 2 C 3 A 4 C 5 A

Exercise 8
1 keep track of 2 said I had to take
3 because she had been late
4 broke my leg 5 he had drunk

Exercise 9
1 B 2 A 3 B 4 B 5 C

Exercise 10
1 A 2 A 3 C 4 C 5 B